TREKKING AND CLIMBING IN
THE ANDES

VAL PITKETHLY
& KATE HARPER

Climbing Consultant: VICTOR SAUNDERS

First published in 2002 by
New Holland Publishers (UK) Ltd
London · Cape Town · Sydney · Auckland

Garfield House, 86–88 Edgware Road,
London W2 2EA, United Kingdom

80 McKenzie Street, Cape Town 8001, South Africa

14 Aquatic Drive, Frenchs Forest, NSW 2086, Australia

218 Lake Road, Northcote, Auckland, New Zealand

www.newhollandpublishers.com

2 4 6 8 10 9 7 5 3 1

Copyright © 2002 in text: Val Pitkethly and Kate Harper, with the exception of individual contributors as listed on page 192
Copyright © 2002 in Health and Safety (by Rachel Bishop & Dr Jim Litch): New Holland Publishers (UK) Ltd
Copyright © 2002 in Mountain Photography (by Steve Razzetti): New Holland Publishers (UK) Ltd
Copyright © 2002 in photographs: Val Pitkethly and Kate Harper, with the exception of individual photographers as listed on page 192
Copyright © 2002 in artwork and cartography: New Holland Publishers (UK) Ltd
Copyright © 2002: New Holland Publishers (UK) Ltd

All rights reserved. No part of this publication may be reproduced, stored in a retrieval system or transmitted, in any form or by any means, electronic, mechanical, photocopying, recording or otherwise, without the prior written permission of the publishers and copyright holders.

ISBN 1 85974 391 9

Publishing Manager: Jo Hemmings
Series Editor: Kate Michell
Editorial Assistant: Anne Konopelski
Editing and Design: D & N Publishing, Marlborough, Wiltshire
Cartography: William Smuts
Production: Joan Woodroffe

Reproduction by Modern Age Repro Co. Ltd, Hong Kong
Printed and bound by Kyodo Printing Co (Singapore) Pte Ltd

The author and publisher have made every effort to ensure that the information in this book was correct when the book went to press; they accept no responsibility for any loss, injury or inconvenience sustained by any person using this book.

Front cover: Camping below La Calzada near Chajolpaya (treks 11 & 12). *Cover spine:* Alpine-style mountaineering on Chopicalqui in the Cordillera Blanca (trek 19). *Title page:* The spires of Cerro Catedral in the Nahuel Huapi National Park (trek 4). *This spread:* A road weaves its way up to Portochuello Llanganuco, with Pisco and Chacraraju in the background (trek 18). *Opposite contents page:* The mighty Siula Grande in the Cordillera Huayhuash (trek 17). *Contents page left:* Local women of the Cordillera Huayhuash (trek 17); *middle:* Llama in the Cordillera Real (trek 11); *right:* The famous ruins of Machu Picchu (trek 16).

CONTENTS

About This Book 6
1 INTRODUCTION TO THE ANDES 8
2 TREKKING AND CLIMBING IN
   THE ANDES 15

3 CHILE AND ARGENTINA 21
Trek 1: Circuit of Torres del Paine 34
PARQUE NACIONAL TORRES DEL PAINE DIRECTORY 40
Trek 2: Around Monte Fitz Roy in the Parque Nacional Los Glaciares 41
FITZ ROY DIRECTORY 46
Trek 3: Around Cerro Castillo 47
COYHAIQUE DIRECTORY 49
Trek 4: Nahuel Huapi Traverse 50
Trek 5: Trans-Andean Trek (Peak: Monte Tronador) 53
Trek 6: Puyehue Traverse 58
SAN CARLOS DE BARILOCHE DIRECTORY 62
Trek 7: Villarrica Traverse (Peak: Volcán Villarrica) 63
PUCON DIRECTORY 67
Peak: Aconcagua 68
MENDOZA DIRECTORY 71

4 BOLIVIA 72
Trek 8: Quimsa Cruz (Peak: Cerro Yaypuri) 82
Trek 9: The 'Other Side' of Illimani (Peak: Illimani) 86
Trek 10: Zongo to Coroico 90
Trek 11: Cordillera Real (Peaks: Huayna Potosí, Condoriri, Pequeño Alpamayo) 94
SORATA DIRECTORY 101
Trek 12: Illampu Circuit (Peak: Illampu) 103
Trek 13: Apolobamba 107
APOLOBAMBA DIRECTORY 111

5 PERU 112
Trek 14: Cordillera Auzungate 119
Trek 15: Cordillera Vilcabamba 123
Trek 16: The Inca Trail 126
CUZCO DIRECTORY 129
Trek 17: Cordillera Huayhuash (Peak: Diablo Mundo) 130
Trek 18: Cordillera Blanca Tranquilo (Peaks: Huamasaraju, Pisco) 134
Trek 19: Cordillera Blanca (Peak: Chopicalqui) 137
Trek 20: Alapamayo Circuit (Peaks: Alpamayo, Huascarán Sur) 140
HUARAZ DIRECTORY 145

6 ECUADOR 146
Trek 21: El Camino del Inca 153
CUENCA DIRECTORY 155
Trek 22: Chimborazo Circuit (Peak: Chimborazo) 156
Trek 23: Papallacta to Cotopaxi (Peak: Cotopaxi) 159
COTOPAXI AND CHIMBORAZO DIRECTORY 162
Trek 24: The Pinan Lakes 163
OTAVALO DIRECTORY 165

7 VENEZUELA 167
Trek 25: Sierra Nevada de Mérida 172
Trek 26: Pico Humboldt (Peak: Pico Bolivar) 175
MERIDA DIRECTORY 177

THE ANDEAN ENVIRONMENT 178
MINIMAL IMPACT TREKKING 181
MOUNTAIN PHOTOGRAPHY 183
HEALTH AND SAFETY 185
SECURITY IN SOUTH AMERICA 187
Bibliography & Glossary 188
Index & Acknowledgements 189

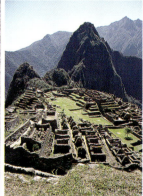

ABOUT THIS BOOK

Covering the Andes from south to north, this book is divided into six countries: Chile and Argentina, Bolivia, Peru, Ecuador and Venezuela.

The first opening chapter provides a brief introduction to all the Andean countries. The second opening chapter covers all the practicalities thereafter – the logistics of setting off on a trek and the possible extra requirements that may be involved in climbing peaks en route.

At the beginning of each country chapter, general information is provided about the history, geography and culture of the country, as well as details of hotels, transport, and so on in and around the country's capital or major arrival city for foreign visitors. Each Andean country is totally different, and the centre you fly into internationally is not always the main base from which you will start your trek/climb. Both trekking and climbing usually entails travelling to another city or town, often by very long bus rides or by internal flights that may require 4–5 hours flying time; this is particularly true of Chile and Argentina. Directories throughout each chapter provide specific listings information. Each country chapter also gives in-depth details of a number of treks, as well as selected climbs that may be accessed during the course of the trek.

The treks and peaks range in difficulty from easy walks to technical climbs, but the majority fall within the ability of any properly equipped and experienced party. Appendices on minimal impact trekking, mountain photography, health and safety, and recommended reading complete the book.

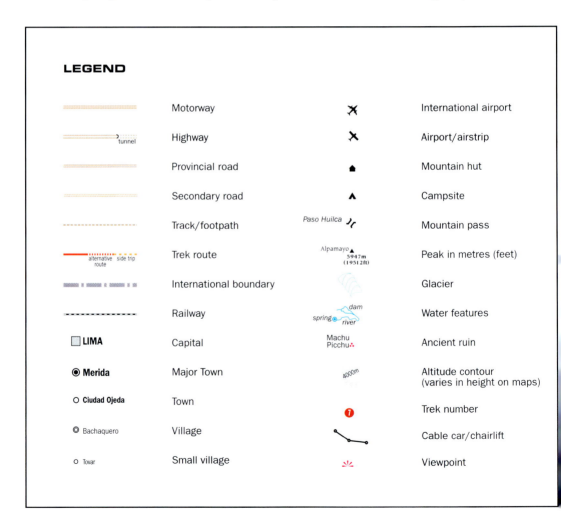

Trek Essentials boxes summarize each trek, including approximate number of days required, means of access to the start and finish, highest elevations reached, trekking style involved and official restrictions, if any. Also mentioned are notable variations on the route.

Top-class **mapping** pinpoints the route of each trek, with ridge lines, selected altitude contours, glaciers, passes and nearest roads included. Also illustrated in fainter dotted lines are alternative trails.

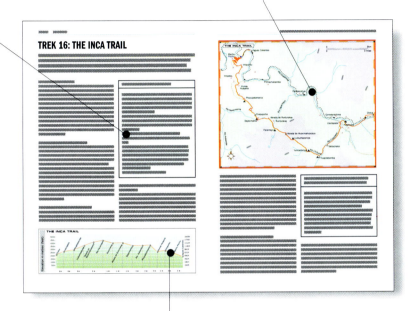

Strip maps illustrate the elevation profile of each trek, including key passes and village spot heights, as well as walking times. (NB Strip maps are illustrative and not designed for cross-reference between treks.)

Specially sourced **topo photographs** show the general approach route to each climbing peak, with the route clearly marked in red. A dotted line indicates where the route goes behind the mountain face shown.

Climb Essentials boxes summarize the characteristics of each climbing route, including summit height, principal camps and grade of climb.

1
INTRODUCTION TO
THE ANDES

The imagination of explorers and mountaineers, scientists, botanists and anthropologists alike have long been captured by the mountains of the Andes. Rearing their spectacular heads in no less than seven countries, these stunning peaks offer some of the wildest terrain on earth, as well as some of the most breathtakingly beautiful.

Moreover, they support an astounding variety of animal and bird life, as well as amazing flowers and plants, in fertile highland valleys that have been home to the native Indian population for centuries.

The colourful traditions and festivals of these people mean that a trip to the Andes will give you a fascinating glimpse into South American culture, as well as offering inspiring scenery, unusual treks and challenging mountaineering.

Las Torres del Paine from the mirador above the Base Camp, Patagonia (trek 1).

THE LAND

The Andes, at almost 7000km (4350 miles) from end to end, is the longest mountain chain in the world, stretching from Mérida in Venezuela to Cape Horn at the southern tip of Chile and Argentina. Although they occupy a relatively narrow strip (generally less than 350km/217 miles, except in Bolivia where this figure doubles), they form the longest uninterrupted high barrier in the world. However, the Andes are not a single high range but a series of ranges or cordilleras, separated by plateaux and elevated basins. Extensive glaciation has left many glacier-fed lakes, including Argentino (Argentina) and Llancahue (Chile) on the eastern flanks and many fjords and islands in the west.

From the south to latitude 27°S, this ribbon of peaks creates a single range with a mean elevation of 3960m (12992ft), including Aconcagua (6962m/22841ft), the highest peak in the western hemisphere. It then splits into three ranges, two of which continue north into Bolivia as the Cordilleras Occidental (western) and Oriental (eastern). Between them lies the Altiplano (a plateau), along with a string of high inter-montane chains. Lake Titikaka occupies the northernmost basin. Major peaks include Ollagüe (5875m/19275ft), Sajama (6520m/21391ft) and Illimani (6439m/21125ft). The Cordillera Occidental veers northwest as the Cordillera Real, at latitude 17°S, the point at which the Andes are widest.

In Peru, the Andes extend northwest to Ecuador (latitude 5°S) as a high plateau with a mean elevation that declines from 4750m (15585ft) to 3050m (10007ft). Above this rise mountains to heights exceeding 6400m (20998ft), including Huascarán at 6786m (22264ft). Tributaries of the Amazon have cut deep gorges into this surface.

In Ecuador, where the Andes narrow to less than 115km (71 miles), the Cordillera Occidental overlooks an inter-cordilleran depression divided into fifteen distinct basins. This double cordillera pattern continues into Colombia, where the Andes fan out into three major northeasterly ranges: the Occidental, the Central and the Oriental, separated by the Cauca and Magdalena river valleys. Major peaks include Cristóbal Colón (5775m/18948ft), Huila (5150m/16897ft) and Tolima (5215m/17110ft). The Cordillera Oriental forks north of Bogotá. One branch continues north as the Sierra de Perijá, to form the west edge of the Maracaibo basin. The other extends northeast to Barquisimeto, as the Cordillera de Mérida, which then continues east as the central highlands, a double row of lower ranges, towards the Sierra de Cumana and the Paria peninsula.

The Andes are second in height only to the Himalaya, with train routes over 5000-m (16405-ft) passes and jeep tracks to the highest ski resort in the world, Chacaltaya, in Bolivia, at 5100m (16733ft). The Andes boast the famous Lake Titikaka, the highest navigable lake in the world at 3800m (12468ft), rich pre-Hispanic ruins, (such as Tiwanaku in Bolivia and the Incan ruins of Machu Picchu in Peru), ancient trails in the countries that flank its spine, and the highest city in the world, El Alto, above La Paz in Bolivia. This all adds up to unlimited opportunities for challenging mountaineering and culturally interesting trekking.

Burros, beasts of burden, are used to transport heavy blocks of ice around the Peruvian city of Huaráz.

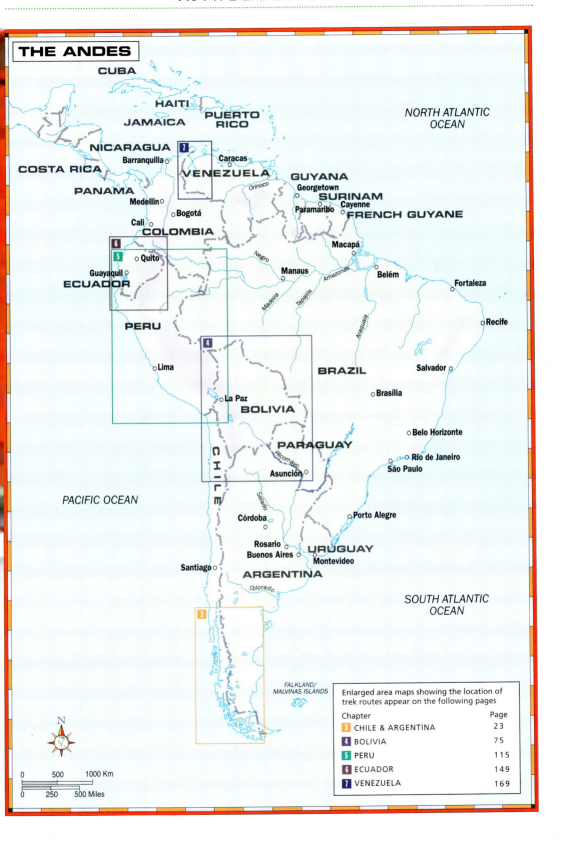

GEOLOGY, CLIMATE, AGRICULTURE AND INDUSTRY

The word Andes means 'metal' in Quechua, the language of the Andean people (who are themselves also known as Quechuas). It is a comparatively young mountain range and is still growing, hence the frequent earthquake activity. Its mountains, forty of which are over 6000m (19685ft), include both active and dormant volcanoes, such as Cotopaxi in Ecuador and Volcán Misti (Volcán Cerro) in Peru. The northern Andes run through Venezuela and Colombia; the central Andes occupy Ecuador, Peru and Bolivia; and the southern Andes are found in Argentina and Chile.

These mountains form a natural barrier that traps clouds from the Pacific Ocean and the Amazon basin. The abundant moisture supports an incredible variety of animal and bird life, along with the most amazing flowers. Annual precipitation exceeds 2540mm (100in) on the Pacific slopes of Colombia and southern Chile, but it drops below 250mm (10in) in the zone extending from southern Ecuador to central Chile, including the highlands of Bolivia. About two-thirds of the Andes lie within the tropics. More significant, however, is the vertical zonation of climates created by changes in elevation. The *tierra caliente* or hot land extending from sea level to 900m (2953ft) has a mean temperature of 26°C (78.8°F), abundant rainfall and tropical rainforest vegetation. The *tierra templada* (from 1800m/5906ft to 3000m/9843ft) has a mean temperature of 21°C (69.8°F) and subtropical forest vegetation. The *tierra fria* (from 3000m/9843ft to 4000m/13124ft) has a mean temperature of 15°C (59°F). Above the *fria* is the paramo (high plateau), extending to the snow line, which is humid, cloudy and too cold for trees, and is instead covered by bunch grass and tundra vegetation. The paramo exists only in Peru, Ecuador, Colombia and Venezuela. In Bolivia, land above 4000m (13124ft) is the high plateau, known as the Altiplano or the puna (high, cold and dry plateau).

Spanish invaders settled the inter-montane basins within the *tierra templada* and *fria*, which had long been occupied by the Indians, including the Incas in Peru and the Chibas in Colombia. About 65 per cent of Andean inhabitants reside in these basins. Subsistence agriculture based on corn, wheat, potatoes and grazing predominates in the *tierra fria*, while in the subtropical *tierra templada* sugar, rice and (especially in Colombia) coffee are grown. Industry, although of increasing importance, focuses primarily on supplying basic goods for local consumption. The heavily mineralized Andes, long mined for gold and silver, are now more valued for copper and tin, along with smaller amounts of lead, zinc and antimony. Colombia and Peru produce small amounts of coal for local use. Snow-capped peaks are an additional source of irrigation water and are scenic attractions for a growing tourist industry.

THE PEOPLE

Andean life is full of festivals and magical music. The people are Indian, Spanish and *mestizo* (mixed), and many retain their traditional clothing and lifestyles. This can be seen on visits to markets such as Zumbaghua in Ecuador, La Paz's Witches Market, the Peruvian markets at Pisac and Huaráz, and at the many festivals held in each country every year. At the Fiesta del Diablo in Bolivia every February, the food is often a resourceful mix of fish, potatoes and meat (guinea pig, beef, mutton, chicken) with vegetable side dishes. The most common alcoholic drink, *pisco*, is a grape brandy, usually sold as a colourless liquid. In Peru and Bolivia you will also find people drinking *maté de coca* (coca leaf tea), which is said to reduce the effects of altitude. In Argentina the locals drink *yerba maté* (the dried leaf of the *Ilex paragueyensis*).

Traditional clothing and working animals continue to be part of daily life for the Andean people who live off the land.

INTRODUCTION TO THE ANDES 13

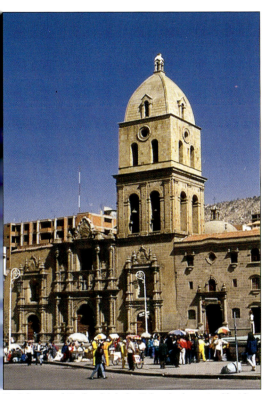

The influence of the Spanish in South America is most evident in the region's churches, like this one in Lima.

VILLAGE LIFE

The local people have developed various protective mechanisms to help them cope, first with their colonization by the Spanish and then with the exploitation of their natural resources by Spain, Britain, Germany and Portugal.

The Spaniards tried to impose Catholicism on the local people who, although seemingly converted, persisted in their use of ritual and their belief in Pachamama (Mother Earth). The fiestas of Colquecruz in the Auzungate area of Peru and Pascuâ (Easter) in Copacabana, Bolivia, are prime examples of this. In highland villages, the way of life is based on rituals relating to Pachamama, the seasons, and the sun, moon and stars.

Each village has its head man (*alcaldo* or *wayaro*) or council chief (*agente municipal*), who carries a ceremonial stick as a symbol of his power, holds office for one year and who must organize traditional fiestas at which he must pay for the musicians and food.

Most rural Indians live outside the money economy and day-to-day life is a case of mutual reciprocity or help. Harvesting, house building and any other major job is done with the help of neighbours, who receive help in return when it is needed. The final roofing of a house is a time for great celebration. A godparent will lay the last tiles or thatch and usually leave some small image in the roof, such as a pottery bull, which represents fertility and is believed to bring good luck.

A baptism, when the children are two years old, is another time of great communal celebration. Friends or family members are asked to be godparents and a fiesta is organized with *cuy* (guinea pig) as one of the principal dishes for the meal. The child's hair will not have been cut until baptism day, when a lock is cut by the new godparents and put in a locket, which is worn for good luck. The child is sprinkled with water – and often a few drops of beer or alcohol. After this, the meal is served to all guests and the singing and dancing begins.

When passing through villages, please remember to be polite and greet the locals with a smile. Most locals will treat you with traditional hospitality and may offer you food or accommodation. You should be sensitive to these offers and, if you accept, make sure you share your food in return. It is courteous to ask permission to camp, if you are near a village. At campsites, you will often be surrounded by curious children (and sometimes adults), who will want to know about your gear, clothing, food and so on. Be polite to the children but don't give out sweets. Be careful of locals who have had too much to drink. To put things into perspective for locals, it is useful to remember how much things cost in your own country. Explain this to them, to help dispel their belief that all Westerners are rich. If local people ask you to move on, please do so quietly, without any fuss, as there is usually a good reason. Remember that you are a guest in their country.

COLOMBIA

The Republic of Colombia, bordered by Ecuador and Peru on the south, and Brazil, Venezuela and Panama on the northwest, is the fourth largest country in Latin America. It has three Andean ranges that cross the country from southwest to northeast, however it has been excluded from this book due to the country's instability. Although agriculture, particularly coffee, continues to be Colombia's basic source of wealth, the illegal trade in drugs is believed to exceed legal exports and threatens the nation's stability. Due to the present political climate of Colombia, various areas of the Andes are held either by guerillas or the army and travel is forbidden within these areas. Sadly, it does not seem likely that this situation will change within the foreseeable future.

2

TREKKING AND CLIMBING IN
THE ANDES

The majestic mountain range that is the Andes offers superb mountain scenery with climbing and trekking options to suit all tastes and abilities. Easy snow climbs can be found on the volcanoes of Ecuador, while the more ambitious can head for the full-on technical climbs of the faces of the Cordillera Blanca and Cordillera Real.

On any trek in the Andes you will come across an amazing wealth of flora and fauna. The variety of climates throughout South America ensures that trekking and climbing will always be possible somewhere on the subcontinent throughout the year. The thing that really makes this region a fantastic place to trek, however, is the people. The diversity of cultures never fails to astound, and you will receive a warmth of welcome never to be forgotten.

Cordillera Raura from Punta Cuyoc, on the Cordillera Huayhuash trek (trek 17).

TREKKING IN THE ANDES

The Andes offer the chance to experience a variety of trekking styles, from fully organized trips with everything carried for you (generally by animals) to backpacking. There is no best way to trek and, whichever way you choose, you will be rewarded with a cultural experience, physical exercise and good mountain views. As in any country, you are often better off travelling with someone else, whether a local or a friend. You can share the responsibility of looking after gear whilst in camps and generally you will be at less risk of theft in those few areas where such crime is a problem. Also, in the case of an accident or illness (particularly at altitude), a travelling companion can be a great source of comfort and help, and can organize a rescue should you require it.

Trekking styles in the Andes tend to vary from country to country. In Chile and Argentina, you will find that the trips described in this book can generally only be done by backpacking. In Peru and Bolivia, many of the treks are at altitude and these would best be enjoyed with the help of burros (donkeys) and *arrieros* (donkey men) or llamas and *llameros* (llama men). Most treks in Venezuela can be easily backpacked and the same is generally true of Ecuador.

There are a few refuges in each country but you will need to have all your gear, including a tent and stove, with you. Also, there are few (if any) chances of resupplying whilst on these trips, so be prepared to take plenty of food and fuel with you. This is particularly true of Peru and Bolivia's high-level treks, such as the Cordillera Huayhuash and the Cordillera Real Traverse. Trekking in the Andes tends to be more remote than in other mountain ranges, such as the Himalaya or the Alps, and there are few villages where you can ask directions, particularly in Chile and Argentina.

Trekking and backpacking are increasingly common in the Andes and it is vital that people develop an awareness of their effect on the environment. Litter and insensitivity to local villagers and their way of life are two of the major problems. Rubbish is a problem on many of the more popular trails and you should try to clean up litter left by others as well as your own. Burn what is flammable and carry out the rest – such as tins and plastic. If employing local *arrieros*, tell them you will pay extra for them to help you clean up campsites along the way and carry the rubbish back to the trailhead. Regarding toilet procedure, defecate away from trails and water supplies. Dig a hole or cover your faeces with a rock, and burn toilet paper or carry it away, along with any sanitary protection, in a plastic bag.

Begging children are another problem. Although people often think they are being kind by giving, they are encouraging begging as a way of getting something for nothing and causing cultural erosion; it is better to use a smile and a greeting instead. Always try to treat the local people as you yourself would like to be treated, and you won't go far wrong.

Arrieros and Their Animals

Many hikers use burros or llamas to carry their camping gear and food, particularly when trekking at altitude or getting to Base Camps for climbs. Animals can only be hired with their owners. Throughout South America, the *arrieros* have organized themselves into associations with set prices (which vary depending on the terrain and altitude).

Ridge walking in Peru's Cordillera Huayhuash (trek 17).

You are also responsible for the *arrieros'* food and accommodation. It is worth drawing up a contract beforehand and it is common to pay an advance at the start of the trip. In some areas of Peru, you must also arrange to obtain a key for the *portada* (gateway) to the valleys. This varies in price and is best arranged in advance. Whenever you employ an *arriero*, try to get a recommendation first.

Guides and Porters

The cost of a guide depends on which country you are in and on whether you are climbing or trekking. In Peru, the UIAGM (*Union Internationale Association Guide de Montagne*) guides in Huaráz use a scale that relates to the peaks' climbing difficulty. Again, try to make sure you have a recommendation before embarking on a trek or climb with a guide.

In Peru, Ecuador and Bolivia, porters can be hired for peak climbs. Check that your porter has the correct equipment; generally, you provide the food and a tent (which can be hired) for them for the duration of the trip. When hiring local help of any kind, make it clear how many days you are paying for, and whether you are paying them for their return journey if you are finishing at a different village. It is best to write a *contracto*, signed by both parties, to ensure that there is no confusion.

Climbing

The grading of difficulty for peaks in the Andes is done in the European style: UIAA (*Union Internationale Association Alpinismo*); F (*facile*/easy); PD (*peu difficile*/slightly difficult); D (*difficile*/difficult); AD (*assez difficile*/quite difficult); TD (*très difficile*/very difficult); and ED (*extrèmement difficile*/extremely difficult). They relate to the normal ascent routes, in normal conditions. Split grades may be used when there is uncertainty, or where glacial changes are known to make a difference to the route.

There are, generally, no peak fees or trekking permits in the Andes (except for Aconcagua). This fact, along with stunning mountain scenery and excellent climbing, make the Andes a very attractive option for climbers and trekkers alike. However, the peaks should not be underestimated. Several have no easy way up. Most treks selected here take the standard (easiest) route and have Alpine grades of F, PD and AD. All of the snow-covered peaks require rope and crampons as well as a knowledge of glacial travel, the use of ice screws and snow stakes or pickets. You will find that most of the necessary climbing equipment can generally be hired in the main centres of each country (with the exception of certain areas of Chile and Argentina).

> ## MAPS
>
> These vary, both in quality and availability. Generally, the best maps are on sale at each country's Instituto Geográfico Militar (IGM), which is usually located in the capital city. The Austrian Alpenverein publishes maps of the Cordillera Blanca and the German Alpenverein offers maps covering the Cordillera Real. Many of the national parks in Chile and Argentina produce their own maps showing the trekking routes.
>
> IGM Offices:
> **Venezuela,** 1st floor, Av Este 6, Edificio Camejo south side, Caracas.
> **Ecuador,** On the hill off Av La Paz y Mino and Av Colombia, Quito.
> **Peru,** Av Aramburu 1190, San Isidro, Lima (it is best to take a taxi and ask it to wait).
> **Bolivia,** Edificio Murillo, Calle Murillo, La Paz (entrance in the alley off Calle Diagonal).
> **Chile,** Dicciocho 369, Santiago (Los Héros metro station).
> **Argentina,** Cabildo 301, Casilla 1426, Buenos Aires.

In Peru, you have the option of hiring fully qualified UIAGM guides. Elsewhere, you will find local guides who know the popular peaks. It is also possible to hire porters in Peru and Bolivia to help you with loads on the higher peaks, such as Huascarán, Chopicalqui and Illimani. In some cases, porters will have their own equipment for glacial travel; you should always check before departing for the climb.

Park Fees and Peak Fees
At present, there are no peak fees in Peru, Ecuador, Colombia, Bolivia or Argentina, with the exception of Aconcagua in Argentina. In Chile, there are fees for the Torres del Paine. There are, however, park fees in all the Andean countries except Bolivia.

BASIC TREKKING EQUIPMENT
Equipment is always a cause for concern and debate. Generally, it is best to use your own judgement and experience as a guide.

BOOTS. Generally, a well broken-in pair of leather boots or Goretex-lined trekking boots will suffice. Remember to keep them waxed and clean.
GAITERS. Essential if you are going on snow.
SLEEPING BAG. For Peru and Bolivia, and if you will be camping on the high peaks in Ecuador and Argentina, a good four-season bag is essential. However, for treks in Chile, Argentina and Venezuela, a three-season bag is fine.

SLEEPING SHEET LINER. A liner is much easier to wash than a sleeping bag. It should be made of cotton or silk.

SLEEPING MAT. Closed cell foam mats are adequate; Thermarest mats are a luxury.

RUCKSACK. For lowland trekking, a capacity of 40 litres should be sufficient. For mountaineering or high-level treks (where you are planning to carry your own food and tent for extended periods), take a 60-litre rucksack. A padded hip belt and padded shoulder straps improve comfort. Make sure that your rucksack fits you properly by checking the back length and ensuring that you can make the necessary adjustments.

STOVE. There are numerous different stoves on offer. An MSR multifuel XGK is one of the best: it works well at altitude and is relatively lightweight. Fuel in South America varies in quality and it is worth taking a filter (coffee filter paper is excellent) in order to filter the fuel before you fill your stove.

CLOTHING. It is best to be prepared for a variety of weather conditions when trekking in the Andes – it is possible to experience all four seasons in one day. You should bring trousers, shorts, socks, fleece jacket, thermal tops and bottoms, and waterproofs (Goretex jacket and trousers are best). A down jacket is useful for high-level treks and climbing.

SUNDRY ITEMS. Sunglasses are important, as the UV radiation is very high in Peru, Bolivia and Ecuador, particularly at altitude. Other useful items include: a head torch and spare batteries; a repair kit; stuff sacks; a sewing kit; a water bottle (minimum 1 litre); a penknife or Leatherman; and a camera and lots of film! An altimeter, although not essential, is interesting for monitoring daily ascent and descent.

It is possible to hire equipment in Huaráz and Cuzco (Peru), La Paz (Bolivia), Quito (Ecuador) and Puerto Natales (Chile). Most major capital cities have little on offer – it is better to hire equipment in the town where you are basing your trip.

Insurance

It is essential to have travel insurance and, if you are travelling alone, it is wise to register with your embassy before departing on treks. Make sure you leave details of your insurance with someone reliable such as La Casa De Guias (the guides school) in Huaráz, Peru. Before going into remote areas, try to locate the nearest telephone or radio transmitters.

RESCUES

Please remember that there is little chance of a helicopter rescue in any of the Andean countries. Basically, you should be prepared to organize your own rescue. This is another advantage of using local people and their animals, particularly on the high-altitude treks and climbs described in this book. Most locals in Peru or Bolivia, for example, are willing to help evacuate someone who has acute mountain sickness using a horse – but you must be prepared to pay for their services.

SAFETY AND SECURITY

It is important to consider safety and security while travelling in South America. On the whole, this is a case of using your common sense and not attracting unnecessary attention to yourself. Due to the disparity in wealth between foreign tourists and locals, petty theft is not uncommon. There has also been an increase of more serious crime over the past few years in various countries, although levels are still lower than those in many cities of Europe and the USA. Travellers should be aware of problem areas and avoid dangerous situations. If you show consideration and behave sensibly you will generally find you are treated likewise.

FOOD AND WATER

The countries of South America offer an extremely wide variety of cuisines, which add a great deal to the traveller's experience. However, hygiene is not always up to scratch so, to avoid major health hassles, try and keep the following precautions in mind.

Drink only bottled or boiled (cooled and iodized) water, and do not use ice cubes unless you are absolutely sure they have been made from clean water. Avoid fruit or vegetables that you canno

---

CLIMBING EQUIPMENT

Plastic boots	Prussik cord
Fleece mitts	Stove
Over-mitts	Fuel
Thin gloves	Lighter
Ski goggles	Ice axe and hammer
Sunglasses	Rope
Hat	Ice screws
Balaclava	Snow stakes
Over-trousers and jacket	Short slings
Fleece trousers	Pegs
Fleece top	Map
Harness	Compass
Crampons	Descender
Karabiners (three screw gates, three snap)	Down jacket
	Gaiters

PERSONAL FIRST-AID KIT

Antiseptic cream	Rehydration salts
Suncream	Glucose tablets
Throat lozenges	Iodine tincture or tablets
Diacalm	Zinc oxide tape
Antibiotics, such as Ciprofloxacin and Flagyl	Safety pins
	Butterfly sutures
Mild analgesics such as aspirin or paracetamol	Cotton wool swabs
	Melolin dressings
Strong analgesics such as Co-proxamol or codeine	Thermometer
	Scissors
Anti-inflammatories	Diamox
Eye drops	Tweezers
Plasters and bandages	

Huayhuash friends (trek 17).

peel or which have not been cooked, and do not eat undercooked meat.

Every country has its traditional dishes, and these are worth trying. Being a vegetarian can be a problem in some of the smaller towns, but generally you'll find the locals very accommodating and keen to help produce some food that you can eat.

The local brews in South America vary from some of the finest wines in the world to hooch such as *aguarte*, a local fire water (brewed from potatoes) that is similar to the Irish *pocheen* – and just as lethal. Beer is generally very good although it tastes more like lager. *Chicha*, a local beer fermented from maize, tastes excellent, but make sure boiled water was used for the brew. *Pisco*, a grape brandy, is particularly popular – and it's well worth trying *pisco sour* (see p.118).

Travelling in Chile and Argentina, however, is as easy as travelling in Europe and food and water are not usually problematic issues.

LANGUAGE

Spanish, or rather Castillian, is spoken throughout the Andes and very little English is understood, especially in out-of-the-way places. Learning some Spanish before you go will greatly increase your enjoyment of the countries. Carrying a phrase book, along with a willingness to attempt a conversation with those you meet, will leave you with some great memories and is often great fun. Being able to count, say 'please' and 'thank you', order meals and drinks, and ask for basic directions will make a big difference to the way the locals treat you. The hill people will usually take the time to speak more slowly, than people in the cities. In Bolivia the main language of the hill people, however, is Aymara.

SPANISH WORDS AND PHRASES

¡Hola!	Hello
¡Buenos días!	Hello/good morning
¡Buenas tardes!	Good afternoon/evening
Por favor	Please
Gracias	Thank you
Con mucho gusto	It's a pleasure
¿Cómo estás?	How are you? (familiar)
¿Cómo está?	How are you? (formal)
Sí	Yes
No	No
¿Dónde?	Where?
¿Cuándo?	When?
¿Cómo?	How?
¿De dónde?	Where from?
A la derecha	To the right
A la izquierda	To the left
¿Dónde está el baño?	Where is the bathroom?
Despacio	Slowly
Mi nombre es...	My name is...
Tengo hambre	I'm hungry
Quisiéra...	I would like...
¿Cuánto?	How much is this?
Muy caro	Too expensive
¿Cuánto cuesta para un burro (arriero cada) dia?	How much for a donkey (donkey man) per day?
Hoy	Today
Mañana	Tomorrow
Ayer	Yesterday
De la mañana	In the morning
De la tarde	In the afternoon
De la noche	At night
Pasado mañana	The day after tomorrow
Para dos semanas	For two weeks

3
CHILE AND ARGENTINA

Patagonia is the name given to the southernmost part of South America, a geographical area spanning both Chile and Argentina. It roughly describes an area of some one million sq. km (0.6 million sq. miles) south of latitude 37°S, which can be subdivided into three regions: **Southern Patagonia, Central Patagonia and the Lake District or Araucanía.**

Linking them all, of course, are the Andes, which stretch for about 2000km (1243 miles), from the volcanoes of the Araucanía in the north to the granite towers of Torres del Paine and Fitz Roy in the south, finally tapering off into the sea at Tierra del Fuego. In Patagonia, the mountains reach a mere average height of some 2000m (6562ft) but, rising as they do from an otherwise flat steppe, they dominate the landscape with their towers, turrets and crenellated ramparts.

Crossing a patch of snow on the Nahuel Huapi Traverse (trek 4).

Southern Patagonia

Southern Patagonia lies at the end of the inhabited world (except for some hardy scientific observers marooned on the ice of Antarctica) and it feels like it. The last time the wind touched earth was on its previous visit to Patagonia, and, what's more, it seems to have speeded up since then.

This is a land of wide open pampas, clouds scudding across blue, freshly washed skies and violent rainbows, where I have seen the wind whirl up the watery equivalent of dust devils from the lake and fling them crashing against a cliff. Needless to say, the ferry did not run that day.

It is also a land almost totally covered by icecaps (the Hielo Norte and the Hielo Sur) and the most extensive area of continuous ice outside the polar regions. The glaciers glide down to the lakes, calve with a roar, a crash and waves enough to swamp any small craft in their path. Icebergs gleam white against the deep green of a glacial lake. Breathtaking!

Patagonia is also a place of pink granite towers, rising up from the pampas, unmistakable in their grandeur, along with deep azure lakes, forests, open meadows, echoing streams. But, above all, there is a sense of untamed wilderness, where you can come and trek, but which you should never take for granted.

Although time has stood still here and the *gauchos* (cowboys) still roam the grasslands, the weather never stops. There can be four seasons in one day, or maybe double that. Make sure your gear is really waterproof and that your tent can withstand a Patagonian wind or dust storm. I have a theory that all tents should be tested down here. If they are still standing after a Patagonian maelstrom, they will stand up to the elements anywhere.

Central Patagonia

Central Patagonia comprises the area south of Puerto Montt on the Chilean side and the western strip of Chubut Province in Argentina. It is the least populated, wildest and, indeed, the wettest of any of the zones, a land of impenetrable temperate rainforests and volcanic activity (the Antarctic, Nazca and South American plates collide at the Peninsula de Taitao here on the west coast of Chile).

Until the 1980s, when the Carretera Austral was finally constructed, the only access to the Chilean part was by boat or long overland routes from Ruta 40 in Argentina. It is still a relatively difficult area to reach, as public transport is somewhat infrequent.

Lake District or Araucanía

The Lake District or Araucanía, home of the Araucarian Indians or Mapuche (and of the monkey puzzle tree), form Northern Patagonia. The Mapuche are one of the few surviving indigenous peoples of Chile and their territory was not incorporated until 1881. The western edge of the Araucanía is dominated by a line of perfectly shaped, conical, snow-capped volcanoes – roughly one every 30km (19 miles). Some are still active.

The southern part of Araucanía includes the stupendously beautiful *Región de los Lagos*, the Lake District, where the lakes form an almost continuous waterway across both countries. It is an area of deep blue lakes, dense lenga forest, thermal springs, alpine grasses, waterfalls and, in Argentina, ski resorts. There is also an abundance of alpine and sub-alpine wild flowers, which are often hidden away in nooks and crannies to escape the elements. The Andes of this region reach greater heights in the Argentinian section than in that of Chile. The two highest peaks, however, Volcáns Lanín and Tronador (both extinct) straddle the border.

Within this area is the Parque Nacional Nahuel Huapi, the first of Argentina's national parks. The park comprises what can justifiably be termed some of the most spectacular mountain, lake and glacier scenery of the Andes, all of which is dominated by the great white bulk of Monte Tronador, the Thunderer (3554m/11660ft).

One of the many granite spires around Laguna Tonchek (trek 4).

ARRIVING IN CHILE
Land and People

Chile, 4300km (2672 miles) long and never more than 200km (124 miles) wide, is wedged between the Andes and the Pacific Ocean and comprises an amazing number of climatic zones, altitudes and varieties of people. It stretches from latitude 56°S (the icy fjords and glaciers of Southern Patagonia), through the temperate Lake District, to the Mediterranean wine-growing central valley of Santiago de Chile, north to the arid Atacama Desert and the Altiplano, bordering Bolivia at latitude 18°S.

A third of Chile's 15-million population live in or around Santiago. The majority of the population is *mestizo* (mixed Hispanic and indigenous), but there are some 1.5 million Mapuche living around Temuco in the Araucanía and 15,000 Aymara people on the Bolivian border. Before the Spanish conquest in 1541, under Pedro de Valdivia, Chile was inhabited by around 15 different Indian peoples, most of whom were wiped out by warfare or disease. Land was given to Spanish settlers under the *encomienda* system, which allocated to the owner rights to the Indians who lived there. There were few women amongst the early Spanish settlers, so the men took Indian wives, with the resultant children becoming known as *mestizos*.

Politics

It was the native-born Hispanics – the *criollos* – and the *mestizos* who rose up against the Spaniards and demanded independence. Simón Bolívar started an uprising in Venezuela and moved on to Peru. An army under José de San Martín marched over the Andes from Argentina and liberated Santiago in 1817. San Martín left his second in command, Bernardo O'Higgins, behind to found the new nation of Chile. Formal independence was declared in 1821 and the main street of Santiago was renamed the Avenida del Libertador Bernardo O'Higgins.

In 1879, Chile waged the War of the Pacific (1879–1883) against Peru and Bolivia, on the pretext of a tax dispute. Chile gained the Taracna region from Peru and, more importantly, the nitrate-rich Atacama Desert from Bolivia. With control of the world's nitrate reserves, Chile's economy boomed, but the expansion of mining created a new working class, and the divide between the landed oligarchy and the ordinary population widened. The opening of the Panama Canal in 1914, coupled with the development of synthetic fertilizers to replace saltpetre, led to a downturn in the economy, which emphasized these differences.

However, copper had been discovered in the Atacama Desert and this became the foundation for Chile's economy, although the mines were under the control of North American mining companies. As the economy expanded again, conditions for the urban workers improved, but the rural workers were still tied to the *hacienda* (farm) owners, who had not improved conditions for decades. The demands for land reform, which had been present for some time, grew.

The 1950s and 1960s saw a variety of presidents all attempting some form of agrarian reform and curtailment of the power of the landed elite, but all failed. The workers became increasingly militant; there were strikes and land seizures by the Mapuche Indians. In 1970, Chile became the first state to freely elect a Marxist president, Salvador Allende. Allende nationalized the copper, banking, rail and telephone industries, and increased public spending in an attempt to boost the economy. Industrialists refused to be nationalized, however, and peasants, who were opposed to the collectivization of land, seized it. The US government, afraid of losing its stake in the copper industry, played a pivotal role in undermining the communist government – capital fled abroad and the economy collapsed.

On 11 September 1973, the military, under General Augusto Pinochet Ugarte overthrew the elected government. Allende died in the coup and Pinochet proclaimed himself president. There followed brutal repression of all leftists or suspected leftists, arrest, torture and even execution without trial. Many thousands of Chileans went into exile during Pinochet's time in power. Today people still grieve for the *desaparecidos*, those who disappeared without trace.

Chile was the first country in which a military dictator voluntarily returned power to the electorate. In 1988, Pinochet accepted a plebiscite decision to reestablish a 'workable democracy' in Chile and stepped down. He remained as commander-in-chief of the armed forces until 1998, when he became a life senator, which should have guaranteed him immunity for life. However, this immunity was stripped from Pinochet on his return to Chile in 2000, after he had spent 18 months under house arrest in England awaiting extradition to Spain to be charged with crimes against humanity. However, at the time of writing, the case against Pinochet had been suspended on the grounds that he was mentally unfit for trial.

Since the return to democracy, Chile has prospered. Copper, gold, fruit, flowers, farmed salmon and wine are all exported and tourism has grown.

TRAVELLING TO CHILE

By Air
Most foreign visitors arrive by plane at the new Aeropuerto Internacional Arturo Merino Benítez in Pudahuel, Santiago de Chile. British Airways is the only airline to fly direct from the UK to Chile. LanChile and Iberia fly here via Madrid; KLM and Lufthansa also fly via Madrid from Amsterdam and Frankfurt respectively; Varig flies via São Paolo; and Aerolíneas Argentinas flies via Madrid and Buenos Aires.

From the USA, LanChile and American Airlines fly direct from New York, Los Angeles and Miami. Aeropéru and LanChile fly in daily from Lima; Lloyd Aéreo Boliviano and LanChile come in from La Paz. Both LanChile and Ladeco offer special multiple internal flight passes, which can only be bought outside Chile.

By Road
The main road entry points into Chile are from Peru, Bolivia and, of course, Argentina.

From Peru
The only crossing is from Tacna to Arica.

From Bolivia
La Paz – Tambo Quemado – Arica (506km/314 miles/18 hrs)
La Paz – Uyuni – Ollagüe – Calama (80km/360 miles/26 hrs from La Paz to Uyuni)
Uyuni – Portezuela del Cajón – San Pedro de Atacama (18 hours on an organized tour)

From Argentina
Mendoza – Los Libertadores – Santiago (6–7 hours)
San Martín de los Andes – Paso de Mamuil Malal (Paso Tromen) – Currarehue – Pucón – Temuco (8 hours)
San Carlos de Bariloche – Paso Puyehué (Los Pajaritos) – Osorno (7 hours)
San Carlos de Bariloche – bus to Puerto Pañuelo – boat to Puerto Blest – bus to Puerto Alegre – boat to Puerto Frías – bus to Peulla – boat to Petrohué – bus to Puerto Montt (8 hours)
El Calafate – Paso Cancha de Carreras – Puerto Natales (6–8 hours)
El Calafate – Río Turbio – Puerto Natales (6 hours)

INTERNATIONAL AIRLINES IN SANTIAGO DE CHILE

Aeroflot, Guardia Vieja 255, of. 1008, tel: (562) 331 0244, fax: (562) 331 0248
Aerolíneas Argentinas, Moneda 756, tel: (562) 639 3922, fax: (562) 639 7923
Aeromexico, Zurich 221, of. 11, tel: (562) 234 4700, fax: (562) 234 4700
Aeropéru, Fidel Oteiza 1953, 5th floor, Providencia, tel: (562) 274 2023, fax: (562) 274 6505
Air France, Alcántara 44, piso 6, tel: (562) 290 9300, fax: (562) 290 9310
Alitalia, Alameda 949, of. 1001, tel: (562) 698 3366, fax: (562) 687 3950
British Airways, Isidora Goyenechea 2934, of. 302, tel: (562) 232 9560, fax: (562) 232 7858
American Airlines, Huérfanos 1199, tel: (562) 679 0000, fax: (562) 672 3214
Avianca, Santa Magdalena 116, tel: (562) 231 6646, fax: (562) 231 8306
Canadian Airlines, Ebro 2740, of. 302, Las Condes, tel: (562) 232 7111, fax: (562) 231 1811
Cubana de Aviación, Aeropuerto floor 3, of. 2, tel: (562) 274 1819, fax: (562) 274 8207
Ecuatoriana, Moneda 1170, tel: (562) 671 2334, fax: (562) 671 1421
Iberia, Bandera 206, piso 8, tel: (562) 671 4510, fax: (562) 696 9479
KLM, San Sebastián 2839, of. 202, tel: (562) 233 0991, fax: (562) 233 0483
LAB, Moneda 1170, tel: (562) 671 2334, fax: (562) 671 1421
Lufthansa, Moneda 970, 16th floor, tel: (562) 630 1655, fax: (562) 630 1636
South African Airways, Santa Magdalena 75, of. 411, Providencia, tel: (562) 335 3272, fax: (562) 335 2718
Swissair, Barros Errázuriz 1954, of. 1104, tel: (562) 244 2888, fax: (562) 244 2890
Varig, Miraflores 156, tel: (562) 693 0940, fax: (562) 693 0928
United Airlines, El Bosque Norte 0177, of. 19, tel: (562) 337 0000, fax: (562) 690 1177

DOMESTIC AIRLINES IN SANTIAGO DE CHILE

Ladeco, Av B. O'Higgins 107, tel: (562) 661 3000, fax: (562) 661 3000 or Huérfanos 1157, tel: (562) 633 8343
LanChile, Américo Vespucio 901, tel: (562) 565 2525, fax: (562) 565 2595, www.lanchile.cl; or Estado 10, 20th floor, tel: (562) 687 2323/2333; or Agustinas 640, tel: (562) 632 3442; or Pedro de Valdivia Norte 0139, Providencia, tel: (562) 232 3448
Transportes Aéreos Isla Robinson Crusoe, Av Pajaritos 3030, tel: (562) 531 4343, fax: (562) 531 3772
Alta, Las Urbinas 030, Providencia, tel: (562) 244 1777, fax: (562) 144 1780
DAP, Luis Thayer Ojeda 1304, Providencia, tel: (562) 334 9658, fax: (562) 334 5843

Visas

Most travellers to Chile (excluding New Zealanders and those from Luxembourg, India, Russia and Poland) do not need a visa. US citizens must pay an entry fee, which is valid for the life of their passport.

On arrival, you will be given a tourist card that is required to exit the country. A 90-day visa is stamped in your passport, which can be extended (for a considerable sum) for a further 90 days at the Departamento de Extranjera, Moneda 1342 in Santiago or in other cities.

It is advisable to carry your passport with you at all times, as the police may ask to see it and you must show it when cashing travellers' cheques or when checking in to a hotel. It is a good idea to keep a photocopy in a safe place back at your hotel.

EMBASSIES

Argentina, Miraflores 285, tel: (562) 639 8617/638 0890, fax: (562) 639 3321

Australia, Gertrudis Echenique 420, Las Condes, tel: (562) 228 5666, fax: (562) 208 1707, http://hq.satlink.com/ausemba/immba.htm

Bolivia, Av Santa Maria 2796, tel: (562) 232 8180, fax: (562) 232 9839, email: cprobolchi@manquehue.net, www.microweb.cl/bolivia/

Brazil, MacIver 225, Piso 15, edificio Banco Exterior, Castilla 1110, tel: (562) 639 8867, fax: (562) 633 6848, email: cobrachi@ctc-mundo.net, www.cobrachi.co.cl

Canada, Nueva Tajamar 481, tel: (562) 362 9660, fax: (562) 362 9663, email: stago@dfait-maeci.gc.ca

France, Carmencita 79, Las Condes, tel: (562) 232 8888/5020/5021, fax: (562) 231 5021, email: ambassade@ambafrance-cl.org, www.france.cl

Germany, Agustinas 785, 7th floor, Stock tel: (562) 463 2500, fax: (562) 463 2525, email: embalem1central@entelchile.net, www.embajadadealemania.cl

Italy, Calle Clemente Fabres 1050, tel: (562) 225 9029/9212/9439, fax: (562) 223 2467, email: italcom@entelchile.net

Netherlands, Las Violetas 2368, Providencia tel: (562) 223 6825, fax: (562) 225 273, email: Nlgov@holanda-paisesbajos.cl, www.holanda-paisesbajos.cl

New Zealand, El Golf 99, Oficina 703, Las Condes tel: (562) 290 9802, fax: (562) 207 2333, email: nzembsgo@ctcreuna.cl

Peru, Andrés Bello 1751, tel: (562) 232 6275

Spain, Av Providencia 1979, tel: (562) 204 0239

UK, Av El Bosque Norte 0125, 3rd floor, Las Condes, tel: (562) 370 3100, fax: (562) 370 4170, www.britemb.cl

USA, Andrés Bello 2800, Las Condes, tel: (562) 232 2600, fax: (562) 330 3710, www.usembassy.cl

---

Customs/Immigration

Duty-free allowances are 400 cigarettes, 50 cigars or 500 grams of tobacco and 2.5 litres of alcohol. Remember that, if you are entering the country from Bolivia or Peru, you will be searched for drugs. Wherever you are coming from, it is illegal to bring in any fresh fruit, vegetables, dairy produce or meat.

At certain crossing points Chilean customs officials put luggage through an X-ray machine, so keep all film in your hand luggage.

There are no restrictions on the import or export of local and foreign currency.

Money

The peso (Ch$) is the unit of currency in Chile. In Chile, and throughout South America, the US$ is more useful than £ sterling. In the small towns you can often change US$ at hotels or shops.

TRANSPORT
In Santiago

The streets of Santiago are lined with yellow buses, although these buses can be very unpleasant, particularly in the winter months when Santiago is enveloped in a dense smog. A cleaner way to travel is by the spotless and very efficient metro. There are now three lines, one running under the Alameda (main street) east to west and two running north to south. Both the buses and the metro are very cheap.

There are also, of course, hundreds of taxis, which are metered, and *collectivos*, taxis with a set route that pick up passengers along the way.

Countrywide
By Air

Since distances in Chile are so vast, the easiest way to travel is by air. LanChile and Ladeco are the main domestic airlines connecting all the major cities. In addition, the smaller airlines, DAP and Alta, serve the smaller communities in Patagonia. Airport tax is payable on international departures and domestic flights.

By Bus

There is a very efficient, frequent and comprehensive system of buses in Chile, linking all the major towns. The buses are fast, comfortable, punctual and very good value. The pullmans have reclining seats or, on those with *salón cama,* the seats go almost flat. Most serve meals and show videos.

The roads in Chile are mainly paved, with the exception of the Carretera Austral south of Puerto Montt. In rural areas, the buses that serve the local population are less frequent and more crowded.

TREKKING AGENCIES IN SANTIAGO DE CHILE

Alpi Exploraciones, Mercedes Marin 7103, Las Condes, tel/fax: (562) 229 3874. Good for mountaineering.
Altue Exploraciones, Encomenderos 83, Las Condes, tel: (562) 232 1103, fax: (562) 233 6799. Good for hiking, rafting and sea kayaking.
Andesescape, Santa Beatriz 84A, Providencia, tel/fax: (562) 235 5225. Runs the refuges in Torres del Paine.
Azimut 360, Arzobispo Casanova 3, Bellavista, tel: (562) 735 8034. For hiking, rafting and horse-riding.
Cascada Expediciones, Orrego Luca 054, Providencia, tel: (562) 234 2274, fax: (562) 233 9768, email: cascada@ibm.net. Rafting, riding, climbing, kayaking.
Chile Eco-Adventure, tel: (562) 234 3439/236 1325, email: www.chilnet.cl. Mountain services.
Mountain Service, Paseo las Palmas 2209, tel: (562) 234 3439, fax: (562) 234 3438. Mountaineering and climbing.
Pared Sur, Juan Estaban Montero 5497, Las Condes, tel: (562) 207 3525, fax: (562) 207 3159. Hiking, riding, rafting, mountain-biking.

There are four bus terminals in Santiago. Buses to the south go from the Terminal de Buses Santiago (also known as the Terminal de Buses Sur), Alameda 3800; buses to Mendoza go from the Terminal los Héroes, Tucapel Jiminez and the Terminal de Buses Santiago; buses to the north depart from the Terminal San Borja, Alameda 3250 (Metro Estación Central); and all pullmans and the Turbus service go from the Terminal de Buses Alameda, O'Higgins 3712.

By Train
The train service to the south only goes as far as Temuco, but the views are superb and the train dates from 1926. Note, however, that the journey can be subject to unforeseen delays.

ACCOMMODATION
As in any capital city, there is a huge number of *hostales, residenciales* and hotels from which to choose in Santiago. Here is a selection:
Youth Hostel, Cienfugos 151, tel: (562) 671 8532, fax: (562) 672 8880, email: histgoch@entelchile.net.
Hostal Rio Amazonas, Rosas 2234, tel: (562) 698 4092, fax: (562) 671 9013, email: amazona@entelchile.net, www.altiro.com/amazonas.
Nuevo Hotel Valparaiso, San Pablo 1182, tel: (562) 671 5698. Recommended, but a bit insecure.
Residencial Londres, Londres 54, tel/fax: (562) 638 2215. Highly recommended.
Hotel Paris, Calle Paris 813, tel: (562) 639 4037. Clean and comfortable.
Residencial del Norte, Catedral 2207, tel: (562) 695 1876. Mid-range.
Hacienda del Sol y Luna, Cuara Hijuela 9978, tel: (562) 601 9254, fax: (562) 601 9663. Near the airport in Pudahuel, handy for transit passengers, provides free airport transfers.
Hotel Principado, Arturo Buhle 015, tel: (562) 222 8142, fax: (562) 222 6065.

FOOD AND DRINK
Food
With such a long coastline, it is no surprise that seafood is Chile's speciality. Try *sopa/cazuela de mariscos* (shellfish stew), *erizo* (sea urchin), *ceviche* (a marinade of raw fish), *chupe de locos* (abalone stew) or even *chupe de congrio* (conger eel stew), not forgetting *curanto* (a mixed stew of shellfish, fish, pork, lamb, beef and potato).

Meat tends to be *parillada* (grilled) and comes in enormous portions. *Lomo al pobre* is a favourite – basically, steak and chips, with two fried eggs. In Chilean Patagonia the main dish, apart from seafood, is the *asado* of lamb, usually six lamb chops on a plate! Santiago is full of fast-food outlets.

Empenadas (a type of pasty) *de pino* (beef) or *de queso* (cheese) and *humitas* (mashed corn wrapped in corn husks) are typical snacks.

Until recently, there was a distinct shortage of vegetables as the growing season was too short, but the introduction of polytunnels has revolutionized the restaurants. Nevertheless, Chile is quite a difficult country in which to be a vegetarian, although there are several veggie restaurants now in Santiago.

If you are going backpacking, the supermarket in the nearest town to the start of the trek is the best place to buy provisions.

In Santiago absolutely everyone eats ice cream, and it is available in any flavour you could imagine – try *chirimoia* (custard apple).

Drink
Chile is, of course, famous for its wine. Indeed, one vineyard keeper sadly claimed that Santiago was built on the best vineyard in South America. Most of the vines were brought over from France before the French vineyards were decimated by blight, so they are the original wine stock.

Pisco is a spirit made from distilled grapes. *Pisco sour* is a traditional welcome drink made of *pisco*, lemon and egg white. There is a variety of light beers, which can also be bought German-style as draft beer, or s*chopp.*

COMMUNICATIONS
Chile's country code is 56 and the code for Santiago is 2. ENTEL is Chile's official telephone network. It provides free internet access at Morande 315, and is open Mon–Fri, 9am–6pm. There are many internet cafes.

The main *correos* (post office) is on the Plaza de Armas, Agustinas 1137 – open: Mon–Fri, 9am–6pm, Sat, 9am–noon. There is a nominal charge for all poste restante items.

LANGUAGE
In order to get by in Chile, you need to be able to speak some Spanish or Castillian (*Castellano*). The only people who tend to speak any English are those in the tourist business. Chilean Castillian is spoken very fast and consonants are often swallowed. Chileans also drop most of the 's' sounds, so 'Buenos dias' becomes 'buen dia' and 'que quieres?' is spoken as 'que quiere?' They are fond of adding 'cito' to the ends of words to turn them into diminutives: 'un café' becomes 'un cafécito', a small coffee. The Mapuche are struggling to hold onto their language and on the Bolivian border the local people speak Aymara.

SECURITY
Chile is a safe country. There is very little street crime, and people are incredibly friendly and helpful. However, pickpockets do operate on the streets of Santiago, especially around the Plaza de Armas and the Alameda, and any other crowded areas.

The toll-free number for the police (*carabineros*) is 133 throughout the country.

USEFUL ADDRESSES

Tourist Agency Municipal, Casa Colorada, Merced 860 - open: Mon-Fri, 10am-6pm.
Sernatur, Av Providencia 1550, (metro Manuel Montt/ Pedro de Valdivia).
BOOKSHOPS
Feria Chilena del Libro, Huerfanos 623.
Libreria Universitaria in the Universida de Chile, Alameda.
MAPS
Maps IGM, Dieciocho 369, south of the Alameda - open: Jan-Feb, Mon-Fri, 8am-2pm; March-Dec, 9am-6pm.
You can photocopy part of a map at the *mapoteca* of the National Library, Alameda (Santa Lucia metro station).

ARRIVING IN ARGENTINA
Land and People
Argentina has a land area of some 2.8 million km^2 (1.7 million sq miles) which can be divided into roughly five geographic areas: the Cuyo and the Andean northwest, where Aconcagua is situated; Mesopotamia and the northeast, a subtropical forested lowland area; the Chaco, the arid western area bordering on Bolivia; the Pampas, the agricultural heartland around Buenos Aires; and Patagonia and the Lake District.

The population of Argentina is 36.3 million, and is essentially a nation of immigrants as the indigenous population was practically wiped out in the Indian Wars of the 1880s. The immigrants came in waves: first the Spanish, then (from the mid-nineteenth century onwards) Italians, Basques, Welsh, English, Ukrainians, Germans, Swiss, Croatians, Bulgarians and Yugoslavs. Later, people arrived from the Middle and Far East. Today, there are around 200,000 Mapuche in the Lake District and some Quechua people on the border with Bolivia.

Politics
The Spaniards were not terribly interested in Argentina. Since the country had no silver or gold reserves, they viewed it as an area for the production of food for the miners of Potosí, and it was ruled from Lima in Peru. However, the horses and cattle they left behind flourished, and the cattle ranch became the cornerstone of the growth of Buenos Aires.

Although prohibited from trading directly with Europe, the city managed to do so clandestinely, and so successfully that by the time of the Napoleonic wars, the *criollos* (native-born Hispanics) of Buenos Aires declared their independence. There ensued a power struggle between the Federalists of the interior (mainly the big landowners, supported by rural peasants), who advocated rural autonomy, and the Unitarists of Buenos Aires, who upheld central authority and looked to Europe for ideas, immigrants and capital. Although Juan Manuel de Rosas, leader of the ranchers, came to power in 1829, he helped to centralize power in Buenos Aires. More importantly, he introduced the *mazorca,* the political police, and the notion of rule by terror. His overthrow in 1852 signified the triumph of Unitarism and its concomitant openness to foreign capital.

Sheep replaced cattle on the big *estancias* (ranches), supplying wool to the mills of the UK and encouraging the immigration of Basque and Irish refugees. The Indian Wars of the 1880s cleared the Mapuche and Telhuelche Indians from the land and opened the way for settlers from Switzerland,

Bad weather in the remote Puerto Frías, on the Trans-Andean Trek (trek 5).

Germany, Italy and France. By 1890, British capital dominated the Argentinian economy. Argentina itself became one of the world's most prosperous countries, although the wealth created went into the hands of landowners. These powerful few were opposed to any attempt at industrialization and were seen to be synonymous with foreign interests. There were calls for reform.

In 1946, Lieutenant-General Juan Perón won the presidency on a programme of domestic industrialization and economic independence. Perón pursued popular nationalist policies, introducing labour reforms and improving conditions and wages for the working classes, nationalizing the railways, and giving women the vote in 1947. His was an autocratic style of government, involving secret police and press censorship.

In 1955, due to soaring inflation and poor economic performance, Perón was ousted by a military coup, which paved the way for 30 years of military government (excluding the brief three-year period of 1973–6, when Perón returned from exile, only to die a year later and be replaced by his third wife, Isabelita, who was again overthrown by the military).

During the 1960s and 1970s, economic and political instability led to strikes and the rise of a left-wing guerrilla group, the *Montoneros*, who carried out an aggressive terrorist campaign. This was countered by the *Guerra Sucia*, the Dirty War, in which it is estimated that some 10,000–30,000 people 'disappeared'. The Dirty War ended only when General Galtieri, facing economic collapse (and in an attempt to unify the nation), decided to occupy the Malvinas (Falkland Islands) and provoked a war with the UK in 1982. The war ended quickly, with the Argentinian army surrendering after 74 days and handing power over to a civilian government.

The years since the return to democracy have seen persistent economic problems, coupled with threats of military takeover. In 1989, Carlos Menem, of the Partido Justicialista, a Perónist party, was elected president. He, surprisingly, pardoned imprisoned members of the junta as well as the leader of the *Montoneros*. There were many charges of corruption levelled against his government, scandals over privatization, and ministers involved in cover-ups. Menem was also criticized for forging links with the USA (he sent troops both to the Gulf War and to Croatia). In 1999 Menem tried to alter the constitution to enable himself to stand for a third term, but the Perónists lost to the Alliance for Work, Justice and Education (Allianza) led by Fernando de la Rúa.

Allianza came to power at a time of rising unemployment. In 1991, the Argentinian unit of currency, the *peso*, had been pegged to the US$, and, for a time the economy was stable, but by early 2002 Argentina had declared itself bankrupt, which in turn led to political crisis and governmental collapse.

TRAVELLING TO ARGENTINA

By Air
Most visitors arrive by plane at Buenos Aires' Aeropuerto Internacional Ministro Pistarini, known as Ezeiza. British Airways is currently the only airline to fly direct from the UK to Buenos Aires. Aeroflot, American Airlines, Air France, All Nippon Airways, Cubana, Japan Airlines, KLM, Korean Air, Malaysia Airlines, Pluna, Quantas, South Africa Airways, Swissair, TAP, United Airlines, Varig and Vasp all fly to Buenos Aires.

LanChile (seven daily flights), Ladeco and Nacional have frequent flights from Santiago de Chile to Buénos Aires, Aeropéru flies in from Peru and Lloyd Aéreo Boliviano from Bolivia.

Special multiple internal flight passes include the Argentina Pass and the Mercosur Pass, which can be bought outside Argentina, often in conjunction with an international flight. In addition, LanChile and LAPA have combined to allow Patagonian circuits via Punta Arenas, Río Gallegos, Ushuaia, Bariloche and Trelew.

By Road
The main road entry points are from Uruguay, Paraguay, Brazil, Bolivia and Chile.

From Bolivia
La Paz – Buenos Aires (48 hours)
La Paz – Villazón – La Quiaca – Salta/Jujuy (36 hours)
Tarija – Bermejo – Aguas Blancas – Salta/Jujuy
Santa Cruz – Yacuiba/Pocitos – Salta/Jujuy

From Chile (see also Arriving in Chile section)
Mendoza – Los Libertadores – Santiago (6–7 hours)
San Martín de los Andes – Paso de Mamuil Malal (Paso Tromen) – Currarehue – Pucón – Temuco (8 hours)
San Carlos de Bariloche – Paso Puyehué (Los Pajaritos) – Osorno (7 hours)
San Carlos de Bariloche – bus to Puerto Pañuelo – boat to Puerto Blest – bus to Puerto Alegre – boat to Puerto Frías – bus to Peulla – boat to Petrohué – bus to Puerto Montt (8 hours)
El Calafate – Paso Cancha de Carreras – Puerto Natales (6–8 hours)
El Calafate – Río Turbio – Puerto Natales (6 hours)

Visas
Citizens of the USA and most European countries, including the UK and Ireland, do not need a visa (although New Zealanders, Australians and South Africans do need one). On arrival, you will be given a tourist card which is required to exit the country. Normally, it is valid for 90 days, although it can be extended for a further 90 days at the office of Migraciones, Av Antardida Argentina 1365, Buenos Aires, or in provincial capitals or a department of the federal police.

It is advisable to carry your passport with you at all times, as the police may ask to see it, and you must show it when cashing travellers' cheques or when checking in to a hotel. You should keep a photocopy in a safe place at your hotel.

Customs/Immigration
Duty-free allowances are 400 cigarettes or 50 cigars, 2 litres of alcohol and 5kg of foodstuffs. Remember, if you are entering the country from Bolivia or Peru, you will be thoroughly searched for drugs. If you are entering from Chile, officials will be

---

INTERNATIONAL AIRLINES

Aeroflot, Av Santa Fe 816/822, tel: (5411) 4312 5573
Air France, Paraguay 610, Piso 14, tel: (5411) 4317 4747
Alitalia, Suipacha 1111, 28th floor, tel: (5411) 4321 8421
American Airlines, Esmeralda 719, Piso 5, tel: (5411) 4394 3925/3674
British Airways, Viamonte 570 Piso 1°, tel: (5411) 4320 6600
Canadian Airlines, Av Cordoba 656, tel: (5411) 4322 3732
Iberia, Carlos Pelligrini 1163, 1st floor, tel: (5411) 4327 2739
KLM, Suipacha 268 – 9th Floor CP C1008AAF, Buenos Aires, tel: (54 11) 4326 8422/8427, fax: (5411) 4326 8429
LanChile, Paraguay 609, tel: (5411) 4387 2222/4316 2200
Lufthansa, Marcelo T. de Alvear 636, tel: (5411) 4319 0600, fax: (5411) 4311 2803
United Airlines, Av Eduardo Madero 900, 9th floor Capital Federal (CP 1106), tel: (5411) 4316 0777; within the country (except Buenos Aires): 0800 888 0777; email: united@unitedargentina.com

DOMESTIC AIRLINES

Aerolíneas Argentinas, Paseo Colón 185, tel: (5411) 4343 2071/2089 or Peru 2, tel: (5411) 4343 8551/8559, free phone: 0810 2228 6527
Austral Líneas Aéreas, Leonardo N Alem 1134, tel: (5411) 4340 7800
Líneas Aéreas del Estado (LADE), Peru 710, tel: (5411) 4361 7071
Líneas Aéreas Prividas Argentinas (LAPA), Pelligrini 1075, tel: (5411) 4819 5272 or (5411) 4114 5272
Sapse Líneas Aéreas, Tucumán 1920, tel: (5411) 4371 7066
Southern Winds, Cerrito 1318, tel: (5411) 4814 1170

EMBASSIES

Australia, Villanueva 1400, 1426 Buenos Aires, tel: (5411) 4777 6590/6585, fax: (5411) 4772 3349, www.australia.org.ar
Brazil, Cerrito 1350, 1010 Buenos Aires, tel: (5411) 4815 8737/8742, fax: (5411) 4814 4689, email: embras@embrasil.org.ar
Canada, Tagle 2828, 1425 Buenos Aires, tel: (5411) 4805/3032, fax: (5411) 4806/1209
France, Santa Fe 846, tel: (5411) 4312 2409, www.embafrancia-argentina.org/
Germany, Villanueva 1055, 1426, tel: (5411) 4778 2500, fax: (5411) 4778 2550
Italy, Calle Billinghurst 2577, 1425 Buenos Aires, tel: (5411) 4802 0071, www.ambitalia-bsas.org.ar/
Netherlands, Edif. Buenos Aires, Av De Mayo 701, tel: (5411) 4334 4000
New Zealand, Carlos Pelligrini 1427, Piso 5, 1011, tel: (5411) 4328 0747, fax: (5411) 4328 0757, email: kiwiargentina@datamarkets.com.ar
Peru, San Martín 969, tel: (5411) 4311 7582. (Consulate: Codoba 1345, tel: (5411) 4871 8960)
Spain, Florida 1943, tel: (5411) 4811 0070. (Consulate: Guido 1760, tel: [5411] 4811 0078)
UK, Dr Luis Agote 2412, 1425 Buenos Aires, tel: (5411) 457622, fax: (5411) 480317
USA, 4300 Colombia, 1425 Buenos Aires, tel: (5411) 7747 601/4772 8526, www.usia.gov/posts/baires_embassy/

looking for electronic goods or any fresh fruit, vegetables, dairy produce or meat, which may be confiscated.

Please also note that at the crossing points of Los Libertadores and Los Pajaritos, Chilean customs officials put luggage through an X-ray machine. Keep all film in your hand luggage.

There are no restrictions on the import or export of local and foreign currency.

Money

The peso (Ar$) is the unit of currency in Argentina. This has been pegged to the US$, so it is just as easy, particularly in the big cities, to pay in US$. Remember, though, that in smaller places, people may not like to be paid in US$ and you will usually get change in Ar$. The exchange rate for changing pesos back to £ sterling is less favourable than that for US$.

TRANSPORT
In Buenos Aires

Buenos Aires is served by a complex system of buses, suburban trains, and the *subte*, an old but efficient metro. Both the buses and the metro are relatively cheap. City bus 86 and two private minibus companies, Manuel Tienda León and San Martín, go out to Ezeiza airport (both of the latter also operate services to Aeroparque Jorge Newberry). Taxis are black and yellow and are quite expensive.

Countrywide

By Air
There are two airports in Buenos Aires, the international Ezeiza, 35km (22 miles) south of the centre, and the Aeroparque Jorge Newberry airport, Costanera Av Rafael Obligado, for domestic flights. Distances in Argentina are so vast that the easiest way to travel is by air, although internal flights are expensive. Aerolíneas Argentinas, Austral Líneas Aéreas, LADE and Sapse Líneas Aéreas all fly to Patagonia. You will have to pay airport tax for international and domestic flights.

By Bus
The main bus terminal is known as the Retiro, and can be found at Av Ramos Mejia 1880, Buenos Aires. Booking a bus ticket here is remarkably organized, as each bus company has its own desk.

The bus system in Argentina is efficient, frequent, comfortable and comprehensive, linking all the major towns, although buses do tend to be more expensive than in Chile. The pullmans have reclining seats or, on those with *salón cama,* the seats go almost flat. Most serve meals and show videos.

BUS COMPANIES

Chevallier (Neuquén and Bariloche), tel: (5411) 4313 3288
Costera (Criolla/Don Otto Río Gallegos), tel: (5411) 4313 2503
El Condor (Neuquén and Bariloche), tel: (5411) 4313 3687
El Sureno (Bariloche), tel: (5411) 4315 288
El Valle (Bariloche, San Martín de los Andes), tel: (5411) 4313 2441
Expreso Pingüino (Río Gallegos, with connection to Punta Arenas), tel: (5411) 4311 5440
La Estrella (Neuquen and Bariloche), tel: (5411) 4313 3051
TAC (Bariloche), tel: (5411) 4313 3742
Via Bariloche (Bariloche), tel: (5411) 4315 3122
Travelling time to Bariloche: 23 hours
Travelling time to Río Gallegos: 40 hours

BUSES TO MENDOZA
Chevallier (San Luis and Mendoza), tel: (5411) 4313 3288
Expreso Jocoli (San Luis and Mendoza), tel: (5411) 4311 8232
TAC (San Luis and Mendoza), tel: (5411) 4313 3627
Travelling time to Mendoza: 13 hours

Guanacos in Torres del Paine National Park (trek 1).

By Train
The Ferrocarriles Argentinos have been privatized and are now much less frequent. Servicios Ferrovarias Patagonicos (Sefepa), a commuter and suburban network, goes from Constitucion, Buenos Aires.

ACCOMMODATION
As in any capital city, there is a huge number of *hostales*, *residenciales* and hotels from which to choose in Buenos Aires. Here is a selection:
Albergue Juvenil, Brazil 675, near Constitución station, tel: (5411) 4300 9321. Need YHA card. Can be noisy.
Juan Carlos Dima, Puan 551, tel/fax: (5411) 4432 4898. Rents rooms in the Universidad de Buenos Aires, good for longer stay. Kitchen, TV.
Hostelling International, Moreno 1273, tel: (5411) 4381 9760. email: bahostel@hostels.org.ar. New in 2001.
Che Lagarto, 1836 Av San Juan, tel: (5411) 4304 7618, email: chelagarto@hotmail.com, www.chelagarto.com.ar. Backpackers hostel. Internet, kitchen.
Hotel Maipú, Maipú 735 Central, tel: (5411) 4322 5142. Friendly.
Hotel Bolivar, Bolivar 886, tel: (5411) 4361 5105. Good value.
Hotel Sportsman, Rivadavia 1425, tel: (5411) 4381 8021.
Hotel Majestic, Libertad 121, tel: (5411) 4435 1949. Colonial style, good value.

FOOD AND DRINK
Food
Argentinians eat a meaty diet – after all, this is the land of the cattle ranch. Steak, *bife de chorizo*, and *parillada*, a mixed grill of steak and every type of grilled meat imaginable (including kidneys, intestines and udders) is popular. Also on the menu are *carbonada* and *puchero* (casseroles) and *pollo con papas fritas*, chicken and chips! In the Patagonian Lake District, trout, boar and venison are specialities, while lamb is favoured further south.

Argentina is not a good place to be a vegetarian. The Italian influence is strong, though, so there is plenty of pizza and all kinds of pasta. Try *fugaza*, a cheeseless onion pizza, or *fugaztta* with cheese.

As in Chile, *empenadas* are eaten as snacks, but they are usually meaty and smaller. Argentinian ice cream is of Italian origin and delicious!

When you go to El Calafate, make sure you buy some jam, made from the calafate berry, but beware; once you taste it, you may have to go back for more!

Drink
You can recognize an Argentinian anywhere in the world by his/her *maté gourd*, a wooden or silver pot,

---

TREKKING AGENCIES IN BUENOS AIRES

Ecology and Adventure Argentina/Adventure Centre, Talcahuano 736, No 1, 1391 Buenos Aires, tel: (5411) 4374 9639/9648, fax: (5411) 4372 9956, 24-hr mobile: (5411) 4477 2531/423 7262. For hiking, climbing and birding.
Trekking Argentina, Paraguay 542, 1057 Buenos Aires, tel: (5411) 4313 6853, fax: (5411) 4311 6853. For trekking, overland trips, rafting, birding, horse-riding.

USEFUL ADDRESSES

Tourist Agency Municipal Office, Sarmiento 1551, 5th floor, tel: (5411) 4372 3612. Open: Mon–Fri, 10am–6pm.
Dirección Nacional de Turismo, Santa Fe 883, tel: (toll free) 0800 50016. Open: weekdays, 9am–5pm. Branch at the Ezeiza airport, tel: (5411) 4480 0224.
BOOKSHOPS
El Ateneo, Florida 340, tel: (5411) 4325 6801.
LOLA, Viamonte, 976, 2nd floor, tel: (5411) 4322 3920. Open: afternoons only, Mon–Fri.
Libreria del Turista, Florida 937.
Fundación Vida Silvestre Argentina, Defensa 245 (1065 Buenos Aires), for books on wildlife.
MAPS
Administración de Parques Nacionales, Santa Fe 690 (at the north end of the Florida shopping mall), tel: (5411) 4311 0303, ext 165.
Instituto Geográfico Militar, Cabildo 301 (*Subte* station Ministro Carranza). Open: Mon–Fri, 8am–1pm.

and silver *bombilla*, or straw. *Yerba maté* is the dried and chopped leaf of *Ilex Paragueyensis*, a type of holly. The pot is filled with leaves, boiled water is poured on and the resulting mixture is drunk through a straw. There is also a ritual involved: first the pot is filled, then it is passed clockwise around a group of friends. Each person drains the liquid in turn and then pours more water on the leaves. Yerba maté is mixed with other herbs and a little sugar in the north, but taken neat in the south. If you are invited to partake, it means that you have been accepted into a group; it would be a shame to refuse.

Argentinian wine is good; the best is produced in the area around Mendoza. As regards spirits, *ginebra bols* and *cana* (cane alcohol) are national specialities. There is a variety of light beers, which can be bought German-style as draft beer, or s*chopp*.

COMMUNICATIONS

Argentina's country code is 54, and the code for Buenos Aires is 11. There are now two telephone networks in Argentina: Telecom, servicing to the north of Buenos Aires; and Telefónica to the south, with Buenos Aires split in half.

The main post office in Buenos Aires is located in Sarmiento 189 and is open Mon–Fri, 9am–7.30pm. Airmail to Europe takes between five and 10 days. Surface mail to Europe takes on average 20–25 days, but can take as long as 50 days, so it is advisable to send everything by airmail. Internal postal services are subject to delay. Post office hours are Mon–Fri, 8am–8pm and Sat, 8am–2pm. There is a charge for poste restante items.

LANGUAGE

In order to get by in Argentina you need to be able to speak some Spanish. More English is spoken in Buenos Aires than in other parts of the continent. Argentinian Spanish is more gutteral, with a heavy 'j' sound replacing the usual 'y' sound for 'y' and 'll'.

SECURITY

Argentina is quite safe. There is very little street crime. However, as in all big cities, pickpockets do operate on the streets of Buenos Aires, especially in crowded areas. In general, the police (*carabineros*) do not have a very good reputation. If there are problems, say you will phone your embassy.

PATAGONIAN UNIVERSALS
Health and Hygiene
Travelling in Chile and Argentina presents no real health problems, and neither country requires any inoculations.

Food and Water
Ceviche, raw seafood, must be cooked and cooled. It is not advisable to drink the tap water in Santiago or Buenos Aires, although you probably would not get sick. It is also recommended to treat or boil the water in the national parks.

Cash Machines
In the cities, it is usually best to use your normal cash card at an ATM (for Cirrus or Plus look for the Enlace sign, or there are Visa machines). The machines give you a menu in either English or Spanish and you can withdraw money in either pesos or US$. Otherwise, you can change travellers' cheques (in US$ or £ sterling) at a *casa de cambio*, or a bank. You tend to get a better rate of exchange for cash than for travellers' cheques.

Time Difference
Both Argentina and Chile are normally three hours behind GMT. However, from mid-December to mid-March – the prime trekking season – the province of Buenos Aires and Chile observes summer daylight savings time.

Electricity
Both Chile and Argentina use the standard current of 220V/50HZ.

TREK 1: CIRCUIT OF TORRES DEL PAINE

Parque Nacional Torres del Paine, 160km (99 miles) northwest of Puerto Natales, is Chile's most famous national park. It takes its name from the pink granite towers at the eastern side of the park and 'paine' (pronounced pie-nee) means pale blue in Telhuelche (the resident Indian tribe), probably referring to the lakes. Some attribute the name, however, to a Welsh woman climber, called Paine. This is an area of outstanding natural beauty, with deep glacial lakes, snow-covered peaks, hanging glaciers, native forests, rushing rivers, and two spectacular mountain features, the 'cuernos' or 'horns' – granite peaks topped with a black sedimentary layer – and the 'torres' – the 'towers' themselves, three fingers of pink granite.

The bus journey from Puerto Natales to the Sede Administrativa (Administration Centre) is a delight in itself. Although only 160km (99 miles), it takes 3 or 4 hours on an unpaved road. You travel from the Ultima Esperanza Sound, with its black-necked swans and stunning views of the snow-capped Monte Balmaceda, across wild and windswept grassland. Here, you will see rheas (birds like ostriches) lifting their skirts and running elegantly through the scrub, noisy caracaras and the rarer black-chested buzzard eagle. Later in the journey, you get your first breathtaking view of the towers rising up out of the plain. It becomes more impressive as the whole massif appears before you.

Park fees are paid at the park entrance. The bus then drives through herds of guanacos, dropping visitors at the Sede Administrativa, where anyone planning to trek should register. Visitors are no longer permitted to hike alone in the park, so you must sign in with at least one other person. Then, you can look around the small exhibition of glacial flora and fauna and buy a map from the shop.

Most guides suggest walking this circuit anti-clockwise, but going clockwise takes advantage of the prevailing westerly winds and makes crossing Paso John Garner less of an uphill struggle.

Sede Administrativa to Lago Grey
The trek proper starts about 1km (½ mile) along the dirt road towards Lago Grey. A line of orange markers leads off across the grassland, and these marker posts will be your guide for the rest of the trek. This is Patagonian pampas at its best, with mile after mile of unbroken coirón (a spiky grass). It's flat here, so the only view is of the ever-changing clouds chasing each other across the sky. This is a time for cursing the inevitable strong headwind and the heavy rucksack.

After about 90 mins you reach the first (free) campsite, Campamento las Carretas, and the Río Grey. At last, a change of perspective, with lenga trees and the first calafate bushes. The path wends its way above the grey-blue river for another hour then heads uphill, to cross the isthmus to Lago Pehoé. Cresting the brow, the view is breathtaking – the Cuernos del Paine (the Horns of Paine) tower over the far side of the unbelievably blue lake. Serried ramparts of yellow-grey granite are topped

TREK ESSENTIALS

LENGTH 6–10 days. 100km (62 miles) excluding side trips. Walking from the Sede Administrativa (Administration Centre) clockwise to Refugio Lago Pehoé, Lago Grey, Paso John Garner, Laguna los Perros, Lago Paine, Hostería Las Torres and back along Lago Nordenskjöld to Refugio Lago Pehoé. Side trips can be made to Torres Base Camp (Campamento Torres) and the Valle del Francés (1 day each).

ACCESS *To start* Bus from Puerto Natales to Sede Administrativa (Administration Centre). *On finish* Launch from Refugio Lago Pehoé over to Refugio Pudeto (weather permitting) and bus to Puerto Natales or retrace steps back from Refugio Lago Pehoé to the start at Sede Administrativa.

HIGHEST POINT Paso John Garner, 1180m (3871ft).

TREK STYLE Backpacking. Although there is a well-developed system of refuges in the park, a tent is necessary for Paso John Garner as the distance between Refugio Grey and Refugio Dickson is too far to walk in one day.

RESTRICTIONS A Park Entry fee of 5,500 pesos must be paid at the Park Entrance. Climbers must pay another 40,000 pesos each, if they want to climb a peak. Everyone must register at the Sede Administrativa. People are not allowed to trek alone. Camping is only allowed at recognized sites within the park. Open fires are no longer permitted, so make sure you carry a stove for cooking.

FURTHER OPTIONS Trek to Mirador Zapata from the Hostería Lago Grey for views of Lago Pingo (2-day return trip).

MAPS JLM 1:100 000 Torres del Paine
Sociedad Turística Kaoniken 1:100 000 Parque Nacional Torres del Paine

TREK 1: CIRCUIT OF TORRES DEL PAINE

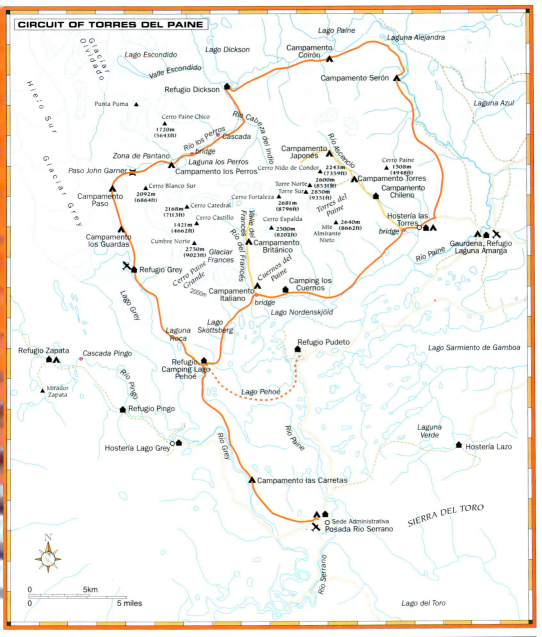

36 CHILE AND ARGENTINA

The 'cuernos' or 'horns' of Torres del Paine – granite peaks topped with a black sedimentary layer – as seen from Lago Skottsberg.

with a layer of burgundy-coloured sedimentary rock.

Another 90 mins or so sees you at Refugio Lago Pehoé, a large pine-timbered building with showers, beds, bar and all modern comforts. The campsite is also well equipped with a toilet and shower block, a shop (selling beer and wine as well as food), individual tent spaces, benches, tables and wind breaks. Be forewarned, though, that the shop also stocks carbon fibre tent poles!

From Lago Pehoé the trail heads northwest, skirting Cerro Paine Grande up a valley full of pink and white foxgloves to overlook Laguna Roca, where silvery grebes nest on the granite slabs around the lake. Look out for the orange *calceolaria uniflora* here, which I call 'hippopotamus flower' – you'll realize why when you see it. Further on, there's a first glimpse of Lago Grey. The glacier, an offshoot of the Hielo Sur, comes right down to the lake, where huge chunks of ice break off and sail away downwind as icebergs. Gnarled seracs of ice stretch as far as the eye can see like some great frozen ocean. The path threads its way above the lake then descends steeply through beech forest to the lakeshore itself, where you'll find Refugio Grey and a campsite. A sandy beach and lapping waves (though perhaps not the icebergs on the shore) add to the seaside feel. It is definitely worth scrambling back up from the campsite to the headland overlooking the glacier, just in case you are lucky enough to witness the awe-inspiring sight of glacier calving.

It is an impressive, if rather chilly, campsite. Parakeets screech in the trees and there is the unmistakable tapping of Magellanic woodpeckers.

Over the Paso John Garner

Onwards from Refugio Grey, the path (which wends its way high above the east side of Glaciar Grey through evergreen coigüe forest) is less well frequented, used only by those completing the full circuit. The second free authorized campsite on this trek, Campamento Los Guardas (formerly Chileno; no facilities), is reached after about 90 mins. Hereafter, the trail becomes quite tortuous. It crosses landslide areas, descending into and rising out of ravines. This is real Hansel and Gretel country – the forest is thick and there are often fallen trees to negotiate. The ladders and fixed ropes that used to be in place to help trekkers over the rocky sections have fallen into disrepair and one area has been destroyed by fire. But the views of Ventisquero Grey and the peaks to the west more than make up for any discomfort.

It takes about 5–6 hours to reach Campamento Paso from Glaciar Grey. This small, free campsite, with no facilities, is tucked away in the forest. It can be quite squalid and overcrowded. The best water supply is above the campsite to the east, but the water will still need boiling.

There is a certain mystique about crossing the Paso John Garner. In good weather, it is very straightforward: just follow the orange markers. In snow storms or poor visibility, it is quite a different proposition. The ground is quite featureless and the only maps available are trekking maps, with the contours at 100m (328ft) intervals. In the past, people have got lost and for this reason trekkers are not supposed to travel alone in the park.

In normal conditions, follow the path rising steeply from the campsite through the forest. After rain, it may become quite slippery, but luckily there are tree roots to use as support. An hour later, the trees end and there are tremendous views of the Hielo Sur. Another hour of trending rightwards sees you on top of the pass, the highest point of the trek and a wild and exposed place. This is usually not a place to linger, although the views of Punta Puma and Cerro Paine Chico to the northeast and Cerro Blanco Sur to the south are superb. It looks no distance at all down to Laguna los Perros, but the terrain is rough. Continue trending rightwards downhill, over rocky bluffs and streams. Then there's an hour of bog-hopping (featured on the map as Zona de Pantano, which is marshland) before you cross the bridge into Campamento los Perros, a welcome sheltered campsite in the woods, where there is now a toilet and shower block and a shop.

Campamento los Perros to Hostería las Torres

This part of the trek, on the north side of the Paine massif, is the most remote. Apart from the new Andescape refuge (Refugio Dickson) at Lago Dickson and the replacement of a couple of rickety old log bridges, little seems to have changed in the past 20 years.

From the campsite the trail leads down along the moraine to the stunning little Laguna los Perros, where the glacier calves directly into the lake. The icebergs change shape, turn turtle or break up as you watch.

The route then crosses the Río de los Perros (named after a herder's dogs, who drowned in the river when it was in spate) on a newish suspension bridge and follows it through thick woods to Lago Dickson, crossing the Río Cabeza del Indio on logs. It is worth making a short detour to watch the cascada thundering down its ravine, and to look back to the now innocuous-seeming Paso John Garner. Look out for orchids and, further on, Magellanic woodpeckers.

At last, the trail starts to descend steeply and there before you lie Lago Dickson, the Ventisquero Dickson and, beyond, the snow-covered jagged peaks on the Chile–Argentina border. It would be possible to follow the glacier from here into Argentina, but this is not permitted. Camping is allowed on the grass outside the refuge. This is one of the park's original refuges, and could be used as an emergency shelter.

It would be possible to spend a day here exploring the hidden Valle Escondido as far as Lago Escondido and Glaciar Olvidado ('forgotten glacier'), although there are no marked trails and you would have to cross the Río de los Perros where it enters the lake.

The trek itself continues across open, flat, wild and windswept pampas, where you are likely to startle snipe and geese. It takes just under three hours to Campamento Coirón, an authorized (free) campsite and another old-style hut (in a poor state of repair). Watch out for mice here, which have been known to chew on anything left outside the tent. There is also a resident *zorro gris* (grey fox), which is hopefully getting fat on a diet of mice.

The path now undulates above Lago Paine. This is the essence of Patagonia: open skies above a turquoise lake, scrub lenga trees, the flash of green parakeets, calafate bushes and, beyond the lake,

A favourite photo spot at the mirador below the Torres del Paine.

The rhea is an ostrich-like native of the Patagonian pampas.

grasslands stretching as far as the eye can see. This land is still worked by the *estancia* (ranch) and you may see a *gaucho* (cowboy) rounding up his cattle in traditional fashion. Here, too, if there are rain showers, you will see the most vivid of rainbows arching across the sky, two- or even three-fold.

After crossing a spur and descending to the tiny horseshoe-shaped Laguna Alejandra, there is a further 2 hours of pampas before reaching Campamento Serón, a private campsite and hut. The surrounding meadows abound in upland geese, ruddy geese, caracaras, Southern lapwings and ibises.

From Campamento Serón, you can either trek to Laguna Amarga, where there is a *guardería*, a basic refuge and a shop (where, if you're lucky, you can even buy bread!) or hike direct to Hostería las Torres via an upper path. The trail junction is unmarked, but if you walk for about 90 mins it leads off uphill in a southerly direction just after the second stream crossing (there are no bridges, but the streams are wide and shallow). As you ascend and traverse the southerly slopes of Cerro Paine, following wire fences, there are excellent views of Laguna Amarga and Lago Nordenskjöld. Finally, you descend slightly through a gap and over moraine to join the dirt road coming up from Laguna Amarga. The Hostería las Torres is the collection of buildings that used to be the old *estancia*, consisting of a refuge, self-catering accommodation, a restaurant, bar, shop and organized grassy campsite.

Most people do a day hike from the *hostería* up to the mirador (viewpoint) to see the towers after which the park is named. Three fingers of pink-yellow granite, the tallest 2850m (9351ft) high, rise up from the glacier below at 250m (820ft) – a vertical height gain of 2600m (8530ft). Many rock-climbers have aspired to scale their heights: some have succeeded, but many have failed, rebuffed by the constant winds and the sudden violent Patagonian storms. The smallest tower, Torre Norte, was first climbed in 1958, while Torres Central and Sur were conquered in 1963.

The path crosses the fast-flowing Río Ascensio on a new suspension bridge, then follows the narrow valley, traversing scree slopes above the river, as far as Campamento Chileno, where there is a new refuge and a rather gloomy campsite on the opposite bank. After following the river for a short while, the path ascends steeply through the forest, crossing streams on log bridges, until it emerges in an open boulder field. The final section involves some scrambling up granite blocks to reach the viewpoint above the glacial lake and below the towers. This is a truly magical spot.

It is probably worthwhile, if you have time, to camp at the Torres Base Camp, Campamento Torres, a free campsite in the forest with a distinct sense of history. There are all sorts of climbers' shelters in place. It is also home to several types of hawks, parakeets and woodpeckers.

The best reason for camping here is the chance to climb up to the mirador in time for sunrise. There are few sights more awe inspiring than watching the sun's first pink rays striking the summits, travelling down their length until the towers glow bright red then turn to yellow as the sun gains in strength.

After breakfast at camp, it is possible to make a day hike to the other climbers' camp, the Campamento Japonés, and up the Valle del Silencio to the west side of the towers for sunset. This valley is well named; it feels very remote and can be exposed and intimidating in bad weather, dominated as it is by huge bare granite slabs, lifeless moraine and the glacier of Fortaleza, the fortress. A truly wild place – probably the wildest of the trip.

Hostería las Torres to Refugio Lago Pehoé, via the Valle del Francés

To return to Lago Pehoé from the suspension bridge over the Río Ascensio, head west along the path above the north shore of Lago Nordenskjöld beneath the ramparts of Monte Almirante Nieto. The mountainside is riven by countless ravines, each with its own thundering waterfall. In the distance, to the south, the great bulk of Cerro Castillo can be seen. After about an hour you will reach a small lake; after another hour you will need to negotiate one of the streams rushing down from Almirante Nieto. This involves some boulder hopping and creative route-finding; picking a way across is affected by the level of the water. A further 2 hours sees you to the campsite by the new refuge, Camping los Cuernos.

The path to the entrance of the Valle del Francés is reminiscent of a coastal path; you can see where you are heading, but it takes an eternity to get there, as you climb up and down, in and out of ravines for a good 90 mins. The stupendous views more than compensate for this. If the weather is good, this section can appear positively Mediterranean: blue sky, blue lake, sun-drenched rock, distant mountains.

The Valle del Francés, the narrow valley between Cerro Paine Grande and the Cuernos, is one of the gems of this trek. The trail leads past Campamento Italiano, up through the forest (look out for parakeets and woodpeckers), to emerge on the lateral moraine, which you will follow to a chasm where the Río del Francés hurls itself down a gigantic water slide. Further on, the path levels out at a natural viewpoint opposite the tremendous Glaciar Francés, with its hanging seracs and icefalls. When gravity takes its toll, these come crashing down with a roar that echoes around the valley. You continue upwards more gradually, the Cuernos towering above you, through a boggy area into the shelter of the forest to Campamento Británico. It was from this camp that a British team made the first ascent of the peak at the head of the valley, Fortaleza, in 1968. It is also possible to hike further up the valley to two small lakes on the tree line (90 mins round trip).

To return, retrace your steps to the trail junction and cross the Río del Francés on a suspension bridge. Here, I once saw five condors circling Cerro Paine Grande. The path then contours around to Lago Skottsberg, a jewel of a lake with the Cuernos as a backdrop. You will see calafate and chaura bushes, laden with berries to stave off your hunger. The Cuernos and the blue lake are thrown into contrast by the red Chilean firebush. You ascend to a spur for a final view back up the valley, the Cuernos glowing red in the sunset, before dropping down to Lago Pehoé and the site of your first night's camp.

The following day, you can take the launch over to Refugio Pudeto (weather permitting) and catch a bus out of the park.

Side trip towards Lago Pingo

If you have extra time (and a sense of adventure), it is worth making the 2-day trek up towards Lago Pingo from the Hostería Lago Grey before you set out on the main circuit. The scenery here is as wild as anywhere and there will be few, if any, other trekkers. The lenga forest is alive with parakeets, Magellanic woodpeckers, and Chilean flickers, while torrent ducks play in the rapids of the Río Pingo. These are the most amazing of ducks: all muscle, they swim upstream against fast flowing water, hunting for fish. Scramble up through the forest to overlook the Cascada Pingo, an impressive waterfall where the force of the water is so great that the spray flies upwards.

Camping is allowed at the Refugios Pingo and Zapata, both of which are old style, delapidated but still usable, huts. It is no longer possible to get to Lago Pingo, as the bridge to it has been destroyed, but you can hike up to the Mirador Zapata for views of the lake, Glaciar Grey and the Hielo Sur.

It is also good value to drop down to the beach at the south end of Lago Grey for a close-up view of the huge icebergs washed up there.

Glaciar Grey as seen from the path towards Campamento Paso.

PARQUE NACIONAL TORRES DEL PAINE DIRECTORY

It's a long way to Puerto Natales, the jumping off point for the Torres del Paine National Park. There are three options:
1. Fly into Buenos Aires, connect with a flight to Río Gallegos (3¼ hours or 5¼ hours), then travel by bus to Puerto Natales (6-8 hours).
2. Fly direct to Santiago de Chile, then on to Punta Arenas (4 hours), then again by bus to Puerto Natales (4-5 hours). This flight covers spectacular scenery – you fly down the length of the Andes, following a chain of volcanoes, then over the northern and southern icecaps, before flying directly above the Paine towers.
3. Fly into Santiago, then fly down to Puerto Montt (2 hours) and take the 4-day boat trip to Puerto Natales. This is brilliant if the weather is good, but a bit miserable otherwise. There is now also a new daily flight with ALTA direct to Puerto Natales from Santiago.

REGIONAL FLIGHTS
Santiago to Puerto Montt and on to Punta Arenas: LanChile, Ladeco or Nacional (daily).
Buenos Aires to Río Gallegos: Aerolíneas Argentinas (twice daily), Austral (daily except Sunday), LAPA (Mondays and Fridays).
Punta Arenas to Puerto Natales (and on to Coyhaique): ALTA (daily).
Puerto Montt to Puerto Natales: ALTA (daily).

REGIONAL TRANSPORT
Punta Arenas to Puerto Natales by bus: Buses Fernández, Bus Sur, Austral Bus (twice daily).
Río Gallegos to Puerto Natales by bus: Quebek Tours, El Pingüino, Interlagos bus companies.
Puerto Montt to Puerto Natales by boat: Puerto Eden, operated by Navimag (takes 4 days).
Puerto Natales to Sede Administrativa by bus: Turismo Zaajh, Servitur, Buses JB, Cayetano, Tour Express bus companies (daily, leaving early in the morning).
There are also tour operators that run daily excursions to the park.

ACCOMMODATION IN PUERTO NATALES
Top end:
Hotel Costa Australis, corner of Costanero Pedro Montt and Manuel Bulnes, tel: (5661) 412000, fax: (5661) 411881. New.
Hotel Capitan Eberhard, Costanero Pedro Montt 25, tel: (5661) 411208, fax: (5661)411209. On the waterfront, with panoramic views. Slightly overpriced.
Hotel Juan Ladrilleros, Pedro Montt 161, tel: (5661) 411652, fax: (5661) 412109. More basic.
Hotel Glaciares, Eberhard 104, tel: (5661) 412189, fax: (5661) 411452. Nothing exciting, but comfortable.
Amerindia Concept, Bories y Pedro Montt.
Budget:
Hospedaje Teresa Ruiz, Esmerelda 463. Recommended.
Residencial Dickson, Bulnes 307, tel: (5661) 411218. Recommended by backpackers. Handy for the ferry.
Residencial Patagonia Adventure, Tomás Rogers 179, tel: (5661) 411028. Dormitory and private rooms. Hires gear.
Hospedaje Elsa Millán, Elcano 588. Home-made bread. Dormitory style. Recommended. No telephone.
Casa Cecilia, Tomas Rogers 64, tel/fax: (5661) 411797, email: redcecilia@entel.chile.net. Delicious breakfasts, but small rooms. Also runs a cheaper annex in summer.

LOCAL ACTIVITIES
Andescape, Eberhard 595, tel/fax: (5661) 413291, website: www.chileaustral.com/pathgone. Provides information and reservation of the refuges in Torres del Paine. Can provide camping equipment, a guide, a cook, horses, etc. Also has an office in Santiago, Santa Beatriz 84A, Providencia, tel/fax: (562) 235 5225.
Andes Patagonicas, Blanco Encalada 226, tel/fax: (5661) 411594, email: alvera@ctc.net. Rents camping gear. Minibus service to the park.
Turismo Paori, Eberhard 577, tel/fax: (5661) 411229, email: paori@chileanpatagonia.com
Knudsen Tours, Blanco Encalada 284, tel/fax: (5661) 411531, email:knudsen@chilesat.net. Daily tours and trekking trips to park.
Onas Patagonia, Eberhard 556, tel: (5661) 414349, fax: (5661) 412707. Rents camping gear. Trekking, sea kayaking and rafting.
Turismo Luis Díaz, Blanco Encalada, tel/fax: (5661) 411654. Rents camping gear. Runs 1- and 2-day trips to the park.

ACCOMMODATION IN THE PARK
Hotels:
Hostería las Torres, tel: (5661) 247050. Access by road from Guardería Laguna Amarga. Restaurant, shop and pet rhea! Located at start of trek up to Torres Base Camp.
Hostería Pehoé, tel: (5661) 411390. Stunning location on an island, connected by a bridge on Lago Pehoé.
Hotel Explora, tel: (5661) 411247. Ugly building at the Salto Chico. Upmarket.
Hostería Lago Grey, tel: (5661) 248220, ext 29. At the southern end of Lago Grey. Access by road.
Posada Río Serrano, near the Sede Administrativa. Older style.
Refuges:
Refugio Lago Pehoé
Refugio Dickson
Refugio los Cuernos
Refugio Grey
Refugio Chileno
Refugio Laguna Amarga
Authorized campsites Listed according to location, clockwise around the park):
Campamento las Carretas, free
Camping Pehoé
Campamento Italiano (Valle del Francés), free
Campamento Británico (Valle del Francés), free
Camping Grey
Campamento los Guardas, free
Campamento Paso, free
Campamento los Perros, free
Camping Dickson
Campamento Coirón, free
Campamento Serón
Camping Laguna Amarga, free
Campamento Chileno (Río Ascencio)
Campamento Torres (Río Ascencio)
Campamento Japonés (Río Ascencio), free
Camping los Cuernos

TREK 2: AROUND MONTE FITZ ROY IN THE PARQUE NACIONAL LOS GLACIARES

The Parque Nacional Los Glaciares is dominated by the Monte Fitz Roy massif, with its host of granite spires and needles. Monte Fitz Roy was originally called 'El Chaltén' (Peak of Fire) by the local Telhuelche Indians, as they thought it was a volcano. Francisco Perito Moreno renamed it after Captain Fitzroy of the Beagle who, in 1834, together with Charles Darwin, was probably the first European ever to set eyes on it. As well as being scenically breathtaking, the area is rich in condors, torrent ducks, Magellanic woodpeckers, and the forest is home to the endangered huemul, a type of sturdy Andean deer and the Patagonian hare, the mara.

On the other side of the continent from Torres del Paine, in Argentina, lies the Parque Nacional los Glaciares and the Monte Fitz Roy massif. After crossing the Chile–Argentina border (coming from Puerto Natales), with all the bureaucratic formalities that only a tiny checkpoint in the middle of nowhere can dream up to justify its existence, there's a journey of some 6 hours through unrelenting Patagonian pampas. Hour after hour passes with flat steppe and an unbroken horizon, but the monotony is relieved by the ever-changing cloudscapes and by flocks of rheas, black-chested buzzard eagles, Southern lapwings, caracaras and the odd Andean fox scampering across the unpaved road. Not to be forgotten are the delights of 'the hotel', which appears like a mirage in the midst of vast emptiness, and which we christened the 'Baghdad Café'.

About 45 mins before arriving at El Calafate on Lago Argentino, the bus turns a corner and reveals the vast bulk of Monte Fitz Roy, a granite mass,

TREK ESSENTIALS

LENGTH 4–6 days. 50km (31 miles). Bus to El Chaltén, trek to Campamento Bridwell, Campamento Poincenot, Piedra del Fraile and return via the Río Electrico and the Valle del Río de las Vueltas to El Chaltén.

ACCESS *To start* Bus from El Calafate to El Chaltén. *On finish* Bus from El Chaltén to El Calafate.

HIGHEST POINT Mirador Laguna Torre, 580m (1903ft). Side trip: North Fitz Roy Mirador, 1400m (4593ft).

TREK STYLE Backpacking or horse assisted. Camping is only allowed at designated sites. It is usually free, but without facilities. Camping los Troncos is the only organized site, and you have to pay. There is a warden, individual covered cooking areas and a small refuge, with shop and bar.

RESTRICTIONS All visitors to the park need to register at the *guardería*, provide a proposed itinerary and list of campsites, and attend an obligatory environmental talk. A park fee is included in the bus fare to El Chaltén.

FURTHER OPTIONS 1. Follow the dirt road north from El Chaltén to Laguna del Desierto, where you can either hike to the north end of the lake, or take a boat. 2. It is also possible, with mountaineering equipment, ice axe, crampons and rope, to make a full circuit of Monte Fitz Roy, by ascending the Glaciar Torre from Laguna Torre, crossing two high cols onto the Glaciar Fitzroy and descending to the North Fitz Roy Mirador and Refugio Los Troncos. This would be a serious undertaking, necessitating all the normal precautions for glacial travel, and depending on good snow conditions.

MAPS Argentinian IGM 1:100 000 Estancia Kaiken Aike No 4972-26, Santa Cruz

Argentinian IGM 1:100 000 Laguna del Desierto No 4972-20, Santa Cruz

Argentinian IGM 1:100 000 Glaciar Viedma Nos 4972-25 and 4975-30

Argentinian IGM 1:100 000 Monte Fitzroy No 4972-19

Zagier and Urruty 1:50 000 Monte Fitz Roy and Cerro Torre – a trekking map showing routes and contours, drawn from the four IGM maps

An old climbers' shelter at Campamento Maestri, from where Maestri made his disputed ascent of Cerro Torre.

42 CHILE AND ARGENTINA

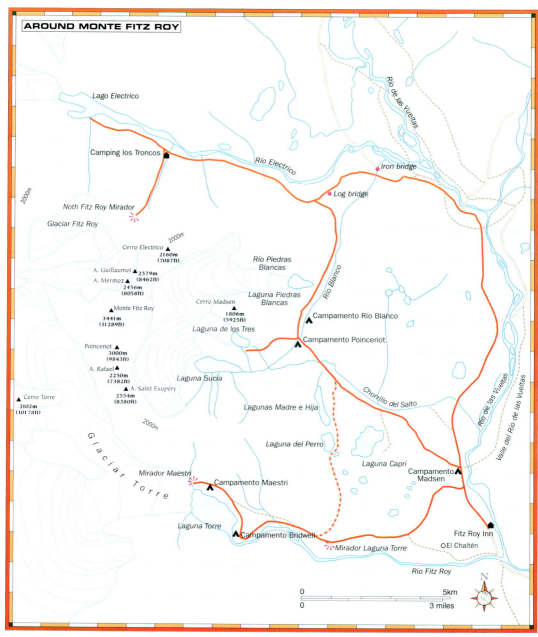

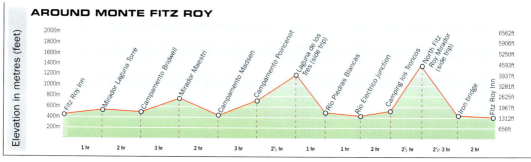

3441m (11289ft) high, rising directly up from the flat steppe at a lowly 300m (984ft).

El Calafate itself is somewhat reminiscent of Keswick in the English Lake District, with its souvenir shops catering for the not insubstantial tourist trade. There's even a 'Patagonia' shop, selling outdoor gear (at vastly inflated prices). Maps and last minute provisions can be bought; the supermarkets are slightly less expensive than the stores in El Chaltén (which is closer to the trail head, but where it would be difficult to get everything you needed).

There are two bus companies operating between El Calafate and El Chaltén. Both leave early in the morning and will pick you up from your hotel. The distance is a mere 220km (137miles), but it takes 4 hours on an unpaved road. However, the drive is spectacular, taking you along Lago Argentino then Lago Viedma, with views of the Viedma Glacier at its head and the snow-capped peaks on the Chilean border. The drivers are keen to stop after 2 hours at another unlikely café in the middle of nowhere, La Leona, where the coffee is good and the home baking even better! The approach to the park is dominated by views of Monte Fitz Roy. On arrival at the *guardería*, however, all eyes are drawn to the perfect granite finger of Cerro Torre, a magnet for rock climbers in the 1950s and 1960s. Cerro Torre was first ascended (without dispute) only in 1974, and it still maintains its allure today.

After stopping to sign in at the *guardería*, the Los Glaciares bus drops you at the Restaurante Senyera in the village. Cal Tur (the other bus company) drops you at the Fitz Roy Inn, about 1km (¾ mile) further along the road.

The Fitz Roy Inn to Campamento Poincenot

The trek starts from the Fitz Roy Inn. It is clearly marked at the white craft shop. Head quite steeply upwards for about an hour to a bluff, the Mirador Laguna Torre, and gaze in awe at the golden snow-topped spire of Cerro Torre at the head of the valley. Look out for condors here. I have seen four in one day. The path then descends gently to the Río Fitz Roy, where torrent ducks have been seen swimming against the current in its raging, icy waters. Follow the path up into the woods to the sheltered Campamento Bridwell, home for a season to many a climbing expedition. The view from the camp is stunning. There is even a perfectly sited bench for watching the sunset over Cerro Torre or for climbers topping out.

From Campamento Bridwell, if you have time, it is worth making the detour to Campamento Maestri and the Mirador Maestri, for an even closer view of Cerro Torre. Head about halfway around the glacial lake until the path zigzags upwards and you reach the now derelict small climbers' refuge, set amidst lenga trees and yellow calceolarias. Continue upwards on a cairned path, which becomes increasingly indistinct, until you come to the Mirador Maestri after about 90 mins with its breathtaking views of Cerro Torre and the Cordón Adela.

An easy crossing of the Río Blanco.

Retracing your steps to the Mirador Laguna Torre, head downhill to the next trail junction and follow the path through a *mallín* (swamp area) down to the road. Then ascend again (steeply), just past Campamento Madsen, on the main waymarked trail to join the Chorrillo del Salto at the turn-off to Laguna Capri, a jewel of a lake set against the backdrop of Monte Fitz Roy. Continue beside the river, through another boggy area, until the path rises through woods to the Campamento Poincenot, beside the Río Blanco, which is sheltered by trees and dominated by the Fitz Roy and Poincenot Peaks.

The short-cut traverse path from Campamento Bridwell to Campamento Poincenot leaves the main trail about 45 mins below Campamento Bridwell. It ascends through thick forest to a ridge, contours to the left of a swamp to Laguna del Perro, then descends to the Lagunas Madre e Hija (home of upland geese and spectacle ducks) to join the Poincenot Trail, at the point where it crosses the Chorrillo del Salto River. The park authorities closed this path for a while, for environmental reasons, but it was reopened in January 2000.

Side trip to Laguna de los Tres

Campamento Poincenot is the starting point for one of the best viewpoints of the trek, the tiny Laguna de los Tres (named after the French threesome who made the first ascent of Monte Fitz Roy in 1952), at the foot of the eastern face of Monte Fitz Roy. Cross the Río Blanco on a precarious log bridge, pass Campamento Río Blanco, the climbers' Base Camp, and ascend steeply on a zigzag path. You should reach the top of the moraine wall after about an hour. The granite tower of Fitz Roy, with its acolytes, Poincenot, St Exupéry and Rafael, rises dramatically before you. Head around the lake to the left and peer down into the green depths of Laguna Sucia. (This lake can be reached directly from camp, but the views are not as panoramic.) It is also possible, but with more difficulty, to ascend Cerro Madsen (1806m/5925ft), the spur to the north of the lake (4–5-hour round trip).

Campamento Poincenot to Camping los Troncos

From Poincenot, cross the Río Blanco again on the log bridge, but this time proceed along the west bank. This route runs partly in the woods, partly over boulders, following cairns and crossing ravines, until you reach the river flowing down from Laguna Piedras Blancas after about an hour. Take the time to scramble and boulder-hop up to this gem of a lake, nestled below ice falls cascading down from the mighty Fitz Roy itself. Great chunks of ice crash into the lake at frequent intervals, the sound reverberating wildly around the rock walls and sending waves to upturn existing icebergs.

The magical Laguna Piedras Blancas below Monte Fitz Roy.

Monte Fitz Roy as seen from the Northern Fitz Roy Mirador.

White rocks, bleached by the sun, white ice and blue sky make this a veritable suntrap. Many an hour can be spent here watching icebergs.

Thread your way back through the boulders and jump across the river, where the rocks almost make a natural bridge, just before the confluence. Continue down the Valle Río Blanco, following cairns as the trail winds its way in and out of the gravelly river bed, as far as the intersection with the large trail coming up the Río Electrico (1 hour from the Piedras Blancas turning). Head up left through the woods, keeping a watchful eye out for Magellanic woodpeckers, Chilean flickers and the green flash of parakeets. The path levels out, continues beside the upper Río Electrico, passes through an open meadow and brings you to Camping los Troncos after 2 hours. This has been built on the site of a huge boulder, the Piedra del Fraile, which shelters the campsite from the glacial wind blowing down from the Hielo Sur. A staircase has been constructed to the top of the boulder, to provide a mirador up to the glacier and the north side of Monte Fitz Roy. The campsite is quite an oasis. There is grass, a toilet and even a hot shower, the water heated by a wood fire.

Side trip to North Fitz Roy Mirador

An enjoyable 'rest' day can be spent here, with a walk up the Río Electrico (watch out for torrent ducks) to Lago Electrico, a wild and bleak place, constantly hammered by the incessant wind blowing from the Hielo Sur (1-hour return trip). This can be combined with a hike up to the mirador for a stunning view of the north face of Fitz Roy, Aguja Mermoz and Aguja Guillaumet, and, to the southwest, the Hielo Sur (90 mins of steep ascent). The return trip can take 3 hours.

If you have more time, and a lot of energy, it is possible to climb up from the glacier leftwards (southeast), scrambling up scree to a col, then trend right below a cliff and ascend to the Cerro Electrico Ridge, for close-up views of Fitz Roy and Cerro Pollone.

Return to El Chaltén

To return to El Chaltén, retrace your steps down the Río Electrico and continue on the main path east, following cairns, to cross the Río Blanco on a log bridge. After rain, it may be necessary to wade across the river, but it is quite broad and shallow, and not too fast-flowing. Face upstream and use a stick or trekking pole for stability, or link arms and move slowly across, making sure each foot is stable before you transfer your weight onto it. The trail continues beside a stream bed, finally reaching the main dirt road through the park at the iron bridge over the Río Blanco after 2–2½ hours. Follow this road through the Valle del Río de las Vueltas back to El Chaltén, where the bus to El Calafate leaves at 4pm.

FITZ ROY DIRECTORY

The starting point for any exploration of Los Glaciares National Park is El Calafate, on the shores of Lago Argentina. Its economy is based on the booming tourist trade, with all the trappings that implies. It takes its name from the calafate berry, *Berberis buxifolia*, which grows in abundance throughout the region. This is a small purple (and very tasty) berry on a spiky stalk. It is said that if once you eat this berry, you will always want more, which will make you return to the area.

REGIONAL FLIGHTS
Buenos Aires to Río Gallegos: Aerolíneas Argentinas (twice daily); Austral (daily except Sunday); LAPA (Mondays and Fridays).
Río Gallegos to El Calafate: El Pingüino (daily); Líneas Aéreas Kaiken (Mondays, Saturdays and Sundays); LADE (Thursdays).
Buenos Aires to Comodoro Rivadavia: Austral (daily).
Comodoro Rivadavia to El Calafate: LADE (Mondays and Wednesdays); TAN (Wednesdays and Fridays).

REGIONAL TRANSPORT
Río Gallegos to El Calafate by bus: Quebek Tours, El Pingüino, Interlagos (daily).
Puerto Natales to El Calafate by bus: Cootra, Del Glaciar, San Cayetano, Buses Zhaaj bus companies. El Pingüino (Mondays, Wednesdays and Saturdays). Many tour operators in Puerto Natales also run minibuses to El Calafate.
El Calafate to El Chaltén by bus: Cal Tur and Los Glaciares bus companies (daily at 6am, returning 4pm).

ACCOMMODATION IN EL CALAFATE
There is not a wide selection of accommodation in El Calafate, as the town caters mainly for day visitors to the Perito Moreno Glacier.

Top end:
Hotel El Quijote, Gregores 1191, tel: (54) 2902 491017.
Hotel Michelangelo, Moyano 1020, tel: (54) 2902 491045. Friendly staff.
Hotel La Loma, Av Roca 849, tel: (54) 2902 491016.
Hostería Kaiken, Valentin Feilberg 119, tel: (54) 2902 491073. Excellent breakfast.

Standard:
Hospedaje del Norte, Los Gauchos 813, tel: (54) 2902 491117.
Cabañas del Sol, Av Libertador 1956, tel: (54) 2902 491439. Highly recommended.
Hospedaje Los Lagos, 25 de Mayo 220, tel: (54) 2902 491170. Also recommended.

Budget:
Albergue del Glaciar, Los Pioneros, tel/fax: (54) 2902 491243. Much recommended by backpackers.
Albergue Lago Argentino, Campaña del Desierto 1050 (near the bus station), tel: (54) 2902 491139. Also highly recommended by backpackers.
Hotel La Loma, Roca 849, tel: (54) 2902 491016. Hostel-style accommodation in the main hotel. More upmarket, but pleasant.

Hospedaje Alejandra, Espora 60, tel: (54) 2902 91328. Highly recommended.
Hospedaje Buenos Aires, Ciudad Buenos Aires 296, tel: (54) 2902 491147.

Campsites:
Camping Municipal, José Pantín. Within easy walking distance from the town.
Camping Los Dos Piños, 9 de Julio 218, tel: (54) 2902 491271. Cheaper, but at the north end of town.

LOCAL ACTIVITIES
APN Intendencia for Parque Nacional los Glaciares, Av del Libertador 1302, tel: (54) 2902 91005, fax: (54) 2902 91755. Open: Dec-Mar, Mon-Fri, 8am-9pm; Sat & Sun, 10am-9pm.
El Calafate's Tourist Office, Terminal de Omnibuses (in the centre of town).
Club Andino Lago Argentino, c/o Hospedaje Avenida, Av del Libertador 902, tel: (54) 2902 491159.

TOUR OPERATORS
Cal Tur, Los Gauchos 813, tel: (54) 2902 491117.
Expediciones Patagonia, tel: 0962 493043.
Fitz Roy Expeditions, tel: 0962 493017.
Interlagos Turismo, Av. Libertador 1175, tel: (54) 2902 491018.
Receptivo Calafate, Av. Libertador 945, tel: (54) 2902 491116.
Tur Aike, Av. Libertador 1080, tel: (54) 2902 491389.

ACCOMMODATION IN EL CHALTEN
Top end:
Fitz Roy Inn, tel: (54) 2902 493062. Also has camping facilities.
Hosteria Fitz Roy, tel: (54) 2902 422436.
Hostería la Quinta, just before the park entrance.

Budget:
Ruca Mahuida, tel: (54) 2902 493018.
Albergue Patagonia, tel: (54) 2902 493091.
Posada Lago del Desierto, tel: (54) 2902 493010.
Albergue los Ñires, tel: (54) 2902 493009.

Campsites:
Campamento Confluencia, across the road from the Guardería Chaltén. Free, but no facilities.
Campamento Madsen, further along the road, past the Fitz Roy Inn. Free, but no facilities.

AUTHORIZED CAMPSITES WITHIN THE PARK
Campamento Bridwell, views of Cerro Torre.
Campamento Laguna Capri, there is also a basic wooden hut here.
Campamento Poincenot.
Campamento Río Blanco, for climbers only.
Refugio and Camping Los Troncos, a privately owned hut and campsite, for which you have to pay – but there's a bar, small shop and hot showers (when the fire is lit!).

TREK 3: AROUND CERRO CASTILLO

The Reserva Nacional Cerro Castillo is situated southwest of Coyhaique in Chile's XI (political) region. It extends over 1340km² (833 sq miles), from Lago Elizalde in the north to the Río Ibáñez in the south. The area is dominated by the basalt spires of Cerro Castillo (2675m/8777ft) which, as its name implies, looks like a medieval castle. Indeed, the reserve is a mass of spires, turrets and ramparts interspersed by glaciers. It is a wild and remote place, home to the endangered huemul, the Andean fox, the chingue, the skunk and the Chilean flicker, or *pitio*, a type of woodpecker.

From Coyhaique, where you should buy all your provisions, buses run south to Cochrane on Tuesdays, Wednesdays, Saturdays and Sundays only, leaving at 8am. There are also private minibuses to Puerto Ibáñez. The journey south takes about 2 hours. You should get off the bus at the hairpin bend on the Río Blanco, where there are a couple of roadworkers' huts, Las Horquetas Grandes.

Las Horquetas Grandes to Laguna Cerro Castillo

Cross the Estero Paso de las Mulas and follow a dirt road, first beside the Río Blanco (going downstream), then west past a farmhouse, to reach a *puesto* after 1–1¼ hours. Now cross the Estero Blanco Chico and, after another 30 mins, the Estero La Lima itself. Head on up the valley, through grassy meadows; cross the Estero Aislado to reach a lagoon (home of black-necked swans), where you bear left at the track junction to avoid the swamp; and cross the rushing Río Turbio after 1½–2 hours. Continue along the valley floor, with great waterfalls gushing down from the glaciers above, and pick up a small trail which leads through lenga forest, then across a scrubby open area (45–60 mins). You can camp anywhere in this wild and remote spot, where you may even see a huemul.

From here, it is worth making the short side trip to the snout of the Glaciar Peñón. Just follow the Río Turbio for 20–30 mins upstream for an impressive view of the castle-like ramparts of Cerro Castillo, then retrace your steps.

> **TREK ESSENTIALS**
>
> **LENGTH** 4–5 days. 62km (38 miles) (including side trips). Walk up the Estero La Lima to the Pasada Peñón, down to the Estero del Bosque, on to Laguna Cerro Castillo, then to Campamento Neozelandés and out via the Estero Parada and the Senda Río Ibáñez to Villa Cerro Castillo.
> **ACCESS** *At start* Bus to Las Horquetas Grandes on the Carretera Austral, 75km (47 miles) south of Coyhaique. *On finish* Bus back from Villa Cerro Castillo to Coyhaique.
> **HIGHEST POINT** Pasada Peñón, 1453m (4767ft).
> **TREK STYLE** Backpacking. There are no huts in the area.
> **RESTRICTIONS** None.
> **FURTHER OPTIONS** 1. Side trip to Glaciar Peñón, a tarn directly beneath Cerro Castillo. 2. A day exploring from Campamento Neozelandés beneath Cerro Castillo.
> **MAPS** Chilean IGM 1:50 000 Lago Elizalde Section I No 132
> Chilean IGM 1:50 000 Balmaceda Section I No 133
> Chilean IGM 1:50 000 Villa Cerro Castillo Section J No 10

To continue the trek, follow the small stream uphill, through a rocky gully and beneath a snowfield up to your right, reaching the Pasada Peñón (1453m/4767ft) after 1½–2 hours. Head for the brilliant turquoise lake visible down to the southwest, descending (with care) down scree slopes. Remember to stop occasionally, or you may miss the spectacular icefalls in front of you: 'When you walk, walk; when you look, look'.

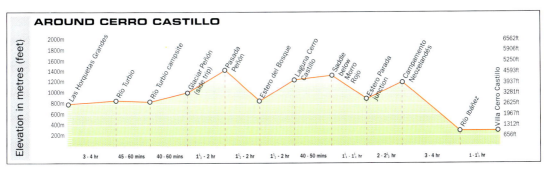

The castellated ramparts of Cerro Castillo as seen from Campamento Neozelandés.

Head downstream and you will reach the Estero del Bosque after another 1½–2 hours. Then go uphill again, threading your way through avalanche debris, keeping to the north bank of the stream, until you reach Laguna Cerro Castillo, cradled beneath Cerro Castillo: an impressive sight (1½–2 hours). Camp at the lake, for the view, or choose one of the more sheltered spots in the scrub, 20 mins walk below.

Laguna Cerro Castillo to Estero del Bosque

Traverse around the lake on a high path to the saddle below Morro Rojo, for stupendous close-up views of Cerro Castillo. From the little tarn to the left, you can see down to Villa Cerro Castillo and

Lago General Carrera.

From here you can either hike directly to Villa Cerro Castillo (3 hours) first heading east down a spur, then southeast to the Río Ibáñez, or take the longer (but more interesting) route up to Campamento Neozelandés, which is the site of the 1976 New Zealand Base Camp. For this option, from the saddle, head west below the rocky turrets of Cerro Castillo, and you will reach a small col after 40–50 mins. Descend the rocky gully with care and after about 30–45 mins walking, pick up a more distinct path coming up the Estero Parada Valley.

Another 2–2½ hours will see you negotiating the bogs at the head of the valley, and looking for a dry campsite (they do exist!). This is a wild and awe-inspiring place, hemmed in on three sides by spires and ramparts – a nice place to spend a rest day, or go exploring.

To get to Villa Cerro Castillo, merely descend the Estero Parada past the path junction where you turned uphill, continuing down the valley past a farm (with its grassy meadows full of ibises) to the Río Ibáñez, which you follow to the Estero del Bosque and the Carretera Austral. You can camp at the bridge over the Estero del Bosque. Buses run back to Coyhaique five times a week

COYHAIQUE DIRECTORY

Coyhaique is the regional capital of Chile's remote XI Province. The name means 'landscape of lakes' in Telhuelche. It is a small city, with a population of 35,000, located in the deep south between Puerto Montt and Punta Arenas. It is situated on the Carretera Austral, built in 1988 as part of General Pinochet's overall plan to link the region with the Chilean heartland. In fact, most traffic goes through Argentina. Coyhaique is the starting point for any exploration of the Cerro Castillo National Park, 75km (47 miles) south.

REGIONAL FLIGHTS
Santiago de Chile via Puerto Montt to Coyhaique: LanChile (daily).
Punta Arenas via Puerto Natales to Coyhaique: ALTA (daily).
Puerto Montt to Coyhaique: ALTA (daily).
Cochrane to Coyhaique: Don Carlos (Mon and Wed).

REGIONAL TRANSPORT
Puerto Aisén to Coyhaique: Don Carlos bus company (eight per day). La Cascada.
Cochrane to Coyhaique: Don Carlos bus company (twice a week); Collectivo Puerto Ibáñez (Mon, Wed, Fri).
Chalten to Coyhaique: Artetur bus company (Thursdays); B y V Tour (Mon, Wed, Fri).
Puerto Montt via Argentina to Coyhaique: Turibus (twice a week); La Cascada (weekly).
Comodoro Rivadavia to Coyhaique: Turibus (twice a week).

ACCOMMODATION
There is not a wide selection of accommodation in Coyhaique. It tends to be either rather expensive or very basic.
Top end:
Hosteria Coyhaique, Magellanes 131, tel: (5667) 231137.
Hotel Luis Loyola, Prat 455, tel/fax: (5667) 234000. Central heating and TV.

Standard:
Hostal Bon, Serrano 91, tel: (5667) 231189. Friendly and clean.
Residencial El Reloj, Baquedano 444, tel: (5667) 231108.
Hospedaje Guarda, Simpson 471, tel: (5667) 232158. Garden. Excellent breakfast.

Budget:
A youth hostel is usually run in one of the schools during Jan and Feb. The school changes each year.
Albergue las Salamandras, 2km south of town in forest. tel: (5667) 211865. Kitchen facilities; camping possible
Hospedaje Pierrot, Baquedano 130, tel: (5667) 221315. Highly recommended. Internet access.
Hospedaje Baquedano, Baquedano 20, tel: (5667) 232520. Allows camping in the garden.
Hospedaje Nathy, Almirante Simpson 417, tel: (5667) 231047. Friendly. Allows camping in the garden.
Hospedaje los 4 Hermanos, Colon 495, tel: (5667) 232647. One of Coyhaique's better value hostels.

Campsites:
There are many campsites in Coyhaique and on the road between Coyhaique and Puerto Aisén.
Camping Municipal, José Pantín. Within easy walking distance of the town.
Camping Alborada, tel: (5667) 238868. Hot shower.

LOCAL ACTIVITIES
Sernatur, Bulnes 35, tel: (5667) 231752, email: Sernatur_Coyhaique@entelchile.net. Open: Mon-Fri, 8.30am-9pm; Sat, Sun 11am-8pm.
Dirección Municipal de Turismo, Baquedano 310, tel: (5667) 232100, fax: (5667) 234051.
CONAF, Bilbao 234, tel: (5667) 212125,
Museo Regional de la Patagonia, Baquedano 310. Historical photos and pioneer artefacts. Open: Jan-Mar, 8.30am-1pm, 2.30-8pm.

TOUR OPERATORS
Expediciones Coyhaique, Portales 195, tel/fax: (5667) 232300. Pricey.
Expediciones Lucas Bridges, Lillo 311, tel/fax: (5667) 233302, email: lbridges@aisen.cl.
El Puesto, Moraleda 299, tel/fax: (5667) 33785, email: inter-media.cl/elpuesto/. Strong on rock and ice climbing.
Turismo Queulat, 21 De Mayo 1231, tel: (5667) 231441. Adventure tourism, fishing.

TREK 4: NAHUEL HUAPI TRAVERSE

Parque Nacional Nahuel Huapi, created in 1922, is the oldest of Argentina's national parks. We have the explorer Francisco Perito Moreno to thank for this. Moreno was given the land for his services to the Argentinian Boundary Commission, but he returned it to the state, on the condition that it was made into a national park. The park stretches from Parque Lanín in the north to latitude 42° south (the edge of the Argentinian Lake District). At its centre is Lago Nahuel Huapi. Nahuel Huapi is said to mean 'Island of the Tiger' in Mapuche and refers to the spotted jaguar that used to roam hereabouts. The whole area lay at the heart of the Mapuche land. This is a high-level trek through a stunning area of granite spires, deep blue lakes, alpine passes and mountain huts.

Two separate companies, Tres de Mayo and Buses Codao, run buses at alternate 2-hourly intervals from Bariloche to Villa Catedral ski village (1030m/3379ft), a journey of some 30 mins.

From here there are two routes to Refugio Frey. One goes via the *teléférico* to Refugio Lynch (1870m/6135ft) and traverses the ridge, following red and yellow paint splashes to the Cancha de Futbol, where it meets the path between Refugio Frey and Refugio San Martín, and then descends, past Laguna Schmoll, to Refugio Frey. There are several disadvantages to this route: first, the expense of the *teléférico*; second, the ridge is very rocky and exposed, can be icy and requires a good head for heights; third, you will need to retrace your steps the following day, back up to Laguna Schmoll, to reach Refugio San Martín (also known as Refugio Jakob).

The second and, to my mind, preferable option is to take the unsignposted old road from the car park diagonally opposite the bus shelter and follow this to the trailhead and a signpost marked 'Frey'. The trail then leads easily above Lago Gutíerrez and ascends through the forest to, after 1½–2 hours, a junction where you turn right. You follow the Arroyo Van Titter, then cross it on a precarious footbridge to reach the Refugio Piedritas, a Hansel- and-Gretel-like wooden house in the forest, built beneath a huge boulder. It sleeps eight, but is always locked as it belongs to the Club Andino Esloveno of Argentina (you cannot stay there unless you are a member). Continue up, more steeply, through the lenga forest to Refugio Frey (1700m/5577ft). The refuge stands at the eastern end of Laguna Tonchek in a tremendous location, with views of both north and south Cerro Catedral. It sleeps about 40 and is

TREK ESSENTIALS

LENGTH 5 days. 50km (31 miles). Trek to Refugio Frey, over the Paso Brecha Negra to Refugio San Martín (Jakob), to Refugio Segré (Italia), to Refugio López and down to the road at Puente López.

ACCESS *At start* By bus from Bariloche to Villa Catedral ski village. *On finish* No. 10 bus from Puente López to Bariloche.

HIGHEST POINT Cerro Navidad, 2060m (6759ft).

TREK STYLE Backpacking, either camping or hut to hut. Camping is officially allowed only at designated sites, (free and without facilities). There is a policy of no fires.

RESTRICTIONS There is a US$5 entry permit, unless you enter by a public road, as at Villa Catedral.

FURTHER OPTIONS Side trips to Cerro Cella and Laguna los Témpanos. Also, you can hike over the Paso Schweizer to Lago Mascardi from the Refugio San Martín (Jakob) (6–7 hours).

MAPS Argentinian IGM 1:100 000 Llao Llao Neuquén No 4172-22

Argentinian IGM 1:100 000 San Carlos de Bariloche Neuquén No 4172-23

CAB 1:100 000 Parque Nacional Nahuel Huapi

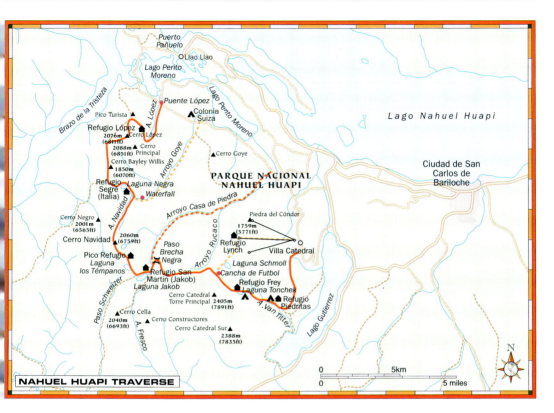

often full of young climbers who come to tackle the superb granite spires here. An area for camping is tucked in the trees beside the lake.

Refugio Frey to Refugio San Martín (Jakob)
From Refugio Frey, head along Laguna Tonchek, then ascend northwest, following red paint splashes, beside the stream to Laguna Schmoll, with impressive views of Cerro Catedral. Keeping this on your right, continue upwards until you reach a wide sandy area and the Cancha de Futbol, situated on a rocky ledge above the Arroyo Rucaco. An arrow and sign saying 'Refugio Jakob' point the way down the other side, heading first left, then back right and, finally, down a great scree run (look out for lizards) to the forest below. From here, the trail leads through a boggy meadow and re-enters the lengas, reaching a camping place after another 25 mins. Continue following the red markings across several streams until the path heads left out of the trees and begins to climb steeply up to Paso Brecha Negra (2025m/6644ft) for breathtaking views of the towers of Cerro Catedral and, below, Laguna Jakob and the San Martín (Jakob) refuge. A further hour of steep descent, first on scree then through bog and, finally, crossing the Arroyo Casa de Piedra, sees you to the hut (1600m/5249ft) with the *guardien*. Camping is permitted a few minutes up from the hut. Water can be collected from the hut tap.

Not to be missed is the side trip to Laguna los Témpanos, a tiny lake that lies in an impressive rocky cirque, whose walls tower 500m (1640ft) above. From the refuge, head up the ridge behind the camping area and cross glacier-scratched limestone slabs, following the ubiquitous red markers, then go down to the lake, with its permanent snowfield. For views of Monte Tronador (3554m/11660ft) and Cerro Catedral, a side trip to Cerro Cella (2040m/6693ft) is recommended. This heads around Laguna Jakob beside the stream into the hanging valley of the Arroyo Fresco, until just before the col, when you ascend on scree to the ridge and follow this to the summit (1–1½ hours from camp).

Refugio San Martín (Jakob) to Refugio Segré (Italia)
From Refugio San Martín (Jakob), it is possible to descend the Arroyo Casa de Piedra directly to the road in an easy 4 hours. If the weather is good, take advantage of one of the excellent swimming pools some 30 mins before the road. Alternatively, spend a day here, exploring the area. Alpine plants abound, tucked away in their own small microclimates among the boulders.

From Refugio San Martín (Jakob), it is worth continuing to Refugio Segré (Italia) on a rather more challenging trail. This is the wildest part of the trek, taking you across rocky ridges, beside pinnacles, up gullies and down scree, with a real sense of being 'out there'. There are none of the familiar paint splashes to follow, although there are sporadic cairns. Route-finding is not always easy, but the warden of Refugio San Martín (Jakob) is usually only too pleased to provide a description and can telephone ahead to the Refugio Segré (Italia) to warn them that you are on your way.

Follow the marked path to above Laguna los Témpanos, but don't descend to the lake. Head right in a north-north-easterly direction up the ridge coming down from Pico Refugio. After about 15 mins you reach a steepening traverse left along a terrace, until a gully slants up right. Ascend this to the ridge, which you now follow in a north-northwesterly direction. At the first pinnacle, descend slightly and walk below its eastern face, then cross a boulder field, always heading for an obvious gap in the crags ahead to the north. At the col, the views of an array of jagged peaks are stunning: Cerro Catedral, Cerro Navidad, Cerro Negro and Monte Tronador. It should take about 2½ hours to here from Refugio San Martín (Jakob).

From the col, it is only another 500m (1640ft) along the ridge to the summit of Cerro Navidad (2060m/6759ft). Once there, descend first north along the ridge, then northeast on scree, to pick up the Arroyo Navidad. Follow this steeply down until (after 2–3 hours) you reach a bivvy site beneath a boulder and the main paint-splashed path coming up the Arroyo Goye. Now for the sting in the tail: an hour's slog up a steep zigzag path through scrub to the ridge, where you are greeted by the welcome sight of Laguna Negra and the Refugio Segré (Italia) just below you. Camping is at the southeastern end of the lake, but remember to go to the hut to tell them of your safe arrival!

Refugio Segré (Italia) to Puente López

It is possible to descend the Arroyo Goye out to the road from here, with the advantage that you will be able to sample the delights of home-baking at the wonderful Salon de Thé (where blackforest gâteau is a speciality!) in Colonia Suiza. But it probably makes more sense to continue on to Refugio López.

Head along the eastern side of Laguna Negra on

One of the more adventurous parts of the second day on the Nahuel Huapi Traverse.

a well-marked path and cross its rocky northern end, where some scrambling is necessary and there is even a fixed rope to aid descent. Follow the markers north, beside a stream, and ascend to the ridge to the south of Cerro Bayley Willis after about 45 mins. Continue heading for a col to the north. From here the views are spectacular; your eyes will be drawn to the mighty glaciated Monte Tronador, which straddles the Chile–Argentine border and, to its north, the distinctive pointed Puntiagudo Peak. Now head downhill, following cairns and paint splashes to the meadows below and a campsite in the lengas beyond a stream. Ascend again, at first gently, then more steeply up a scree-filled gully, to yet another shattered ridge to the north of Cerro Principal. Turn northwest for the summit of Cerro López and marvel again at the panorama before you: the perfect textbook volcano of Osorno, Tronador and, below, Bariloche and Lago Nahuel Huapi. If you continue north to the slightly lower Turista Peak, you will find a seat from which to gaze in comfort. You may also be rewarded by the sight of condors soaring overhead. Retrace your steps along the ridge and it is only about an hour of following red and white arrows down the rocky spur to Refugio López, visible far below. Take care near the bottom, however, as some downclimbing is involved. The hut sleeps 100 and is the most popular and comfortable of all the huts in the area, in a great location overlooking Lago Nahuel Huapi. It certainly gets busy, especially at weekends. There is camping down the Arroyo López, some 15 mins below the hut, in a clearing in the woods.

It is an easy 2-hour hike down the east bank of the Arroyo López to Puente López on Ruta Nacional 79. The number 10 bus back to Bariloche goes past here every 2 hours until evening.

TREK 5: TRANS-ANDEAN TREK

The Trans-Andean Trek, as its name implies, crosses the Andes. It can be done in either direction, from west to east (Peulla in Chile to Pampa Linda in Argentina) or (as here described) from east to west. There is a well-known tourist trip that crosses the Andes, using a combination of boat and bus through the lakes of the Lake District, known as the *Traversia*. However, it is quite expensive and, as in all organized tours, you tend to be herded around somewhat, with no time to explore for yourself. This trek more or less follows that route on foot, though from the finish at Peulla, you will have to take a boat across Lago Todos los Santos. The scenery is superb – that wonderful combination of water and mountains – and you will see few other people, except, of course, where the tourist boats and buses disgorge their passengers.

Two companies run daily buses to Pampa Linda from Bariloche in the summer season, leaving at 8am and 9am respectively. The journey takes 2½–3 hours. Several tour operators also offer day excursions. There are two campsites at Pampa Linda, one free (with no facilities), and that of the CAB (Club Andino Bariloche), which has hot showers.

Pampa Linda side trips

From Pampa Linda, there are two possible side trips before you start the trek. The first merely requires you to continue up the dirt track from Pampa Linda

The climbers' bus to Pampa Linda.

TREK ESSENTIALS

LENGTH 5–6 days. 49km (30 miles), or 100km (62 miles) including side trips. Trek up the Río Alerce to Paso de las Nubes, down the Río Frías to Puerto Frías (Argentinian border post), on to Paso de Pérez Rosales, then Casa Pangue (Chilean border post) to Peulla.
ACCESS *To start* By bus to Pampa Linda from Bariloche. *On finish* 2-hour boat journey across Lago Todos los Santos from Peulla to Petrohué, then bus to Puerto Montt.
HIGHEST POINT Paso de las Nubes 1335m (4356ft)
TREK STYLE Backpacking. Horses can be hired for the ascent to Refugio Otto Meiling.
RESTRICTIONS Entry permit of US$5. A tent must be carried as there are no huts en route. Camping is only permitted at designated sites. A passport is needed to cross the border between Argentina and Chile. Raw agricultural products and dairy produce may not be carried across the border.
FURTHER OPTIONS Side trips to: Salto Garganta del Diablo and Piedra Pérez/Filo Clerk, Refugio Otto Meiling, from Pampa Linda; Laguna Alerce, from the first campsite; Glaciar Peulla, from Casa Pangue; Laguna Margarita, from Peulla; ascent of Monte Tronador (3554m/11660ft), from the Refugio Otto Meiling.
MAPS CAB 1:100 000 Parque Nacional Nahuel Huapi Argentinian IGM 1:100 000 Llao Llao Neuquén No 4172-22 Chilean IGM 1:50 000 Monte Tronador Section H No 46

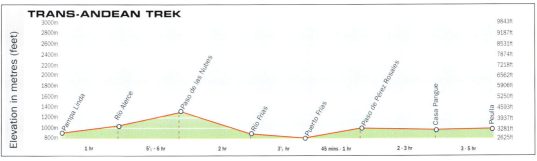

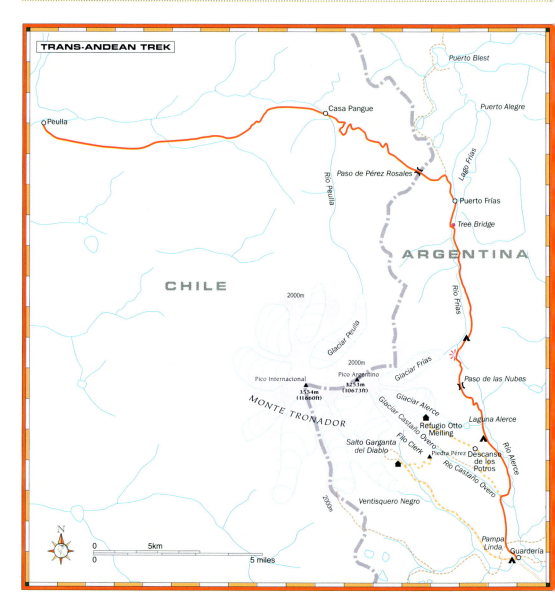

to the Salto Garganta del Diablo (The Devil's Throat), continuing to Piedra Peréz/Filo Clerk. The second side trip is to the Refugio Otto Meiling, the starting point for an ascent of Monte Tronador.

If you decide to take one of the *excursiónes* to Pampa Linda, a visit to the Ventisquero Negro (Black Glacier, with black icebergs in the lake below!) and the *confiteria* (tea shop) below the Salto Garganta del Diablo will almost certainly be included in the fare. Be warned, though, that there are whole months when the regular buses stop running, and you have no choice but to take an *excursión*. Hitchhiking is almost impossible, as there is virtually no traffic on the road to Pampa Linda.

The Refugio Otto Meiling, which belongs to the Club Andino Bariloche (CAB), is well worth a visit, situated as it is on a rocky ridge between the Castaño Overo and Alerce glaciers beneath Monte Tronador. It serves meals and sleeps about 60. It is named after Dr Otto Meiling, renowned local Andinist and founder of the CAB. It is clearly signposted from the *guardería* at Pampa Linda. Head northeast, crossing the Castaño Overa river after about 20 mins (on a new wooden bridge), then follow the dirt road, which zigzags its way uphill to the ridge. Continue along this to a grassy area, the Descanso de los Potros, where the road ends at the tree line (2½ hours from Pampa Linda). The views from here are

The Ventisquero Negro (Black Glacier) below Monte Tronador is as black as its name implies.

superb: great rock walls with thundering waterfalls, hanging glaciers and seracs. (Note that horses cannot ascend beyond this point.) Now follow the trail as it winds its way first left then right, through a boulder field to the ridge, and you will arrive at the refuge after 60–90 mins. A stunning spot.

You can hire a guide at the hut to make an ascent of either Pico Argentino or Pico Internacional (see Tronador Climb Essentials). Descend by the same route to Pampa Linda.

Pampa Linda to the Border

After spending some time doing these side trips, you may be keen to get started on the Trans-Andean Trek itself. From the *guardería* at Pampa Linda follow the marked trail towards the Refugio Otto Meiling as far as the bend in the dirt road where there is a three-way signpost. Take the path to Paso de las Nubes, down through avenues of bamboo and coigües to the Río Alerce, which you follow on the west bank, sometimes crossing fallen logs and side streams, until you reach a camping area at the edge of a swamp.

From here you can make a 2-hour side trip to Laguna Alerce, a spectacular glacial lake at the foot of the hanging Glaciar Alerce. At a fork in the trail, follow the true right bank (that is, the right bank of the stream flowing downhill) of the Río Alerce up to the base of a cliff and then over slabs into the hanging valley and on to the lake. You return to the camping area at the edge of the swamp by the same route.

To continue the trek from here, you first need to cross the Río Alerce, then the bog, following plastic markers and often jumping from log to log. After heavy rain you are almost certain to get your boots wet! The path then zigzags its way up steeply through thick forest, contours round to the north, crossing several side streams, and then heads leftwards up a gully, following cairns. It then levels out again and reaches a meadow after 3 hours. Cross this meadow, go through a thicket of lenga, cross one more meadow, then head left up to an indistinct high point, the Paso de las Nubes.

You only realize that you have reached the top when the path (follow the red splodges) immediately starts to descend steeply down the other side. It can be slippery after rain. Down you go into the forest, with occasional glimpses of ice and cascading water ahead. After 90 mins of steady descent you come to one of the most impressive lookout points I have ever seen. Standing on a rocky outcrop of granite slabs opposite the east side of Tronador, with Glaciar Frías and its three spectacular waterfalls thundering down the rock wall of the cirque in front of you, you have an eagle's eye view of the Río Frías and the valley below. It's a breathtaking sight.

The path weaves its way cunningly down 500m (1640ft) to the valley below, where you cross the stream and arrive at a beautiful campsite in the woods. This would be a wonderful place to spend a rest day, scrambling around on the rocks or merely soaking up the amazing atmosphere.

You spend the next 3 hours of the trek on a trail that can only be described as character building! A stick or trekking pole is definitely an advantage. You head down the valley through almost impenetrable bamboo and rainforest (dripping with epiphyte): clambering over, under and around fallen tree trunks; negotiating bogs by balancing on logs or hanging onto bamboo for support; crossing streams on bridges that are soon to be no more. This is your very own fitness trail, and adventure trekking at its best. The interest is always maintained as there is a new obstacle around every corner.

Finally, you reach the river, where the large fallen tree, used as a bridge (complete with wire handrail), seems a positive anticlimax. From here, it is only 30 mins to Puerto Frías, which consists of a jetty and border post on the shores of the ultra-green lake. Spare a thought for the two Argentinian officers whose plane crashed here in 1952 and whose memorial you will pass.

TORRENT DUCKS (*Merganetta Armata*)

Torrent ducks can be found in the unlikeliest of habitats – the fast-flowing mountain streams of the Andes. I have seen them in the Parque Nacional Torres del Paine, in Los Glaciares and on the Río Manso (on the way to Pampa Linda near Bariloche). They are said to inhabit the Parque Nacional Puyehue in Chile, the Río Pelechuco in the Apolobamba region in Bolivia, and the high rivers of Peru and Ecuador. They can also be found as far away as Colombia and Venezuela. In short, torrent ducks inhabit any area of the Andes that has rushing mountain streams – the colder the better, even straight out of the glacial lakes of Southern Patagonia.

Torrent ducks are usually seen in pairs, the male black and white with a striped head, and the female a vibrant slatey grey, with a red belly. Both have red bills and reddish legs. They stand erect on rocks in the middle of a set of rapids, some 42cm (1ft 4ins) tall and pure muscle. They dive into the raging waters in search of fish, swimming upstream or flying over the surface with legs racing, looking for all the world as if they are running on water. Then, they ride the wild torrent down, using the current, swooping and leaning – the envy of any kayaker. No one could deny that they are having fun!

Unfortunately, as the wild areas are disappearing and the rivers are becoming more polluted, torrent ducks are becoming increasingly rare. This is a pity, as they are a joy to behold, if only as an example of how to enjoy yourself!

There is camping in the trees, where you'll find wild raspberries in summer. If you want to stop earlier in the day's trek, there is one possible camping area 2 hours down along the trail (an obvious flat, open area) and another just before you cross the fallen tree bridge.

The Border to Peulla

You must obtain an exit stamp (from Argentina to Chile) from the border police at the checkpoint, who are very helpful. It is possible to return to Bariloche by a combination of boats and buses from here: catamaran across Laguna Frías to Puerto Alegre, bus to Puerto Blest, catamaran to Puerto Pañuelo and then bus back to Bariloche.

To cross the Andes, however, you need to follow the dirt road for 26km (16 miles) to Peulla in Chile. Take the road along the southwest side of Laguna Frías and ascend to the Paso de Pérez Rosales (1000m/3281ft). Then descend past a deserted farmhouse through coigüe forest for 2–3 hours to the Chilean checkpoint at Casa Pangue. It is sometimes possible to camp here. The view of Tronador is superb. From here you can make a 20-km (12-mile) return day hike following the Río Peulla, to the Glaciar Peulla. Just follow the path on the east bank of the river.

Otherwise, cross the Río Peulla on a suspension bridge after a further 3km (2 miles), then head west

The easy way to end the Trans-Andean Trek is by the bus and boat *traversia* through the Patagonian Lake District to Puerto Montt.

along the flat valley for another 2–3 hours before crossing a large expanse of wet pampas and heading south to the customs post outside Peulla. You must have your passport stamped again here.

Some people choose to pay for a ride in an excursion bus between the two checkpoints, to save the 6–9 hour hike, but it is expensive.

There is a CONAF (Corporación Nacional Forestal) campsite (without facilities) at Peulla, as well as several moderately priced *hospedajes* and the upmarket Hotel Peulla. While in Peulla you can visit the Cascada de los Novios waterfall or hike up to Laguna Margarita (3-hour return trip).

From Peulla, take the 2-hour boat journey across Lago Todos los Santos to Petrohué and catch a bus to Puerto Montt via Ensenada and Puerto Varas.

PEAK: MONTE TRONADOR

The approach from Refugio Otto Meiling, and the ridge. Monte Tronador is climbed from the other side of the ridge.

Monte Tronador (3554m/11660ft) is the majestic triple-summited peak whose unmistakable white bulk dominates the surrounding landscape. As the summits' names imply, Pico Chileno lies in Chile, Pico Argentino in Argentina and Pico Internacional, the highest point, straddles the border itself. Although an extinct volcano, its glaciers and seracs creak, groan and come tumbling down with crashes and a roars, giving rise to its name, the 'Thunderer'.

First climbed in 1934, it is definitely one of the more interesting mountains in the area and is a mecca for climbers. The Club Andino Bariloche built the Refugio Otto Meiling at its base and uses this as a centre from which to run mountaineering courses. The refuge sleeps up to 60 people, has a resident *guardien* in summer and serves meals. The location is stunning, situated as it is on a rock ridge between Glaciars Castaño Overo and Alerce, with panoramic views of Cerros López, Bonete, Righi, Catedral and, below, the valleys of Pampa Linda and Paso de las Nubes.

Follow the route description from Pampa Linda to the hut found in trek 5. If you enjoy partying, then go up there on a Saturday night and join the youths of Bariloche, who arrive armed with guitars and bottles of wine.

Leave early from the hut, as once the sun is on the glacier it can feel very unstable. There are huge crevasses to be avoided. Cross the Glaciar Castaño Overo towards the Motte Ridge, then descend slightly left towards the Vieja Ridge. From here, depending on snow conditions, it is possible either to pick a way downwards skirting the ridge and avoiding the bergschrund, or to make a short abseil to the glacier below. Then head towards the obvious depression ahead and climb up to the col between Argentino and Internacional Peaks, avoiding the very large crevasse. At the col, cross the crevasse and continue towards the ridge coming down from the summit. Cross the bergschrund and ascend a 40° slope for two rope lengths to the ridge. Once there, it's a scramble and an exposed snow slope, both short-lived, to the summit. Marvel at the views across Chile and Argentina. You will feel, as they say, on top of the world.

Descend by the same route. It takes 4 hours to the depression, 1–2 hours to the summit and is a 9–10-hour round trip.

CLIMB ESSENTIALS

SUMMIT Monte Tronador, Pico Internacional 3554m (11660ft)
PRINCIPAL CAMP Refugio Otto Meiling 1850m (6070ft)
GRADE Alpine Grade AD+

TREK 6: PUYEHUE TRAVERSE

Once part of the land of the Mapuche Indians, Puyehué (pronounced poo-yay-way) means 'place of the puye', which itself was the name for a small fish found in the freshwater lakes and rivers of the Lake District. The Puyehué National Park attracts 50,000 visitors a year, due in part to its ease of access. Most Chileans and Argentinians seem to head for the hot springs at Aguas Calientes, but those from further afield make for the wild, desolate, volcanic plateau, with its fumaroles, thermal springs, bubbling mud pools and geysers.

TREK ESSENTIALS

LENGTH 4–5 days. 75km (47 miles) including side trips. Trek to Refugio Volcán Puyehue, across the volcanic plateau to Los Baños Nuevos, down the Río Contrafuerte, and out to Riñinahue.
ACCESS *To start* By bus from Bariloche or Osorno to Guardería Anticura. *On finish* Bus from Riñinahue to Osorno.
HIGHEST POINT Volcán Puyehue, 2236m (7336ft).
TREK STYLE Backpacking. It is also possible to hire horses and a guide from El Caulle.
RESTRICTIONS Entry to the private land of El Caulle costs 5000 Chilean pesos, but staying in the well-equipped Refugio Volcán Puyehue, which belongs to the landowner, is free. You must carry a tent as there are no other huts en route. Remember, if arriving from Bariloche, that raw agricultural products and dairy produce may not be taken across the border into Chile.
FURTHER OPTIONS Side trips: Salto del Indio (1 hour from Guardería Anticura); Volcán Puyehue; Los Geiseres (4 hours from Los Baños Nuevos). NB. It would be possible to hike up to the Refugio Volcán Puyehue, base yourself there, do a series of day hikes around the area (ascent of Volcán Puheyué, visit to the hot springs and so on), then return to the Guardería Anticura and pick up one of the many daily buses between Osorno and San Carlos de Bariloche to continue along the international highway.
MAPS Chilean IGM 1:50 000 Volcán Puyehue Section H No 27
Chilean IGM 1:50 000 Riñinahue Section H No 17
CONAF 1:250 000 Parque Nacional Puyehue (main trekking routes)

This is a land of intense volcanic activity, where the magma is a mere 2–4km (1¼–2½ miles) below the surface. The Cordón de Caulle consists of 18 craters along a 4.3-km (2¾-mile) line running northwest from Volcán Puyehué, which erupted in 1960, covering the plateau with pumice and black lava.

Several buses run each day from Osorno in Chile or Bariloche in Argentina to the starting point at the Guardería Anticura, where you need to register. There is also a CONAF campsite there.

It is worth making the 1-hour side trip up to the 6-m (18-ft) waterfall Salto del Indio from here. Salto del Indio is said to derive its name from the story that a Mapuche Indian managed to evade the conquering Spaniards by hiding behind its curtain of water. Follow signs to La Princesa up through the laurel forest, past a deep pool and on to the waterfall. Instead of returning the way you came, you can follow signs to 'Salida 215', which brings you out further up the highway.

Guardería Anticura to the Summit of Volcán Puyehué

To start the trek proper, hike from Guardería Anticura along the road towards Osorno for 20 mins, until you get to the second bridge over the Golgol River, and turn right at the El Caulle sign. This is private land and there is an entrance fee of 5000 Chilean pesos, payable at the tollhouse. This initially seems an astronomical sum, but on arrival at the new Refugio Volcán Puyehue, with its 16 bunk beds, wood-burning stove, saw, axe, broom and, most important, its weather-proof roof, the money seems well spent.

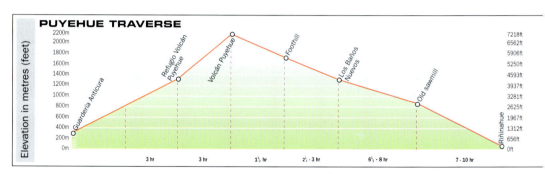

It is definitely a good place to sit out a storm (I speak from bitter experience!) and you can stay for as long as you like.

From the tollhouse bear left at the first fork in the trail, continue beside the electric fence through one gate, and on to another gate, where the track turns left through a cow pasture and finally starts to ascend up through the rainforest. This is a distinct path, gentle at first, then zigzagging steeply to reach the tree line and the hut after 3 hours. There are plenty of places for tents among the trees by the hut.

Water is rather a problem, as the streams seem to run underground, but if you go up the hill behind the hut, drop down to the stream and follow it upwards you should come to running water. Take a cup, though, as the water collects in shallow pools.

It takes 2–2½ hours to reach the summit of Volcán Puyehué (2236m/7336ft) from the hut. Head up the path as far as the turn-off to Los Baños, then continue up the spur, contour to the right and cross three small streams, coming out on a rocky ridge which leads up and around, above the crater, to the top.

The views are spectacular. The barren volcanic plateau stretches away to the north and the rocks gleam bright red and orange below you. The double summit of Volcán Choshuenco and the Cerros de Lipinza lie to the northeast, whilst the blue of Lagos Puyehué and Rupanco, Volcán Casablanca and the triple-summit of snow-capped Tronador lie to the south.

The Descent

Descend the way you came and, at the signpost, head towards Los Baños. The trail contours beneath the volcano, crosses gullies (with or without streams) and leads upwards onto the plateau, below the fumaroles. At this point, you will probably feel gratitude towards the landowner for marking the way with orange-tipped wands. It is a featureless wasteland, with ball bearing-like gravel underfoot, and seems interminable. You head north around the west side of Volcán Puyehué until you come to a trail junction marked Riñinahue. Here, you head northwest between the first distinctive features of the hike – two streams with green vegetation in the bottom. Then you ascend a ridge, descend, re-ascend and finally go down past old fumaroles to a stream and a sheltered camping spot. This is the site of the former hot spring 'Los Baños', now dry. Now cross the stream on an iron grid and

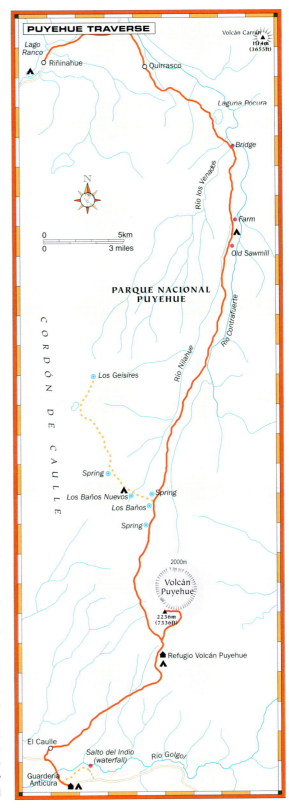

Crossing the Volcán Puyehue plateau can be a very snowy experience, and will require full winter-weather gear.

follow the path for 15–20 mins, across another small stream and hillock, to Los Baños Nuevos, a veritable oasis in the desert or, more aptly, a thermal spring in a volcanic wilderness. Running water, steam rising, green vegetation against a backdrop of reds, oranges and browns, birds twittering and fumaroles smoking above make this place quite idyllic. The thermal pool, which is at the junction of the small and large streams, may need digging out, as it gets silted up, but there is a shovel to hand. There is good camping here, too.

Side Trip to Los Geisires

The 4-hour side trip up to Los Geisires is well worth doing from here. Follow the river northwest. Where it turns west, continue northwest, heading for a distinctive orange-red rock face. Cross two streams, then you'll need to wade the main river (45 mins from camp). Continue heading north, following cairns, until you ascend onto a ridge, where there's a marker. Follow the ridge, then descend to a lake, contour round to the right and ascend the ridge at the east end. From here, you head in the direction of the steaming red rocks, first round to the right, then descending slightly to a boggy basin, with a final steep ascent to the geysers. You'll find a devil's cauldron of bubbling pools, geysers and brilliantly coloured rocks. Be careful where you tread. Return the same way.

To Riñinahue

Retrace your steps to the trail junction marked Riñinahue. Follow the markers along barren pumice ridges, then descend steeply above the eastern branch of the Río Nilahue, and finally go down to cross the stream and climb up the opposite bank, reaching a disused dirt road after 30–45 mins. Continue down into the rainforest, where the trail becomes very overgrown, with fallen trees and bamboo. Descend on a broad ridge between the Río Nilahue on your left and the Río Contrafuerte on your right. After 2–3 hours cross and recross the Río Contrafuerte, then climb back up to the ridge top and follow the slightly more distinct trail for another 3–4 hours until you come to a larger four-wheel drive track. Follow this past an old sawmill and camp 60–90 mins further on in a meadow by the Río Nilahue.

Follow the road to a farm and a bridge over the Río Nilahue, then ascend steeply through the woods (and the occasional patch of grazing land) for 3–4 hours, until you cross the Río los Venados bridge. Continue past several small farms and Laguna Pocura on the right. The valley opens out and finally you come to the small village of Quirrasco. The road now follows the Río Nilahue to where it meets the main Riñinahue–Lago Ranco road. Turn left and head for Riñinahue, where there is one *hostería* and a good bus service back to Osorno.

PUYEHUE VOLCANISM

Volcanoes occur when molten rock (referred to as magma) in the earth's mantle moves upward through fissures or conduits to erupt at the surface. Magma rises because it is less dense than the deeper rocks. Chemical reactions and expanding gases propel the liquid rock towards the surface.

Volcanic eruptions take different forms, depending on the composition of the magma when it reaches the surface. Lava is the name for fluid magma, which can be light and frothy (producing pumice), or heavier and more viscous (resulting in slow-moving ropy lava called *pahoehoe*). Pyroclastic rocks are formed from the solid fragments ejected in an eruption and are named according to their size: volcanic ash, if sand-sized or smaller; volcanic blocks or bombs if bigger.

Most volcanoes only erupt for brief and irregular periods, remaining dormant for the majority of their lives. When active, their effect on the landscape and the local population can be very dramatic. The formation of volcanoes, lava flows, craters, fumaroles (vents from which hot gases escape) and geysers are directly related to volcanic activity. Add to these such side effects as earthquakes, tidal waves and mudflows and you have the potential for widescale disasters.

The most recent eruption of Puyehue, in May 1960, is of particular interest to geologists as it immediately followed, and was probably triggered by, a devastating earthquake measuring 8.9 on the Richter scale. This is one of the few cases of earthquake-triggered volcanic eruptions. The eruption began with explosive activity from numerous craters. Molten rock was blown high into the air to form an incandescent fountain. Lava then continued to rise in the vent and flow out of the crater to ooze slowly down the mountainsides. This extrusion of lava continued for more than a month.

Volcán Puyehue lies on the 965-km (600-mile) long Liquiñe-Ofqui fault line, which runs parallel to the Andes. This crack in the earth's crust is responsible for the highest concentration of hot springs in the country. There are more than 70 separate springs lying hidden in the mountains and fjords of the Lake District and Northern Patagonia. The locals contend that the pools are very good for curing rheumatism.

An incredible black lava flow and fumaroles on the snow-covered Puyehue plateau after an autumn storm.

SAN CARLOS DE BARILOCHE DIRECTORY

San Carlos de Bariloche is situated at 760m (2493ft) on Lago Nahuel Huapi, the largest lake in the Argentinian Lake District. With an economy based purely on tourism, Bariloche is now the largest town in the Patagonian Andes, with a population of some 77,600. It was founded in 1895 by Germans from the Chilean Lake District, and even today there is a Teutonic feel about the place, with its Swiss/German architecture. It can get very crowded in the summer months and also, of course, at the height of the ski season. Prices are high. Bariloche is the starting point for any trek into the Nahuel Huapi National Park, an ascent of Monte Tronador, the Trans-Andean Trek and the gateway to the Puyehue National Park in Chile.

REGIONAL FLIGHTS
Buenos Aires to Bariloche: Aerolíneas Argentinas (twice daily); Austral (daily); Dinar, LADE, LAPA, Sapse, Southern Winds (most days).
El Calafate to Bariloche: TAN (twice weekly).

REGIONAL TRANSPORT
Buenos Aires to Bariloche: Chevallier, El Canario, El Sureno, El Valle, La Estrella, TAC – all buses via Bariloche (daily).
Buenos Aires to Bariloche: Train (twice weekly).
Puerto Montt via Osorno to Bariloche: Andesmar, Bus Norte, Cruz del Sur, La Flota Amiga de la X Region, Río de la Plata, TAS Choapa bus companies (daily).
Puerto Montt to Bariloche via the 'traversía': a bus/boat combination (daily).
Bariloche to Villa Catedral: Codao, Omnibus 3 de Mayo (hourly).
Bariloche to Pampa Linda: Trans RM, Cerros Patagónicos (daily).

ACCOMMODATION
Accommodation can be arranged through the tourist office, where the staff are incredibly helpful (phone number below).
Top end:
Hosteria la Sureña, San Martin 432, tel: (54) 2944 422013. Clean and quiet.
Hotel Internacional, Mitre 171, tel: (54) 2944 425938. Central.
Hotel Carlos V, Morales 420, tel: (54) 2944 425474. Upmarket.
Standard:
Hotel Argentino, Av Costanera 12 de Octubre 655, tel/fax: (54) 2944 425201.
Hosteria del Inca, Gallardo 252, tel: (54) 2944 422644. Recommended.
Residencial Lo de Gianni, Elflein 49, tel: (54) 2944 433059. Good value.
Budget:
Albergue Patagonia Andina, Morales 564, tel: (54) 2944 421861, www.elpatagoniaandina.com.ar. Very central. Excellent breakfast.
Albergue Mochilero's, San Martin 82, tel: (54) 2944 423187, fax: (54) 2944 436117.
Periko's Youth Hostel, Morales 555, tel/fax: (54) 2944 522326, email: perikos@bariloche.com.ar, nicolas@bariloche.com.ar or cecilia@bariloche.com.ar. New. Films, free internet, laundry, hires mountain bikes, arranges tours.
Albergue Alaska, Av Bustillo, 7.5km, tel/fax: (54) 2944 461564, email: alaska@bariloche.com.ar. Kitchen, laundry, hires mountain bikes, arranges tours.
Rosan Arko, Güemes 691, tel: (54) 2944 423109. Rents rooms.
Albergue Rucalahué, Güemes 762, tel: (54) 2944 430888. Kitchen, laundry. Very friendly and helpful owners.
Albergue Ruca Hueney, Elflein 396, tel: (54) 2944 433986, fax: (54) 2944 617416.
Campsites:
All are on Av Bustillo, heading out west along the lake shore:
Selva Negra, (2.9km).
El Yeti, (5.6km).
Petunia, (13.5km).

LOCAL ACTIVITIES
Secretaria Municipal de Turismo, Centro Civico, Av Bartolome Roca, tel: (54) 2944 423022, www.bariloche.org. Open: in summer Jan-Mar, Mon-Fri 8.30am-9pm; Sat, Sun 10am-9pm.
Club Andino Bariloche, 20 de Febrero 30, tel: (54) 2944 424531, fax: (54) 2944 24579, www.clubandino.com.ar. Information and maps. Organizes excursions and the Pampa Linda bus. Open: Jan-Mar, Mon-Sat 8.30am-2pm, 5-8.30pm; Sun, 8.30am-noon, 6-8pm.
APN (Administrative Centre for Parque Nahuel Huapi), San Martín 24, tel: (54) 2944 423111. Open: Mon-Fri, 9am-2pm.
Museo de la Patagonia, Centro Civico, tel: (54) 2944 422309. Open: Tue–Fri, 10am–noon, 2-7pm; Sat, Mon, 10am–1pm.
Rafting:
Aguas Blancas, Morales 564, tel/fax: (54) 2944 432799.
Rafting Adventure, Morales 362, Piso 1 Local 5, tel/fax: (54) 2944 432928, email: aventura@bariloche.com.ar, www.mercotour.com/adventure.
Rafting and kayaking, raftkayak@cpsarg.com.
Horse-riding:
Cabalgatas, Tom Wesley, Av Bustillo 8000, tel/fax: (54) 2944 448193.
Carol Jones, tel: (54) 2944 26508.
Mountain Biking:
Bike Way Mountain, V.A. O'Connor 867, tel/fax: (54) 2944 424202.
Lengal Mountain Bike, tel: (54) 2944 67346, fax: (54) 2944 61650.
Diving:
Arum Escuela de Buceo, Av Bustillo, tel: (54) 2944 523122.
ASAP Diving Centre, Mitre 171, tel/fax: (54) 2944 427088.
Parapenting:
Parapente Bariloche, tel/fax: (54) 2944 42154.
Bookshop:
Librereía Cultura, Elflein 78, tel/fax: (54) 2944 420193.

TOUR OPERATORS
Adventure World, tel: 068 308603, fax: (54) 2944 433260, email: adventure@bariloche.com.ar.
Andes Patagónicos y Nestor H Lujan, Mitre 125, Local 5, tel: (54) 2944 426809, email: andespatagonicos@bariloche.com.ar.
Amuncar, San Martín 82, Piso 1, tel: (54) 2944 431627, fax: (54) 2944 423187.
Cumbres Patagonia, Villegas 222, tel: (54) 2944 423283, fax: (54) 2944 431835.
Lauquén Turismo y Aventura, Mitre 86, Local 5, tel/fax: (54) 2944 442484.
Safari Patagónico, Alaska Youth Hostel, Av. Bustillo, tel/fax: (54) 2944 461564, email: alaska@bariloche.com.ar.

TREK 7: VILLARRICA TRAVERSE

Parque Nacional Villarrica was established in 1940. It takes its name from the still active and smouldering Volcán Villarrica, whose perfect cone dominates the landscape. Villarrica's last major eruption, in 1971, changed the course of several rivers and destroyed the village of Coñaripe. The park comprises 60,000 hectares and stretches from Pucón in the west to Puesco on the Argentinian border in the east. It takes in active and inactive volcanoes and a barren volcanic plateau of lava flows, scoria and pumice, studded with azure alpine lakes.

Below 1000m (3050ft) the hillsides are richly forested with varieties of southern beech trees, rauli, roble and coigüe; at a higher level, lenga and nire predominate, with stands of auracaria, the monkey-puzzle tree, from which this region, the Araucanía, gets its name. This is the land of the Mapuche Indians. Indeed, the Mapuche name for Volcán Villarrica was Rucapillán, meaning 'house of the spirits', home to the ancestors. This trek traverses the breadth of the park, passing beneath Volcáns Villarrica and Quetrupillán and across the plateau to the Argentinian border, to Volcán Lanín, through a landscape of Mapuche names.

Refugio Villarrica to Río Pichillaneahue
From the Refugio Villarrica, head up towards the large tin shed at the top of a ski tow and pick up the four-wheel drive track, which weaves its way below another ski tow. Cross a dry stream bed and follow the foot trail across open heath just above the tree line, through lava fields, finally ascending more steeply leftwards up a rocky spur to reach a ridge after 1½ hours. The route continues above the trees, crossing more lava fields and gullies, not to mention the odd snow patch, then descends through magnificent auracaria forest to the path junction at the Zanjón Pino Huacho (a stream), where a trail comes up directly from Villarrica. Notice the wooden water pipe, down in the bottom of the canyon.

Cross the stream and continue round the mountain, sometimes in forest, sometimes over lava fields and gullies, until you come to a particularly large old monkey-puzzle tree at another path junction. Take the right-hand path, over two more dry stream beds, to a running stream, the Estero Challupen, which you cross. Then, its up through lengas to the Estero Ñilfe, where there are good campsites in the trees on the northern bank. Enjoy the great views of Volcán Choshuenco to the south.

Next, follow sporadic cairns across the open hillside round to the left of a knoll, crossing ridges and streams, always heading for the pass between two volcano cones (points 2006m/6581ft and 1616m/5302ft), which you reach after 1½–2 hours. From here, you get your first views to the southeast of Volcán Quetrupillán and the mighty snow-capped Volcán Lanín.

Descend the ridge down to the right, cross a tiny stream and then head down another ridge to reach the Estero Traico. You need to cross this, then head east across a 1-km (¾-mile) wide lava field towards a stand of auracarias that are visible on the horizon. Climb up to the ridge top and

TREK ESSENTIALS

LENGTH 6–8 days. 88km (55 miles), including side trips. Trek anti-clockwise from the Refugio Villarrica around Villarrica, across lava fields to Palguín/Coñaripe and the Termas de Palguín. Then, continue on towards Volcán Lanín on a high-level route, past Lagunas Azul, Blanca and Abutardas to Puesco, with its *guardería*, customs post, basic campsite and Environmental Education Centre.
ACCESS *At start:* Either get a taxi, walk (2–3 hours on foot) or get a ride from one of the adventure tour operators heading for Volcán Villarrica, from Pucón to Refugio Villarrica. *On finish:* Local bus from Puesco back to Pucón at 8am and early afternoon most days. International buses to Junín and San Martín de los Andes. These may be more problematic, as you will not be on their list for a border crossing. You may need to hitch a ride to the border and get on the Argentinian bus there.
HIGHEST POINT Volcán Quetrupillán, 2382m (7815ft).
TREK STYLE Backpacking. The only accommodation is at the Refugio Villarrica, the Hostería Termas de Palguín and the Hospedaje Agricultor (2km/1¼ miles beyond Puesco at the end of the trek).
RESTRICTIONS Entry fee to the National Park, where camping is only permitted a day's walk or more from the nearest road.
FURTHER OPTIONS Side trip to Volcán Quetrupillán. Climb Volcán Villarrica (2847m/9341ft).
MAPS Chilean IGM 1:50 000 Pucón Section G No 104
Chilean IGM 1:50 000 Villarrica Section G No 103
Chilean IGM 1:50 000 Liquiñe Section G No 113
Chilean IGM 1:50 000 Curarrehue Section G No 105
Chilean IGM 1:50 000 Paimun Section G No 114

64 CHILE AND ARGENTINA

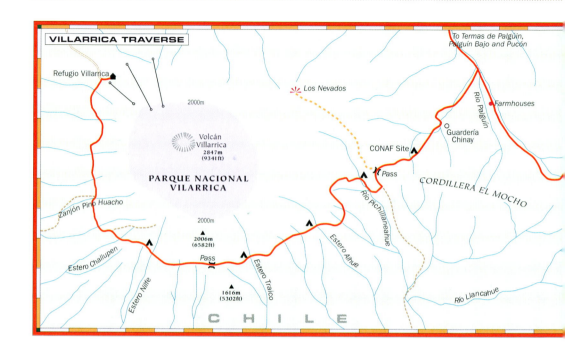

View of Volcán Lanin from Villarrica.

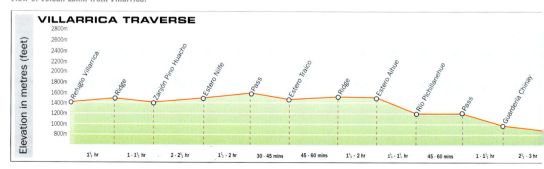

TREK 7: VILLARRICA TRAVERSE

continue in a mainly easterly direction to reach the Estero Aihue after another 2–2½ hours. Now head for the stand of monkey-puzzle trees, situated above the tree line, where you pick up the trail again, following the cairns and red paint up onto wildflower-strewn meadows (make sure you take the higher trail here). Next, head north, contouring around the mountainside and crossing several small streams, until you descend eastwards again into the trees, finally zigzagging down steeply into coigüe forest and bamboo to the Río Pichillaneahue, which you need to ford. Camp on the east bank.

Río Pichillaneahue to Termas de Palguín

From here head downriver for 600m (1969ft), then cross a small ridge to come out on the Palguín–Coñaripe road. Turn left onto it and ascend to a pass. It is possible to make a 10-km (6½-mile) return side trip to a mirador on the broad snow plateau on the northeast slopes from here – follow the road signposted 'A Los Nevados'. Otherwise, continue on down the road past the CONAF campsite to the Guardería Chinay and the boundary of the national park. Keep on going for another 3km (2 miles) to a road junction, where you bear left and arrive at the Termas de Palguín, after another 3km (2 miles), for a well-earned bathe in the hot springs! There is a *hostería* at the Termas, but no official camping, although it is possible to continue on the road towards Palguín Bajo – take the turn to Salto El Léon and camp there. Alternatively, you could camp at the CONAF site in the Upper Cañadon de Chinay and make a side trip down to the hot springs.

It is also possible to hike out from the springs to the road at Palguín Bajo in 2–3 hours. There are buses back to Pucón every hour.

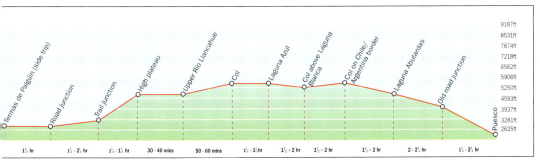

PEAK: VOLCAN VILLARRICA

The much-climbed route to the summit of Volcán Villarrica.

Volcán Villarrica has had more ascents made on it than any other Chilean mountain. It is a perfect conical shape, capped by snow. An active volcano, its most recent eruption was in 1984, and it is said that the next eruption is long overdue. The crater belches forth noxious sulphurous fumes, and molten lava is clearly visible. One of the most striking sights is that of the summit glowing in the darkness.

Technically quite straightforward, the ascent does require a good level of fitness. Crampons and an ice axe are essential. It is a 6–9-hour round trip from the Refugio Villarrica.

The park authorities now demand that everyone, except trained mountaineers with qualifications to prove it, or members of a climbing club, makes the ascent with an approved guide, and there are a plethora of companies in Villarrica only too ready to guide you to the summit. Make sure that your equipment is in good condition and that a mask (to keep out the fumes) is included.

From Refugio Villarrica follow the line of the ski lift uphill on volcanic ball bearings to the top station and the summer snow line (2000m/6562ft). Then head up the well-worn track in the snow to the summit. Near the top, the snow ends and you're back on volcanic grit. The views from the top are tremendous, both down into the glowing crater and out onto the broad panorama of almost all the peaks of the southern Araucanía and Lake District. Descent is by the same route, but the volcanic scoria, so laborious to ascend, makes a great scree-run down!

CLIMB ESSENTIALS

SUMMIT Volcán Villarrica, 2847m (9341ft)
PRINCIPAL CAMP Refugio Villarrica, 1420m (4659ft)
GRADE Alpine Grade F

Termas de Palguín to Laguna Azul

To continue with the traverse trek, however, head back up the road from the Termas to the road junction and take the left fork, which leads into private property, marked by a large gate and cottage. Luckily, the owner does not object to trekkers on his land. Follow the track across the Río Palguín, past some farmhouses, then ford the river and continue straight ahead through a clearing, re-entering the national park at a log gate. Look out for a path, marked with red paint, heading right after 300m (984ft) or so. Follow this up through coigüe forest to a ridge, keep on ascending (first east, then southeast) through auracaria trees and lengas until you come to two small streams and an open plateau. Savour the impressive, unimpeded view of Volcán Villarrica, smoking away to the northwest.

Now cross the plateau, keeping to the left of a rocky volcanic plug, and head southeast over meadows and volcanic waste to reach the upper Río Llanchaue. From here, it is a 3-hour return trip to the crater of Volcán Quetrupillán.

The path then leads downhill for about 10 mins, then up and over ridges, across open slopes (always following red paint markings) to a rocky col, with tremendous views of the volcanoes to the north.

As you descend you will spot Laguna Azul, the next objective, away down to your right. Keep high for a while, then zigzag down to it. It is a brilliant blue jewel of a lake, as its name implies. Camp on the southeastern shore of the lake, or continue round the lake and across the stepping stones to the other side of the outlet stream, to a spot below the remains of Refugio Azul (this is more exposed, however). It is possible to hike along the Río Llancahue to the Palguín–Coñaripe road from here.

Laguna Azul to Laguna Abutardas
From Laguna Azul, the trail continues east, then northeast, across yet another lava field, up and down, finally reaching a small col, with a view down to Laguna Blanca, nestled in a barren volcanic wasteland. Head down to the lake (if you like), then continue south, with Volcán Choshuenco ahead. Follow the rim of an extinct volcano, before heading east again across a spur marking the Chile–Argentina border. Contour northwards, descend into a desolate valley, then ascend northeast back onto the border ridge to re-enter Chile.

The panorama is magnificent. Ahead, there are a selection of tiny tarns, with the spiky peaks of the Cordillera de las Carpas behind and, further east, the saw-toothed La Peineta, the 'dress comb'. Here, you have your last view of Volcán Lanín.

Zigzag down, following the stream, but avoiding cliffs, finally crossing it below a waterfall. Head up again on the other side, to reach a ridge, which you follow to just before a rocky outcrop. Here, the path plunges steeply down through forest, emerging at one clearing, then another, then a grassy marshland area inhabited by buff-necked ibises, at the western end of Laguna Abutardas. Follow the trail across the marsh and up above the steep north side, descending, finally, to the grassy east shore where there is good camping. Don't miss the lovely sandy beach, which is excellent for swimming.

Laguna Abutardas to Puesco
From the lake, descend northeast through lenga and bamboo forest, reaching a *mallín* (swamp) after 30–40 mins. Pick your way through this, looking for markers to the right, where you re-enter the trees. Continue northeast, until you come to an old road. Turn right and follow this, above the rushing Río Puesco to the Pucón to Junín de los Andes international highway (edible strawberries and cherries can be found here, depending on the season). Turn left at the highway and cut off the road's zigzags using trails in the woods, reaching Puesco after 40–50 mins. You need to sign in at the customs post and tell them that you have not come from Argentina. There is a CONAF campsite at Puesco.

PUCON DIRECTORY

Pucón lies at the heart of Chile's Araucanía district, where it has become a thriving centre for outdoor activities. It is ideally located on a lake of the same name as the town, with views towards Volcán Villarrica.

REGIONAL FLIGHTS
There are daily flights to Temuco (66 miles/110km away) from Santiago de Chile on Lanchile and Ladeco.

REGIONAL TRANSPORT
Santiago de Chile to Pucón: Buses Jac, Tur-Bus, Buses Power, Buses Lit (daily; usually via Temuco and Villarrica; 10 hours). *Temuco to Pucón*: Buses Jac (every 15mins; 1 hour).

ACCOMMODATION
There is a wide selection of accommodation in Pucón.
Top end:
Hotel Antumalal, 2km west on road to Villarrica, tel: (5645) 44101/44102; fax: (5645) 44103; email: antumal@lazos.cl. Small, chalet-style hotel in picturesque setting. Heated swimming pool and access to lake.
Gran Hotel Pucón, Clemente Holzapfel 190, tel: (5645) 441001; email: info@granhotelpucon.cl. Luxury on the lake.
Standard:
Hostería El Principito, General Urrutia 291, tel: (5645) 441200. Friendly and clean; recommended.
Hostería Casablanca, Palguin 136, tel: (5645) 441450. Good.
Hostería Millarahue, O'Higgins 460, tel: (5645) 441610. Clean. Inexpensive seafood restaurant.
Budget:
La Tetera, General Urrutia 580, tel: (5645) 441462; email: info@tetera.cl; www.tetera.cl. Good breakfasts. Friendly. Internet. Recommended.
Hospedaje Eliana, Pasaje Chile 225, tel: (5645) 441851. Clean and friendly. Kitchen.
Residencial Lincoyón, Lincoyón 323, tel: (5645) 441144. Clean and friendly.
Hostería Ecole!, General Urrutia 592, tel: (5645) 441675; email: trek@ecole.mic.cl. Dormitory accommodation and double rooms. Vegetarian restaurant. Information on activities. Spanish classes.

TOUR OPERATOR
Sol y Nieve Expediciones, O'Higgins 192, tel/fax: (5645) 441070, email: solnieve@entelchile.net, www.chile-travel.com/solnieve.htm.

PEAK: ACONCAGUA

Aconcagua at 6962m (22841ft), a mere 38m (125ft) short of the mighty 7000m (22966ft), is the highest mountain on the American continent. Indeed, it is the highest outside the Himalaya. Almost on the border between Chile and Argentina, it could be said to be the greatest natural barrier between two of the best wine-growing valleys in the world!

Although a technically straightforward climb, the ascent of Aconcagua by the Ruta Normal should not be underestimated. Firstly, it is very high and, secondly, it is very cold. Altitude sickness, hypothermia, exposure and frost bite are all too common. Winds can reach 240km (149 miles) per hour and temperatures drop to –35° C. Each year, several people die on the mountain.

The key to success, as on any high mountain, is to acclimatize slowly, stay hydrated, eat plenty of carbohydrates, wear the correct clothing and have time in hand, so that you can wait out bad weather. Remember that the weather can change extremely rapidly. Descend immediately if you see a lenticular cloud forming on the summit, as this means bad weather is imminent.

The mountain is best approached by bus from Mendoza, as you need to get your peak permit there, although you can, of course, take a bus

Aconcagua is *the* South American challenge for mountaineers and climbers.

across the border from Santiago de Chile.

There are three main routes up Aconcagua: the Ruta Normal (Normal Route); the Ruta Glaciar los Polacos (the Polish Glacier Route); and the Pared Sur (the South Face). The normal route can be attempted by any fit individual with winter hillwalking experience, who knows he or she can cope at altitude. The Polish Glacier route is for those with alpine glacial experience, and the South Face is steep and technical, for experienced ice climbers only. It is, however, worth hiking up to the Base Camp at Plaza Francia for a stunning close-up view of this awesome face.

The Normal Route

For the Ruta Normal and the Pared Sur, you catch the bus from Mendoza to the Puente del Inca, a natural rock bridge over the Río Mendoza, where there are three shops and a couple of *hosterías*. Burros can be hired here. Then start the hike up the Horcones Valley. The scenery is uninspiring – there is no water, no wildlife and no vegetation. A dead, dreary and dusty landscape, as you would imagine the moon. It is advisable to make a halfway camp at Confluencia, to aid acclimatization. From here, either hike up the right fork of the Horcones, if your destination is the Plaza Francia, or take the left fork, the Horcones Superior, to continue for another 22km (14 miles) to the Plaza de Mulas, the Base Camp for the Ruta Normal. It is a veritable tent city in the main climbing months, January and February, with up to 400 tents at any one time. There is also now an upmarket hotel and restaurant.

Climbing Aconcagua is big business for the local agencies. The best campsites are reserved for the local guides and their parties, as are often the best toilets!

It is worth spending a couple of days acclimatizing at the Base Camp. Several peaks can be climbed as training, including Cerro El Manso (5500m/18045ft, F) Cerro Cuerno (5462m/17920ft, PD/AD) and Cerro Mirador, which is best climbed from the Horcones Valley (6089m/19977ft, PD). Many people acclimatize by moving up to the next camp, leaving a stash of gear, then descending to sleep: 'climb high, sleep low'.

The route up to the next camp, the Nido de Condóres at 5350m (17552ft), is clearly visible from the Plaza de Mulas, zigzagging its way up the scree. There are also poorer campsites at 4900m (16076ft) and at 5200m (17060ft). From here, the summit and the Canaleta, a scrappy, loose, boulder-filled gully, are visible. Head east to gain the north-northwest ridge and reach Campamento Berlin at 5950m (19521ft). You can either camp here, or ascend to White Rocks Camp at 6000m (19685ft). Most people summit from here or Campamento Berlin in one long day, but you could camp at the ruined Refugio Independencia at 6500m (21325ft). This would leave you with less ascent, but probably more of a headache!

From Independencia, continue up the ridge, cross above the Gran Accareo (great scree slope) and ascend the Canaleta, keeping as far as possible to the right, or on snow. At the top, turn east along the Cresta del Guanaco – where the remains of a guanaco, presumably sacrificed by the Incas, were found in 1947 – and head for the summit Madonna. Descend in two days by the same route to Plaza de Mulas.

The Polish Glacier Route

The Polish Glacier Route starts from the Punta de Vacas. Head up the Vacas Valley and camp at the ruined hut and ranger station at Las Lenas after 18km (11 miles; 5 hours). Cross the Vacas River here (only possible without mules in the mornings), then continue for another 18km (11 miles) past the Refugio Gonzalez to Casa de Piedra and camp (6 hours). Make an easier crossing of the Vacas River and head west up the Arroyo Relinchos, crossing it a couple of times, for a further 15km (9¼ miles) to the Base Camp at Plaza Argentina (4250m/13944ft).

From here, the path weaves its way over *penitentes* and moraines to a camp at 4900m (16076ft) at the top of a steep slope. Then follow scree and gain the northeast rib, just left of the Ameghino Col (it is possible to camp here at 5600m/18373ft). Follow the rib, passing rock pinnacles on the left, and reach the High Camps at the foot of the Polish Glacier itself (5700–5900m/18701–19357ft).

From here, it is normal to reach the summit in one long day. Keep to the left of the glacier, passing beneath the Piedra Bandera, a strangely banded rock which looks like the Argentinian flag. The glacier goes up at about 40°, with a steeper angle over to the right. Finish by climbing the east ridge. Descent is usually by the normal route.

An Alternative Route

An alternative route would be to reach the Polish Glacier High Camp, then make a rising traverse across scree and snow to join the Ruta Normal below Independencia (Grade F). The advantage of this would be to avoid the congestion at the Plaza de Mulas; the disadvantage, the extra expense of hiring burros for longer.

CLIMB ESSENTIALS

SUMMIT Aconcagua, 6962m (22841ft)
Ruta Normal
CAMPS Base Camp (Plaza de Mulas) 4200m (13780ft); Camp One (Nido de Condóres) 5350m (17552ft); High Camp (White Rocks) 6000m (19685ft).
GRADE Alpine Grade F
Polish Glacier Route
CAMPS Base Camp (Plaza Argentina) 4250m (13944ft); Camp One 4900m (16076ft); Camp Two (Ameghino Col) 5600m (18373ft); High Camp (Start of Polish Glacier) 6000m (19685ft).
GRADE Alpine Grade PD

MAPUCHE INDIANS

The Mapuche ('people of the earth') live in the Araucanía, on both sides of the Andes. In pre-Hispanic times they were the first inhabitants of half the area now known as Chile and Argentina. About two million of them occupied a vast territory in the southern part of the continent. They now number approximately 1.5 million (constituting over 10 per cent of the total population) in Chile, and 200,000 in Argentina. The Mapuche constitutes the third largest indigenous society in South America.

The Mapuche had a well-developed social structure, were renowned for their impressive artwork and were accomplished warriors. This latter fact may well explain why the Mapuche were never defeated; in fact, they were the only Indian tribe the Spaniards failed to conquer. Rather, the Mapuche secretly observed the Spanish style of fighting, learned from it, and in turn used it against the invaders. Only six months after the founding of Santiago de Chile by the Spaniards in 1541, the Mapuche nearly decimated it, and in 1553 they defeated the Spaniards in the battle of Tucapel and killed their leader, Pedro de Valdivia.

They led many uprisings against the *conquistadors*, the most notable being the general rebellion of 1598, with the result that the Spaniards never seriously contested Mapuche control of the area south of the Río Biobío. Attempted settlements were immediately reduced to ashes during the 17th and 18th centuries, so that by the mid-19th century the Spaniards had abandoned most of the area except for Valdivia. Indeed, foreign travellers referred to 'Arauco' as a separate country.

It was not until Chile had gained its independence from Spain, and waged the military campaigns of the Conquista del Desierto in the 1870s and 1880s, that a treaty with the Mapuche was signed in 1881. Only then was the land settled by immigrants from Germany, Italy, Switzerland and Croatia.

The Mapuche people, although clearly great guerrilla fighters, were not necessarily a violent people. Rather, they were fiercely independent and afraid of losing their land – and with good reason, for eventually, of course, like the native Americans to the north in the USA, they did indeed lose much of it to large estates and have since been restricted to small reserves.

Today, several hundred thousand Mapuche live in the provinces between the Río Biobío and the Río Tolten, still known as La Frontera. The main city for the area is Temuco. They still speak their own language but, having lost most of their land, must now earn a precarious living from small-scale agriculture and selling crafts. The Mapuche are extremely pro-active in their attempt to preserve their native language, along with their dances, their magic, and their agrarian way of life.

From 1965 to 1973 land reform did improve the Mapuche peoples' position, but the military coup of 1973 reversed many of their gains. Since the restoration of democracy in 1989, the Mapuche have been militant in asking for the return of their lands. In 1998 they took their case to the Commission on Human Rights at the United Nations, demanding recognition of their rights and putting forward the notion of cultural diversity for Chile. They have continued campaigning for the restoration of their lands and an end to deforestation, and against the damning of the Río Biobío.

The Mapuche peoples' spiritual beliefs are closely linked to the land and their natural environment, from which they believe the power of life emanates. They believe that people should live in harmony with the natural environment, not destroy it. The Mapuche also have a deep sense of commitment and responsibility to other people in their tribe. Great importance is still attached to family bonds, despite the increased breakdown of the extended family as individuals leave their homes in Araucanía to seek employment and wages in the cities.

More information on the Mapuche people can be found at:

Mapuche Inter-Regional Council, No. 4 2439, P. Ercilla, Temuco, Chile, tel: (5645) 405661, fax: (5645) 275493, email: aanguita@uctem.cl.

Mapuche International Link, 6 Lodge Street, Bristol BS1 5LR, England, tel/fax: (44) 0117 927391, email: mapulink@aol.com.

MENDOZA DIRECTORY

Founded in 1561 and named after the Chilean Governor García Hurtado de Mendoza, it was from here that Simón Bolívar and José de San Martín crossed the Andes in 1814 to liberate Chile. In 1861 it was completely destroyed by an earthquake and fire, and was rebuilt with low, modern buildings and parks, squares, gardens and tree-lined streets. It is now Argentina's fourth largest city, with a population of some 700,000. Situated at 760m (2493ft) in the rain show of Aconcagua, the climate is dry and gentle, but with enough snowfall on the mountains to provide irrigation for the now famous vineyards of the valley of the same name. The Fiesta Nacional de la Vendimia (wine festival) takes place in February and March.

Mendoza is the starting point for any ascent of Aconcagua, as climbing permits need to be bought here. It is also an ideal location for all types of outdoor activities, from skiing in the winter, to trekking, mountain biking, white-water rafting, and more.

REGIONAL FLIGHTS

Buenos Aires to Aeropuerto Internacional Plumerillo, Mendoza: Aerolíneas Argentinas, LAPA (2 hours, twice daily); Dinar (2 hours, daily); Austral (2 hours, 3 times a week).
Santiago de Chile to Mendoza: LanChile, Ladeco (twice daily).

REGIONAL TRANSPORT

Buenos Aires to Mendoza: Bus Chevallier, TAC, Empresa Jocoli, (several daily); Empresa Senda (daily).
Santiago de Chile to Mendoza: Chile Bus, Cata, Tur Bus, Tas Choapa, TAC, Ahumada (6-8 hours, daily); also daily minibus (6 hours).
Mendoza to Puente del Inca (for Aconcagua): Expreso Uspallata (3½ hours, two a day, leaves in the morning, returns in the afternoon).

ACCOMMODATION IN MENDOZA

There is a wide selection of accommodation in Mendoza.
Top end:
Gran Hotel Huentala, Primitivo de la Reta 1007, tel: (54) 261 420 0766. Four-star. Good.
Hotel Balbi, Las Heras 340, tel: (54) 261 423 3500. Pool, helpful staff.
Hotel Del sol, Garibaldi 80, tel: (54) 261 420 4296. Highly recommended.
Middle:
Hotel Petit, Péru 1459, tel: (54) 261 423 2099. Recommended.
Hotel Horcones, Las Heras 145, tel: (54) 261 425 0025. Good value. Recommended.
Hotel Pacifico, San Juan 1407, tel: (54) 261 423 5444. Modern, good value.
Hotel San Remo, Goday Cruz 477, tel: (54) 261 423 4068. Roof-top terrace, TV, quiet, highly recommended.
Budget:
Resdencial Savigliano, Palacios 944, tel: (54) 261 423 7746, email: www.savigliano.com.ar. Near bus terminal, kitchen, laundry facilities, roof-top terrace. Internet. Recommended.
Hospedaje Eben-Ezer, Alberdi 580, tel: (54) 261 423 3635. Quiet.

Hotel Mariani, Lamadrid 121, tel: (54) 261 423 9932. Laundry, heating, good value.
Hotel Galicia, San Juan 881, tel: (54) 261 423 2619. Central, clean, friendly.
Hotel Vigo, Necochea 749, tel: (54) 261 423 0208. Central, garden.
Youth Hostels:
Campo Base, Mitre 946, tel: (54) 261 429 0707, www.campo-base.com.ar. Shared rooms, kitchen and laundry facilities, internet, bike rental, information on Aconcagua, helpful.
Hostel Internacional Mendoza, España 343, tel: (54) 261 424 0018, www.hostelmendoza.net. Central, shared rooms, internet, climbing wall, information on outdoor activities.
Campsites:
In Parque General San Martin, El Challo, 6km (3½ miles) west of city centre. Take No. 110 bus to El Challoa.
Atsa, tel: (54) 261 429 6656. Swimming pool. Friendly, but can be noisy.
Camping Suizo, Av. Champagnat, tel: (54) 261 444 1991. Pool, barbecues. Friendly.

LOCAL ACTIVITIES

Subsecretaria de Turismo, Av. San Martin 1143, tel: (54) 261 420 2800. For permits for Aconcagua. Open 7am-9pm.
Club Andista Mendoza, Pasaje Lemos, tel: (54) 261 424 1840.
Centro de Información y Asistencia Turismo, Paseo Sarmiento/Garibaldi y San Martin, tel: (54) 261 424 5333. Open 9am-9pm. Good maps, English spoken.
Centro do Información, Las Héras 670, tel: (54) 261 429 6298.
Bookshops
Y Libros, Av. San Martin 1252, tel: (54) 261 425 2822
Rubén Simoncini Libros, San Juan 1108, tel: (54) 261 420 2988

TOUR OPERATORS

Andesport, Rufinofi, Ortega 390, tel: (54) 261 424 1003.
Aymará Viajes y Turismo, 9 de Julio 1023, tel: (54) 261 420 0607, fax: (54) 061 420 5304, email: aymara@satlink.com. Adventure travel in general, trekking, climbing, rafting, horsepacking, mountain biking, windsurfing.
Cuyo Travel, Paseo Sarmiento 133, Local 14. Trekking and climbing on Aconcagua.
Cumbres Andinas Turismo, Rivadavia 234, tel: (54) 261 438 0505.
Fernando Grajales, José F. Moreno 898, tel/fax: (54) 261 429 3830. Local guide, organizes climbs on Aconcagua.
Hunuc Huar Expeditions, España 1340, piso 8, oficina 7. Trekking, climbing.
Huera Pire, Emilio Civit 320. Climbing Aconcagua.
Inka Turismo Avenutura, Juan B. Justo 343, tel: (54) 261 425 1281, www.orviz.com. Trekking, climbing, horse-riding, rafting.
Rudy Parra, Aconcagua Trek, Gürraldes 246, Dorrego, tel/fax: (54) 261 424 2003. Mountain guide.
Vida y Aventura Travel, San Martín 1070, tel: (54) 261 420 3663/0654. Trekking, climbing, mountain biking, rafting, windsurfing.

4
BOLIVIA

The Andes stretch the length of Bolivia, from Peru in the northeast to Chile in the south. On the Peruvian border lies the Apolobamba Range, a wild and remote area, where the condors fly and you can still stake a claim to the odd gold mine! Its highest peak is Chaupi Orco, at 6044m (19829ft).

All the treks in this chapter are within relatively easy reach from La Paz. The main range, the Cordillera Real (the Royal Range), lies in western Bolivia and divides the Altiplano from the Yungas. It runs for roughly 150km (93 miles) from Illampu in the north to Huayna Potosí in the south, with five peaks over 6000m (19685ft).

South of Huayna Potosí, and dominating La Paz, stands the mighty Illimani, at 6439m (21125ft) and, further south again, the Quimsa Cruz is a small but significant mountain range of crenellated granite peaks and glaciers.

Passing below Chairoco, one of Bolivia's 6000-m (19685-ft) peaks (trek 12).

Land and People

Bolivia lies at the heart of the Andes. It is a country about the size of France and Italy put together, but with a population of only eight million, of whom 70 per cent live on the Altiplano at the foot of the Andes. It is landlocked, much to the chagrin of Bolivians, since they lost their access to the Pacific Ocean to Chile in the War of the Pacific in 1884.

Although Bolivia was the first country to attempt to overthrow the Spaniards (in the failed revolution of 20 October 1808 in what is now called Sucre), it was in fact the last country to gain its independence – in 1825 – as Spain was keen to keep hold of this wealthy country, which provided silver from mines in Potosí and looted Incan gold. Bolivia can be divided into five distinct geographic areas: the Altiplano, the high valleys, the Yungas, the Chaco and the rainforests of the Amazon basin. This chapter is only concerned with Bolivia's high mountains, the Andes, and the high plateau, the Altiplano, at their feet.

The best time for trekking and climbing in Bolivia is the winter (June to September), when the weather is at its most stable, with clear days and cold nights.

Even though 60 per cent of the population do not speak Spanish as a first language, but rather Aymara, Quechua or one of the other Indian languages, the leaders of Bolivia have been drawn from members of the population who are of Spanish descent or from the *mestizo* (mixed race) class.

Politics

It was not until 1952 that the indigenous people, who were either locked into an almost feudal system of *pongaje* (living and working on the farms of large landowners for no pay), or employed on minimal wages in the mines (which often had absentee owners), rose up in the April Revolution and defeated the military. The MNR (Movimiento Nacional Revolucionar) duly came to power under Victor Paz Estenssoro, nationalized the mines and ended *pongaje*, giving the *campesinos* (peasants) the right to own their land. The MNR ruled for 12 years, after which Bolivia's governments were marked by instability, corruption, bloody power struggles, coups d'états and dictatorships until 1982. Fortunately, since 1982, there has been a return to democracy and stability, although in 1997 Hugo Banzer Suarez, an ex-dictator of the 1970s, was elected president. Banzer's government was characterized by a failing economy and increasing civil unrest. Banzer resigned in 2001 due to ill health and was replaced by Jorge Quiroga who has the difficult task of holding together an unlikely coalition government, but also of appeasing the Aymara people, who have finally found their own leader in another Quiroga known as 'el Mallku' (the Condor).

ARRIVING IN BOLIVIA

La Paz must be one of the most dramatic cities in the world. However you travel, whether by air or by bus, you arrive first at El Alto on the Altiplano. Although it is South America's fastest growing city, El Alto is still obviously in the process of being built, with half-finished buildings and much squalor. First impressions are not terribly favourable. From El Alto, however, the road reaches the rim of the Altiplano and there before you, filling the valley below, lies the city of La Paz. Towering above, dominating the scene, is the great bulk of the mighty snow-covered Illimani. It is breathtaking.

El Alto sits at 4000m (13120ft), but La Paz lies at a mere 3600m (11811ft). This can be a shock to the system if you come by air direct from sea level. Make sure you spend at least a couple of days acclimatizing in La Paz. Walking around the streets of the city at a slow pace is ideal: just watch the Bolivians! From the Prado, the main avenue, all the streets run either up or down. Remember that it is quite natural to feel breathless. Drink plenty of water and try to eat lots of carbohydrates. Coca tea is also said to be a good remedy for *la soroche* (the effects of altitude).

Making camp at Chajolpaya, with La Calzada in the background (treks 11 and 12).

BOLIVIA

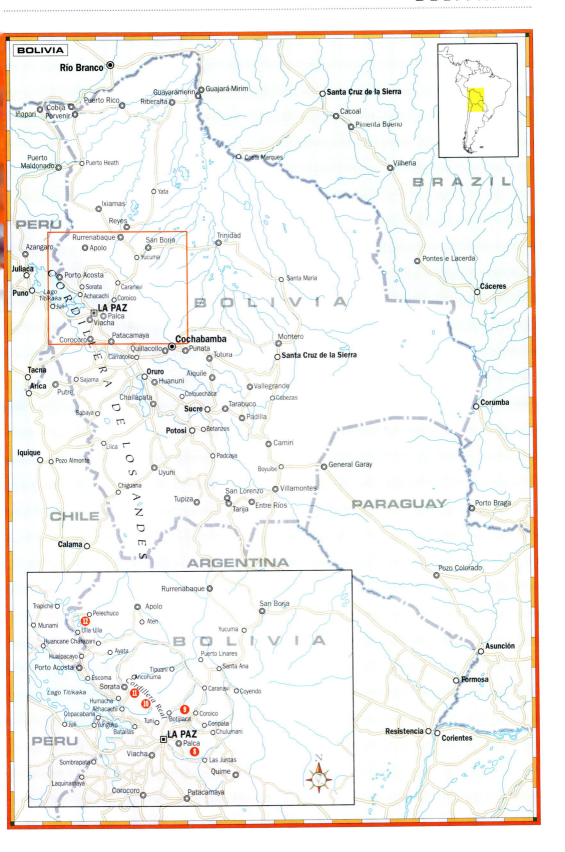

Although Sucre is the official judicial capital of Bolivia, La Paz is the largest city, the centre of finance and commerce and the seat of government (the president's palace). La Paz is, to all intents and purposes, the real capital, and all the foreign embassies are there.

TRAVELLING TO BOLIVIA
By Air
Most foreign visitors arrive by plane at El Alto Airport, La Paz. Very few international airlines, however, actually fly into El Alto, as the airport is at too high an altitude to take jumbo jets. Most carriers fly either via Miami, Río de Janeiro and São Paulo, Lima, Santiago de Chile or Santa Cruz and transfer their passengers onto a smaller plane. American Airlines, Varig, LanChile, Aeropéru and Lufthansa all fly here. Aerolíneas Argentinas now uses Lloyd Aéreo Boliviano for the final leg from Santa Cruz. Bolivia's other airline, Aerosur, also flies in from other cities in Bolivia. There is a distinct shortage of flights into and out of La Paz during the busy time of year, Bolivia's winter. This keeps prices high and means that you must book well in advance. Airport tax is payable on domestic flights and international departures.

By Road
There are various road entry points into Bolivia from Chile, Argentina and Peru.

From Peru
Puno – Copacabana – La Paz (8 hours)
Puno – Desaguadero – La Paz (10 hours)

From Chile
Arica – Tacna – Desaguadero – La Paz (14 hours)
Arica – Tambo Quemado – La Paz (18 hours)
Charaña – La Paz (8 hours)
Calama – Ollagüe – Uyuni – La Paz (26 hours)

From Argentina
Bermejo – Tarija (6 hours)
Tartagal – Yacuiba – Tarija (112 hours)
La Quiaca – Villazón – Potosí – La Paz (30 hours)

Visas
You must have a passport that is valid for at least six months. On arrival you will be given a tourist card which is required to exit the country. Normally, a 30-day visa is stamped in your passport, but you can request a 90-day visa on arrival, or it can be extended at the immigration office, Calle Camacho 1433, corner of Calle Loaza. This is free of charge for EU citizens, but US citizens and some others must pay. It is a legal requirement for you to carry your passport with you at all times, and you must show it when cashing travellers' cheques or at any police checkpoint. It is advisable to keep a photocopy in a safe place back at your hotel.

Customs/Immigration
Your bag will be searched on arrival at El Alto airport. Officials are primarily looking for drugs.

Time Difference
Bolivia is 4 hours behind GMT. After daylight savings, however, the country is 5 hours behind UK time.

Money
The Boliviano (Bs) is the unit of currency in Bolivia, which is divided into 100 centavos. In Bolivia, and throughout the whole of South America, however, the US$ is more useful than £ sterling.

In the cities, it is probably best to use your usual cash card at an ATM (for either Cirrus or Plus, look for the Enlace sign, or there are Visa machines), from where you can withdraw Bolivianos or US$. Otherwise, you can change travellers' cheques (in US$ or £ sterling) at a *casa de cambio*. Alternatively, you can change US$ on the street, where there are recognized traders. The rate is the same.

INTERNATIONAL AIRLINES

Lanperu, Av 16 de Julio No. 1490, Edif Avenida, 1er piso, of. 2, tel: (591 2) 315832/358337, fax: (591 2) 392051
Lan Chile, Av 16 de Julio (El Prado), tel: (591 2) 358390, fax: (591 2) 392051, email: lanbol@ceibo.entelnet.bo
Varig, Av Mariscal Santa Cruz 1392, Edif Cámara Nal. de Comercio, tel: (591 2) 314040/314086, fax: (591 2) 391131
American Airlines, Plaza Venezuela No. 1440, tel: (591 2) 351360/372009, fax: (591 2) 391080
Lufthansa, Av 6 de Agosto, Edif Illimani, No. 2512, tel: (591 2) 431717/810078, fax: (591 2) 431267

DOMESTIC AIRLINES

Lloyd Aéreo Boliviano (LAB), Av Camacho No. 1456-60, tel: (591 2) 371020, toll free: 0800 3001, fax: (591 2) 813415
Aerosur, (5L), Av 16 de Julio No. 616 El Prado, tel: (591 2) 313233/343043, toll free: 0800 3030, fax: (591 2) 300457
TAM (Transporte Aéreo Militar), Av Montes 738, tel: (591 2) 379285/379286. A military airline that flies to regional airports in the lowlands.

In small towns, you can often change money (US$ in cash) at hotels or shops.

TRANSPORT
In La Paz
Within La Paz there are large buses, called *micros*, and a plethora of minibuses, each with a young lad hanging out of the window, shouting the name of the destination. There are also taxis, which are supposed to be metered, but in practice you should negotiate a price before you get in. Then there are the *collectivos*, taxis with a set route which pick up passengers along the way.

The streets of La Paz are very busy. The traffic only stops when there is a transport strike, demonstration or a fiesta! Buses and minibuses run until late at night, then there are always taxis.

Countrywide
By Air
Domestic airlines connect all the major cities.

By Bus
The roads in Bolivia are mainly unpaved. The exceptions are the main road between Arica in Chile and La Paz, and the newly paved road to Copacabana on Lake Titikaka. Journeys are usually long and dusty. Buses are cheap but have not been designed with the larger Westerner in mind! There are buses between all the major cities and there is also a less frequent service to most of the villages. Mining roads have carved a path into the Andes themselves.

It is wise to take food and drink with you and, if you are crossing the Altiplano, a down jacket and/or sleeping bag. Overnight travel can be very cold.

La Paz's central bus station (*terminal terrestre*) for buses to the south and east is at the corner of Av Uruguay and Av Peru. Other buses, generally to the north, leave from the city's cemetery. Buses to other smaller villages leave from a variety of locations (see individual trek guides for information about where to catch a bus for your particular destination.)

By Truck
Local people tend to travel either by bus or by truck. These are used in the same way as a bus, but do not have seats! If there is no bus, and you don't mind a crush, they are a cheap and reliable form of transport.

By 4×4
For a more comfortable, albeit expensive, journey you can hire a 4×4 from a trekking agency. This is

TREKKING AGENCIES

Andean Summits, Calle Armaza 710, tel/fax: (591 2) 422106, email: andean@latinwide.com. Experienced guides; gear for hire.

Andes Expediciones, Av Camacho 1377, tel: (591 2) 319655/ 32091, fax: (591 2) 392344, email: andesexp@ceibo.entelnet.bo. The oldest trekking agency in La Paz.

Azimut Explorer, Calle Sagárnaga 173, tel: (591 2) 333809/ 452482, fax: (591 2) 329465, email: azimexbo@caoba. entelnet.bo or bolivia@azimutexplorer.com, www.azimutexplorer.com. Guide for trekking and climbing; gear for hire.

Club Andino Boliviano, Calle Mexico 1638, tel: (591 2) 324682. Information on trekking and skiing.

Colibri, Calle Sagárnaga 309, tel: (591 2) 371936/378098, fax: (591 2) 355043, email: acolibri@ceibo.entelnet.bo. Trekking and climbing; gear for hire.

Colonial Tours (Hostal Austria), Calle Yanacocha 531, tel: (591 2) 316073, fax: 0811 3419-316073, email: colonial@ceibo.entelnet.bo. All types of tours, treks and climbs.

Nuevos Horizontes, Calle Arturo Borda 1871, tel: (591 2) 416596, email: newhorizons20@hotmail.com. Experienced.

Refugio Huayna Potosí, Hotel Continental, Av Illampu 626, tel: (591 2) 323584, fax: (591 2) 378226. Guide to Huayna Potosí.

TAWA, Calle Sagarnaga 161, tel: (591 2) 825796/329814, fax: (591 2) 391175, email: tawa@caoba.entelnet.bo. Treks and climbs.

Arriving at the start of the Apolobamba trek (trek 13).

EMBASSIES

Argentina, Calle Aspiazu 497, tel: (591 2) 369266/353233
Australia, Av Arce 4829, Edif Montevideo, tel: (591 2) 440459 (consulate only)
Brazil, Av 20 de Octubre 2038, tel: (591 2) 440202
Canada, Plaza España, Edif Barcelona, 2do piso, No 2678, tel: (591 2) 4151541
France, Av Hernando Siles 5390, tel: (591 2) 786125/786114
Germany, Av Arce 2395, tel: (591 2) 440088/440606
Italy, Av 6 Agosto 2575, tel: (591 2) 434929/434955
Netherlands, Av Arce 3031, tel: (591 2) 444040
Peru, Av 6 de Agosto, Edif Alianza 110, tel: (591 2) 442052/440631
Spain, Av 6 de Agosto 2827, tel: (591 2) 431203/430118
UK, Av Arce 2732, tel: (591 2) 432397/433424
USA, Av Arce 2780, tel: (591 2) 430251

sometimes the only (and certainly the quickest and easiest) way to get into some of the mountainous areas. Travel in Bolivia is always a lengthy business!

It is also possible to hire a driver directly, with his own 4×4. Make sure that the driver knows where he is going. It is usual to pay for the outward journey when you arrive at your destination and to pay for the return trip when you get back to La Paz. There are several recommended drivers in La Paz with their own 4×4s:
Vitaliano Ramos, tel: (591 2) 416013
Jorge Escobari, tel: (591 2) 417353
Ramon Flores, tel: (591 2) 721789
José Ayala, tel: (591 2) 483121

ACCOMMODATION

There are a huge number and range of *hostales*, *residenciales* and hotels to choose from in La Paz; here is a selection:
Hostal Austria, Calle Yanacocha 531, tel: (591 2) 408540. Popular, clean, friendly. Kitchen, double rooms and dormitory.
Hotel Torino, Calle Socabaya 457, tel: (591 2) 406003. Central, popular with backpackers.
La Paz City Hotel, Acosta 487, near Plaza San Pedro, tel: (591 2) 322177. Popular with Peace Corps volunteers.
Hostal Sucre, Colombia 340, Plaza San Pedro, tel: (591 2) 492038. More upmarket, also has ensuite accommodation.
Hotel Andes*, Calle Manco Capac 364, tel: (591 2) 455327. Friendly, quite popular with backpackers.
Estrella Andina Hostal,** Av Illampu 716, tel: (591 2) 456421, fax: (591 2) 451401. Nice rooms, friendly, clean, family run.
Hotel Sagárnaga,** Calle Sagárnaga 326, tel: (591 2) 351158/350252, fax: (591 2) 360831. Central clean and safe. TVs.
Residencial Rosario,** Calle Illampu 704, tel: (591 2) 451341/451658, fax: (591 2) 451991. Clean and popular, especially with groups. Restaurant.
Hostal República,** Calle Commercio 1455, tel: (591 2) 202742/203448, fax: (591 2) 202782. Historic building, courtyard and garden. Friendly.
El Rey Palace Hotel**,** Av 20 de Octobre 1947, tel/fax: (591 2) 393016, email:hotelrey@caoba.entelnet.bo. What you would expect from a four-star hotel - Jacuzzis, etc.

FOOD AND DRINK
Food

Traditional Bolivian food tends to be quite bland. Bolivians consume a lot of meat – especially chicken, beef, llama and mutton – and carbohydrates (to keep warm).

Since La Paz is a city of street traders and markets, so it is the 'Comedor Popular' in the market that provides the cheapest meals. You can buy a meal consisting of meat, rice and potatoes, plus coffee, for 2Bs. The hearty soups and stews are also worth a try.

LAND OF THE POTATO

In Bolivia there are reckoned to be some 140 different varieties of potato - there are probably as many words for 'potato' in Bolivian as there are for 'snow' in the Inuit language! The people of the Altiplano have perfected the art of freeze-drying potatoes. When trekking, you will come across a series of circular holes, full of water, beside the streams. Potatoes are put in the water overnight (or left for several nights), brought out, trodden on to remove any excess water and left to dry for days, sometimes weeks, in the sun. The dried potatoes are then carried by the local people as a snack or rehydrated for dinner. It is, however, an acquired taste.

What you will not see in the market is *cuy* (guinea pig), a cheap, swift breeding, valuable source of protein eaten by peasants, or *campesinos*, especially around Lake Titikaka and the Charazani area.

Salteñas (a type of spicy pasty), *empenadas* (another type of pasty), *tamales* (made from corn flour) and *humitas* (corn mush) are all typical snacks, which are normally eaten mid-morning.

Since the mid 1990s, a whole range of cosmopolitan eating houses have sprung up. You will now find restaurants selling food from all over the world. However, Bolivia is, like all Latin American countries, quite a difficult country in which to be vegetarian, although there are a few veggie restaurants now in La Paz.

If you are backpacking, the markets can provide all the food you need at a reasonable price. In recent years, some supermarkets have opened. It is best to do most of your shopping in La Paz, as the choice is limited elsewhere.

Drink

Being at such a high altitude means that it doesn't take much to get drunk. Most of the big cities have their own brewery, producing a lager type of beer. There are two in La Paz itself, Huari and Paceña.

Wine is produced in the Tarija region, with more or less success.

Singani is a spirit made from distilled grapes. At fiestas you will see the *cholitas* ladling out *chuflay* (*singani*, Seven-up and lemon with beaten egg white) from a foaming vat, or sipping *té con té*, hot tea laced with *singani*.

Chicha – a brew made from fermented corn – is the drink of choice for most *campesinos*. In the Apolobamba region, one of the jobs of the Kollowaya medicine men is to make the *chicha* for the fiestas.

Water

Only drink water that has been boiled or treated with iodine, or bottled mineral water.

COMMUNICATIONS

In La Paz there are several internet cafes and phone and fax offices, all providing cheap services. Some of the hotels in Sorata have internet facilities, but those in Charazani or Pelechuco do not.

ENTEL is the telephone network in Bolivia. The main office in La Paz is located at Calle Ayacucho 267; open: 7.30am–10.30pm daily.

The *correos* (post office) in La Paz is at Av Mariscal Santa Cruz, at the corner of Calle Oruro; open: Mon–Fri, 8.30am–8pm; Sat, 9am–7pm; Sun, 9am–noon. Postage is relatively expensive for letters abroad. Poste restante is free.

ELECTRICITY

Bolivia uses a standard current of 220V/50HZ, except in La Paz, where it is 110V. There is no shortage of power in La Paz or Sorata, but electricity can be scarce in Charazani and Pelechuco.

LANGUAGE

In order to get by in Bolivia you need to be able to speak some Spanish or Castillian. The official language of Bolivia is Spanish, yet 60 per cent of the population speak it only as a second language, after Aymara, Quechua or one of the Amazonian languages. As you trek through Bolivia you will find that the local people speak Aymara in the Cordillera Real and Kollowaya, and Quechua in Apolobamba. They are all, however, taught Spanish from an early age.

SECURITY

Bolivia is a relatively safe country. However, as anywhere, it is best to be aware and take precautions. Each year, there are a few muggings late at night near tourist hotels in La Paz, or bags are snatched on a crowded street. Pickpockets from far and wide descend on any fiesta, especially when there are big crowds. It is best not to carry all your money and papers with you. Take very little and lock the rest in the hotel safe.

When travelling, put your rucksack in a blue jute bag (it will look just like all the other Bolivian bags) and put it on the top of the bus. Just keep what you need for the journey with you. Remember not to leave this bag on the bus if you get out for a break, though. Travellers are relatively rich and Bolivians are not.

Some of the popular treks experience spates of thieving. Don't leave anything outside your tent overnight. If confronted, be polite. If someone demands money, make sure you keep a little separate, so that you never have to hand it all over.

OTHER USEFUL ADDRESSES

Tourist agency, Sernatur, Plaza del Estudiante, tel: (591 2) 367442, fax: (591 2) 374630.
Amigos del Libro, Calle Mercado 1315. The best bookshop in La Paz; sells maps.
IGM, Oficina 5, Calle Juan XXIII 100. This is behind the main post office, a dead end off Calle Rodriguez, between Calle Murillo and Calle Linares. Maps are available either immediately, or with 24 hours notice.

BOLIVIAN FIESTAS

Bolivia is the land of fiestas. Not only do the inhabitants celebrate Catholic festivals, but all the Aymara and Quechua ones as well, not to mention notable political dates – and, of course, the foundation of their own particular village. This makes Bolivia a remarkably colourful place, and you'll find processions of people dressed in local costumes dancing on the streets, accompanied by bands, at the slightest excuse. Bolivians definitely know how to enjoy themselves!

CALENDAR OF FIESTAS
1 January New Year's Day.
24 January The day of the *alasitas* – people buy miniature versions of the items they most hope to acquire in the coming year, including consumer goods such as cars, houses, minibuses, trucks, American dollars or Bolivian passports. They have these *cha'lla'd* (sprinkled with *alcohol potable*) by an Aymara priest (often to be found in the door of a Catholic church!), take them home, place them in a prominent position on a shelf and wait for the arrival of their good fortune. This day is dedicated to Ekeko, the God of Abundance, whose likeness is to be found in most houses. He is a happy little character, all strung about with consumer goods and often a guitar.
1st week of February Celebration of the Virgin of the Candelaria in various towns throughout Bolivia. The biggest event is in Copacabana on Lake Titikaka. It is customary for people to make a pilgrimage, take mass, then join in the general revelry and dancing.
February/March (last week before Lent) Carnival throughout Bolivia, similar to the famous carnival of Río de Janeiro, which includes traditional dances in colourful costumes, masked dancers, carnival queens and water bombs (passing tourists make a good target!). The most spectacular celebrations are held in Oruro and in Santa Cruz.
2nd Sunday of March *Fiesta de Phujllay* takes place in Tarabuco. *Campesinos* (peasants) from the surrounding area descend on the town to commemorate the victory of their ancestors in a battle against the Spaniards in 1816. There is much dancing and traditional music, and a mass is held in the Quechua language.
19 March *Fiesta de San José*, formerly celebrated only in Beni, but today enjoyed as Father's Day.
21 March Autumn equinox. Harvest festival is especially celebrated in the rural areas.
March/April Holy Week (*La Semana Santa*) is celebrated throughout Bolivia, but notably in Copacabana. Hundreds of pilgrims walk there from La Paz for the Good Friday night-time procession up Calvary Hill, when the Black Madonna and other effigies are carried from the church.
March/April Easter Day is devoted to dancing and music-making in the town square, in what also appears to be a type of harvest festival.
13 April Big Sunday market in El Alto, selling agricultural products.
15 April *Efemerides de Tarija* commemorates the battle of La Tablada with processions, dancing and music. This culminates in the 'Rodeo Chapaco', recalling the city's *gaucho* (cowboy) roots.
1 May International Workers' Day.
3 May *Fiesta de la Cruz*, commemorating the cross on which Christ was crucified, is not as mournful as it sounds; in fact it is quite a party. It is celebrated mainly on the Island of Suriqui on Lake Titikaka, Copacabana, Cochabamba, Santa Cruz and Tarija, where the festivities last for 15 days!
25 May Commemoration of the first (failed) attempt to overthrow the Spaniards in Sucre.
27 May Mother's Day, celebrated in memory of the *heroinas de la coronilla*, the women of Cochabamba, who defended their homes in the battle of 1812.
May/June (7 weeks after Holy Week) *Fiesta de Gran Poder* – one of the most important festivals in La Paz, with processions and floats, masked dancers, bands, traditional costumes and dances, La Morenada, La Diablada, Los Caporales. Celebrations go on from morning until night!
21 June Winter solstice and start of the Aymara New Year. Aymara ceremonies welcome the rising sun at Tiwanaku.
24 June *Fiesta de San Juan*. There is dancing during the day. At night, great bonfires used to be lit to symbolize the burning of the old year, but when people started putting tyres on the fires, the bonfires were banned and only fireworks are now allowed. It is a spectacular sight if you are in La Paz, as you see fireworks going off on both sides of the valley.
29 June *Fiesta de San Pedro y San Pablo*, celebrated in La Paz, Tiquina, Huarina and Huatajata.
16 July Big celebrations in La Paz to commemorate the failed revolution of Murillo against the Spanish in 1809; include military parades and a mass in the cathedral.
16 July In El Alto there are huge celebrations in honour of the Virgin of Carmen, the protector of

La Paz. Traditional masked dances of *morenos* (Negroes), *diablos* (devils) and llamas. Ethnic groups come to La Paz, dressed in their own traditional costumes.

25 July *Fiesta de Tata Santiago*, with traditional dancing in the streets in La Paz, Copacabana and Isla del Sol.

July At this new fiesta, the Entrada Universitaria puts on a big procession of floats depicting all the various ethnic groups in Bolivia, with (of course) music and dancing!

2 August *Dia del Indio*. A day to celebrate Pachamama and to *challar* (bless with alcohol) the house, vehicles etc.

5 August Celebration of the Virgin of Copacabana. Pilgrimages to Copacabana are followed by Catholic religious ceremonies and traditional dances. This is now mainly a Peruvian festival.

6 August Independence Day (public holiday). Military parades, mass in the Cathedral, big firework displays.

10 August *Fiesta de San Lorenzo* in San Lorenzo, Tarija, with traditional Chacapa dances and musical instruments.

15 August Celebration of the Virgin of Urkupina in Cochabamba. Pilgrimages, traditional dances.

End of August *Fiesta del Chutillo* in Potosí, dedicated to the different dances and music of Bolivia (and indeed of all Latin America) is increasing in importance, and now attracts international dance troupes and musicians.

August is also the month for fiestas in the villages.

1st Sunday of September *Fiesta de San Roque* in Tarija, with eight days of processions, traditional dances and costumes, and typical food and drink. Most noted for the mixed age groups of dancers.

8 September Bull running in the streets of Viacha, 20km (12 miles) from La Paz. Traditional dancing.

14 September Big fiesta in Sorata, with traditional costumes and local dishes.

14 September Commemoration of the failed attempt at revolution in 1810 in Cochabamba.

21 September Spring equinox, celebrated at Tiwanaku. The Aymara leaders predict the weather and the success of the crops. There is also bull running.

24 September Commemoration of the failed attempt at revolution in Santa Cruz.

29 September *Fiesta de San Miguel*, celebrated in Uncia, and noted for the bloody *Tinku* fights, which can get out of hand.

1st week of October Celebration of the Virgin del Rosario in various locations, including Viacha in La Paz, Santa Cruz, Cochabamba, Tarabuco, Potosí and Oruro.

20 October Commemoration of the foundation of La Paz in 1848. It was actually founded on this date in Laja and moved to the present site three days later. Processions and dancing.

1–2 November All Saints (*Todos los Santos*) (public holiday), especially celebrated on the Altiplano.

1 November Breads are made in the shapes of figures and horses, known as *t'ant'a wawas*. If someone they know has died within the past two years, people prepare that person's favourite food and leave an extra place at table. The next day, they go to the cemetery to decorate the graves, and this is followed by a wake for the deceased, with much drinking and dancing.

10 November Foundation of Potosí.

21 December Summer solstice, with great celebrations in the countryside.

25 December Christmas (public holiday). Some of the more colourful festivities take place in Sucre and San Ignacio de Moxos (Beni).

Typical fiesta scene – colourful costumes and traditional folk dancing.

TREK 8: QUIMSA CRUZ

The Quimsa Cruz (meaning 'three crosses' in Aymara) is a spectacular little mountain range to the southeast of La Paz. Only 40km (25 miles) long and 15km (9¼ miles) wide, the cordillera contains around 80 peaks from 4900m (16076ft) to 5800m (19029ft), mostly unclimbed. It is an area ripe for exploration. The peaks to the north of Viloco are predominantly granodiorite spires, and look somewhat similar to the famous Chamonix aiguilles, while the snow peaks are to the south.

The Quimsa Cruz area is stunningly beautiful: a mass of snow-covered peaks or granite spires, brilliant blue lakes, alpine meadows and a wealth of wildlife. Very few people venture up into these mountains; so few, in fact, that it was not until 1999 that the remains of an Incan sacrifice were discovered on one of the higher peaks of the range. It is definitely a place for those who like to go exploring in wild and remote regions. You just need to be self-sufficient in food, fuel and camping equipment.

Access to the Quimsa Cruz is easy as it was one of Bolivia's main tin-mining areas before the great tin crash of 1985, and is well served by roads and tracks. Viloco, whose heyday was in the 1920s, is a rather depressed and depressing mining village, but there are a few shops and you can get a bed and a meal at the Catholic parish office. Tin is still mined throughout the Quimsa Cruz today, but on a much smaller scale. It does mean, however, that for climbers wanting to move Base Camp it is relatively easy, as there are plenty of mining vehicles.

Viloco to Laguna Chatamarca

To start the trek, head east from Viloco up the valley and pick up a good path on the south side of the stream. Follow this up to the pass between Nevados Salvador Apacheta and Knori Chuma and descend to camp in the valley below the pass (there is a flatter area below the path).

The next morning, take up the path again and follow it as it hugs the slopes of Cerro Bengala and rounds the spur to a gem of a lake beneath Cerro Chiar Loma. Now head southeast up the next valley towards Cerro Mina Kholu Grande. Cross the pass, with fantastic views of the glaciated Nevados San Lorenzo and San Felipe. Drop down to Laguna Chatamarca, where there is good camping in an idyllic spot, surrounded by snow-covered mountains.

TREK ESSENTIALS

LENGTH 3–4 days. 24 km (15 miles). From Viloco on a good trail across the cordillera to Mina Caracoles.
ACCESS *To start* Buses leave for Viloco from Calle 5 in El Alto (near the Plaza Juana Azurdoy) at 7am everyday except Thursdays and Sundays. The journey takes 10–12 hours and costs around US$4. Alternatively, you can hire a jeep with a driver or arrange private transport with one of the agencies. The journey by 4×4 takes only 6 hours, but costs about US$250–350 each way (for up to six people). *On finish* Bus (everyday except Thursdays and Saturdays), truck or private transport from Mina Caracoles to La Paz.
HIGHEST POINT Unnamed pass, 5190m (17028ft).
TREK STYLE Backpacking or burro/llama assisted.
RESTRICTIONS None.
FURTHER OPTIONS The whole area is ripe for exploration, with many paths leading into remote cirques and valleys. Climbing opportunities: Cerro Yaypuri (5566m/18262ft). There are countless peaks in the area, both snow peaks and pure rock, at a variety of grades. Most of them are still unclimbed.
MAPS Bolivian IGM 1:50 000 Mina Caracoles.

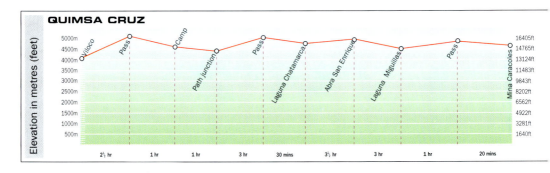

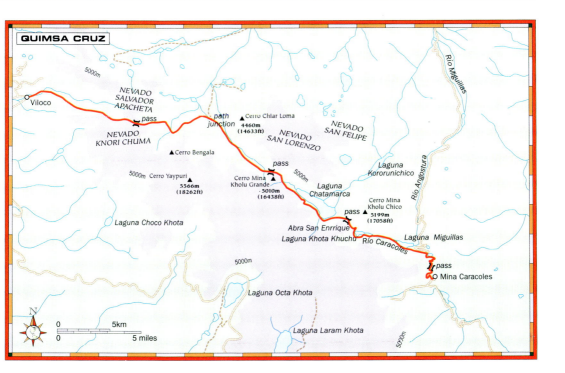

Laguna Chatamarca to Mina Caracoles

On your final day, follow the path around the south side of the Laguna Chatamarca and up to the Abra San Enrrique to the south of Cerro Mina Kholu Chico. Descend to Laguna Khota Khuchu and follow the Río Caracoles to Laguna Miguillas, where you pick up the road, go over a pass and head down to Pacuni and Mina Caracoles from where there are buses back to La Paz.

The deep blue waters of Laguna Chatamarca make a wonderful backdrop to an idyllic camping spot on this trek.

CERRO YAYPURI

The west flank of Cerro Yaypuri.

The Khori Chuma Cirque, at the head of the Laguna Choco Khota Valley in the north-western end of the Cordillera Quimsa Cruz, provides access to a whole range of pleasant routes in a fairly remote setting. The west peak of Cerro Yaypuri gives an enjoyable introduction to the alpine peaks of the Quimsa Cruz. There are excellent views from the summit, right across the cordillera – a panorama of largely unexplored and unclimbed peaks, as far as the eye can see!

Continue on past Viloco to two large lakes, go over a high pass at 4820m (15814ft), and, on descending this, the Laguna Choco Khota Valley comes into view on the right hand side. Continue down for another 8km (5 miles) to where, at a sharp right-hand bend, a track leads off up the valley to the right. Follow this to its end at the Laguna Choco Khota.

Laguna Choco Khota Base Camp (4400m/14435ft) can be made pretty much anywhere around the shores of the lake. You can, if you want, camp where your transport drops you off, but a more agreeable campsite can be found amongst the boulders, at the northern corner of the lake.

Most of the routes in the area can be done in a single day from the Base Camp, but a High Camp or a bivi is an enjoyable aspect of a high-altitude ascent. A comfortable High Camp can be made at the bottom of the Yaypuri Glacier at around 4900m (16076ft). To reach the High Camp first walk northeast to the head of the valley. On the right-hand side a cairned moraine ridge takes the easiest line up through some very difficult and tiring moraine. Just below the start of the glacier are some wide sandy bays. The second bay you come to is the best place to camp, as it has running water.

West Peak of Cerro Yaypuri by the Southwest Flank and North Ridge

From the base of the Atoroma Glacier, go up the right-hand side of the glacier, which is initially straightforward. After a short while head for the right-hand side of an isolated rocky buttress on the glacier. From here ascend a short steep slope (50 degrees) for about 50 metres, after which the angle eases. From this point pick a line through the obvious crevasses, heading towards the ridge line and slightly rightwards. Once on the ridge, make directly for the summit via a small easy rock step. Beyond the summit a traverse to the east summit looks tempting, but the rock is very poor and the best descent is to reverse the route. Allow 2½ hours to get from the Base Camp to the glacier, 4½ hours from the base of the glacier to the summit, and another 2 hours for the descent.

CLIMB ESSENTIALS

SUMMIT Cerro Yaypuri 5566m (18262ft)
CAMPS Base Camp (Laguna Choco Khota) 4400m (14435ft); High Camp (edge of the glacier) approximately 4,900m (16075ft).
GRADE Alpine Grade PD+

MINING IN BOLIVIA

The Incas were the first to exploit the mineral wealth of the Bolivian Andes. They found gold which they used for artefacts and in the buildings of Cuzco. This gold came primarily from mines on the Río Tipuani, near Sorata, and from the area around what is now Sunchuli in the Apolobamba area.

The Spaniards were only interested in the vast silver riches of Cerro Rico (the Rich Hill) in Potosí, southern Bolivia, which were discovered in 1545. This silver financed the Spanish Empire for two centuries, but provided little benefit to the miners, who were forced to work under the most appalling conditions. If they were not killed by a mining accident, they often died from pulmonary silicosis, a disease of the lungs caused by inhalation of silica dust. By the time of independence, the silver had run out, leaving Potosí (one of the 'happening' cities of South America) a ghost town, and Bolivia itself impoverished.

Tin was the next major mineral to be exploited. This was found primarily in the heart of the Cordillera Real, sometimes at very high altitudes. By 1900 it accounted for 50 per cent of Bolivia's exports. This time, the wealth was accrued in Bolivia by three tin-producing giants, Simon Patino and the Aramayo and Hothschild families. By the 1930s, the major boom was over, although tin was still mined profitably (mainly by absentee English owners) until nationalization in 1952 and the formation of COMIBOL (Corporación de Minera de Bolivia). This followed the 'April revolution', an armed revolt by the miners, which took place when it looked as if the party they had just elected, the MNR, would be prevented from taking power by a military coup.

After 12 years in power, the MNR *was* ousted by a military coup and a period of political instability followed when miners' conditions and wages deteriorated again. In the 1980s, the bottom dropped out of the world tin market and, in 1985, when the price of tin fell by half, many unprofitable mines were closed. Some 70 per cent of those who were employed by COMIBOL in 1985 (around 18,500 people) had lost their jobs by 1986. There was widespread unemployment and migration to towns, or to the Chapare region (where they started to grow coca). Some of the mines, however, were taken over by the workers and run as cooperatives, often with quite dangerous conditions.

Today, the Cordillera Real is littered with abandoned tin mines and mine workings. Indeed, we have the tin producers to thank for many roads into the mountains (dirt tracks though they are) and for the paths over high passes linking the valleys. The road to the Quimsa Cruz only exists because of the tin mines at Viloco and Mina Caracoles.

Gold is still mined on a large scale at Aguas Blancas, on the way to Pelechuco, and a new mine has opened on Lago Suches. Workers' cooperatives own the mines of Sunchuli and Hilo Hilo. In addition, there has been a minor 'gold rush' in the Tipuani Valley and throughout the Apolobamba, where small groups of men can be seen with wheelbarrows and pickaxes on remote mountainsides. As in the old days in Alaska, you merely have to stake a claim in La Paz. The sign *Compro Oro* (Gold Bought) can often be seen in Pelechuco's shops.

It is estimated that 100,000 people work as small-scale miners today, with some 500,000 people depending on it for a living. That is a fairly large proportion of an overall population of 8 million people.

Bolivia is, moreover, still a major producer of tin, zinc, silver, tungsten and gold. The mining sector accounts for about 90 per cent of the country's legal export earnings.

Small-scale gold mining in Apolobamba (trek 13).

TREK 9: THE 'OTHER SIDE' OF ILLIMANI

Illimani is the mountain to which all eyes are drawn on arrival in La Paz. This trek traces a route around the 'back' of the mountain, exploring the not normally visited 'other side'. You will see few, if any, trekkers, except at Puente Roto, Illimani's Base Camp. To the north, the trek takes you through a greener, more agricultural landscape than in the Cordillera Real proper, but it is still dotted with either working or disused mines. It is a mixture of mining communities and big working *estancias* (ranches), with their cattle, donkeys, horses and llamas. The whole area is, however, all the while dominated by the triple-summited bulk of the majestic Illimani.

Cohoni to Puente Roto
From Cohoni, follow the road back towards La Paz for 5 mins, then head uphill on a broad track to a ridge, where there is a tremendous view of the west side of Illimani. Keep going up the path, keeping to the right of the Río Huacanasca, until you reach the wide-open meadow known as the Puente Roto (broken bridge), the Base Camp for an ascent of Illimani. No one seems to know where the bridge originally was, as there is no sign of it now, but the meadow is sure to be full of climbers' tents. People often leave a camp here, whilst making a 2-day ascent of the mountain. Even if you do not want to attempt the summit, it is normally possible to ascend the ridge to Nido de Cóndores, Illimani's High Camp without mountaineering equipment. This is a 6-hour round trip from here.

Puente Roto to Tres Ríos
From Puente Roto, follow the old mining road around the western side of Illimani, crossing the Río Pinaya Jahuira by Laguna Laram Khota. Keep on contouring, in and out of ravines, crossing various rivers and passing numerous disused tin mines, until you reach the La Paz–Lambate road. Head up right to the Abra Pacuani and descend on paths to the right to Estancia Totoral Pampa, where camping is possible in the pampas just before the village.

Follow the road down to the village of Tres Ríos, which boasts two bars, one with a pool table and dance floor, two shops, a good-sized school, but no *alojamiento*. The economy of the village is tied to its wolfram mine, the Bolsa Negra, which is thriving. There are tremendous views of Mururata to the north and Illimani's awe-inspiring northern face to the south.

TREK ESSENTIALS

LENGTH 4-5 days. 51 km (32 miles). From Cohoni to Puente Roto (Illimani's Base Camp), then on a disused mining road round the west side of Illimani, continuing with a traverse below the northern and eastern faces of Illimani to Lambate.

ACCESS *To start* By bus or private transport to Cohoni. Buses run to Cohoni twice daily, except Sunday, from the Calle Luis Lara, near the Plaza Linares in San Pedro at 1pm and 3pm – a 4-hour journey. *On finish* By local bus or private transport back from Lambate to La Paz. Buses run Monday to Saturday.

HIGHEST POINT Pass above Mina Bolsa Blanca, 4800m (15748ft).

TREK STYLE Backpacking or burro/llama assisted.

RESTRICTIONS None.

FURTHER OPTIONS Side trip to Nido de Cóndores (Illimani High Camp); climb to Illimani (Pico Sur) at 6439m (21125ft). The trek could be continued from Lambate on the Yunga Cruz trail to Chulumani (5 days).

MAPS DAV 1:50 000 Cordillera Real Süd (Illimani)
Bolivian IGM 1:50 000 Cohoni 6043 IV
Bolivian IGM 1:50 000 Palca 6044 IV
Liam O'Brien 1:135 000 Cordillera Real

TREK 9: THE 'OTHER SIDE' OF ILLIMANI

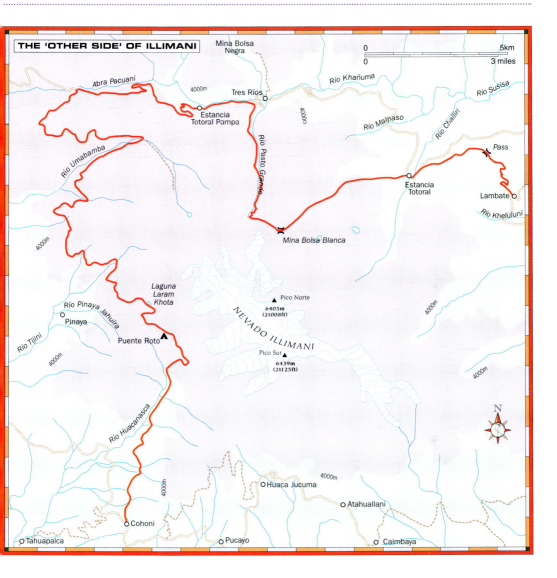

Tres Ríos to Lambate

From the village, take the mining road up along the Río Pasto Grande. There are places to camp as you start the ascent. It takes 3 hours to reach the pass above the Mina Bolsa Blanca, from where you get a bird's eye view of the valley and look across to Mururata again. Descend to the Río Malpaso; the trail becomes more and more distinct. There are more campsites, in a truly remote and idyllic setting, 2 hours down from the pass, or you can continue down the valley, on the right-hand side of the river, to camp above Estancia Totoral Pampa.

Head down to the *estancia*, then follow the road as far as a bridge over the Río Challiri, where a path on the right first crosses a broad pass, then leads down to the tiny village of Lambate.

Illimani Base Camp at Puente Roto.

PEAK: ILLIMANI

Illimani is the southernmost and highest peak of the Cordillera Real. Its giant snow-capped bulk dominates the city of La Paz. All eyes are drawn to its gleaming whiteness. It has a continuous summit ridge of over 6000m (19685ft), which runs for 8km (5 miles). There are five main summits, three visible from La Paz, including the highest, Pico Sur, on the right. Illimani was first climbed in 1898 by Sir Martin Conway, who started the first topographic survey of the Cordillera Real. The first full traverse was accomplished in 1979 and has only been repeated two or three times, as it involves at least two bivouacs above 6000m (19685ft).

The route to Illimani's highest summit, Pico Sur.

Illimani is usually climbed from the La Paz side. There are two basic approaches to the Base Camp at Puente Roto: either from Estancia Una via Pinaya, or from Cohoni.

For details of buses to Cohoni and a route description to Puente Roto see trek 9. Catching a bus to Estancia Una is more complicated. Buses for Quilahuaya leave at 5am from Calle Max Paredes, near the Comedor Popular. From Quilahuaya, it is a 2-hour walk to Estancia Una, or sometimes the bus continues on to below the aqueduct, leaving you a walk of 30 mins. From Una, it is a further 4-hour walk up through the village of Pinaya to Puente Roto, though it is possible to hire burros.

Most climbers prefer to arrange private transport with one of the trekking agencies. This shortens the hiking time to a mere 2 hours to Base Camp. It is also possible to hire burros in Pinaya.

From Pinaya, follow the well-trodden path uphill, past several small farms, eventually arriving in a flat area, crossed by streams, below a disused mining road. From Puente Roto you have a grandstand view of Illimani's central and southern summits and Huayna Potosí. At night, the lights of La Paz twinkle below.

From Puente Roto, it is a 4–6-hour slog up to the High Camp at Nido de Cóndores. Porters can, however, be hired from both Una and Pinaya, to carry heavy equipment on this section. Hike along the disused mining road for 15 mins, then follow the obvious path up to the left, beside the stream, towards the screes (below the rock ridge) that come down from the Nido de Cóndores. Follow this past a rock band on the right and continue upwards to the start of the ridge. Follow the crest, which becomes steeper and more exposed (some scrambling is necessary), to the rocky platform which is the Nido de Cóndores.

It is best to leave High Camp at 4am, in order to get down before the snow softens. Unfortunately, it is always cold, as this is the west side of the mountain.

From the High Camp, follow the ridge as it narrows and rises steeply, then levels again. The crevasses en route are usually obvious. There is one steep section (50°) before the route swings left, crosses a crevasse (which can sometimes be an ice pitch), then heads towards a notch in the ridge. Once on the ridge, turn right and follow the broad slope, past one false summit to the Pico Sur (6–8 hours).

The views are magnificent, with the whole of the Cordillera Real to the north, the Altiplano and Lake Titikaka, La Paz itself and the unmistakable, jagged peaks of the Quimsa Cruz to the southeast.

Descend by the same route (2–3 hours). It is possible to arrange for porters to come up to Nido de Cóndores that day, so that you can descend in another 2–3 hours to Puente Roto.

CLIMB ESSENTIALS

SUMMIT Illimani, Pico Sur 6439m (21125ft)
CAMPS Base Camp (Puente Roto) 4400m (14436ft); High Camp (Nido de Cóndores) 5450m (17881ft).
GRADE Alpine Grade PD

TIWANAKU

Everyone has heard of the Incas, with their great feats of architecture and irrigation and their worship of the Sun God. But in Bolivia, or Alto Peru, as it was then called, their empire was short-lived. It lasted a mere 70 years, from 1476 to 1531, when the Spanish conquistadors arrived.

The pre-Incan civilization of Tiwanaku is of much greater significance, since it existed from around 1500BC to AD1200. It is characterized by a great knowledge and development of architecture, science, astronomy, mathematics and agriculture, coupled with a socio-economic and political organization unsurpassed in modern-day structures. The Tiwanaku civilization is considered by many to have been as advanced as that of ancient Egypt.

The ceremonial centre of Tiwanaku was situated some 70km (44 miles) outside La Paz on what is now the Altiplano, but which was then the shores of Lake Titikaka, which has since receded. It is normal to speak of three distinct periods, based on the carbon-dating of artefacts found:

1580BC to AD133   The village or formative period
AD133 to AD700   The urban or classical period
AD700 to AD1200   The imperial or expansive period

Carved heads in the Templo Semisubterráneo.

The Village Period
This was characterized by the domestication of plants and animals, the first attempts to construct dwellings and the use of adobe as a building material and basis for ceramic work. There was no social stratification.

The Classical Period
This was Tiwanaku's heyday. Methods of agriculture were perfected and intensified to feed a growing population. Stone was used as a building material and ceramic work, which was predominately anthropomorphic (depicting men, women, pumas and serpents), was glazed. The population built an impressive infrastructure of roads, irrigation canals and agricultural terraces, even constructing wooden boats to transport stone for temples across the lake. The division of labour was introduced, and with it a more hierarchical social structure. A form of aristocracy emerged among the religious leaders.

The main impetus of this era was the building of large temples, of which three main temples have been excavated thus far. There were three levels: 1. the Akapana, a kind of pyramid with seven storeys which rose above the ground, and which seems to have served both as ceremonial centre and observatory; 2. the Kalasasaya, a rectangular temple on the ground with seven entrances, the main entrance being to the east, perhaps as a means of keeping track of the changing seasons (this temple contains three important statues: the Sun Gate, showing what appear to be distinct calendar markings depicting 12 months, the Ponce Monolith, named after the architect who discovered it and the Friar's Monolith); and 3. Templo Semisubterráneo, a semi-subterranean temple with an array of carved heads.

The three levels symbolize the Tiwanaku view of the world, namely their belief that human beings had to maintain the harmony between the Alaxpacha, God the creator, in the stars and Acapacha, or Pachamama, below the earth. Hence the three temples. Tiwanaku culture was essentially peaceful, built on trade and religion.

The Imperial Period
The imperial or expansive phase seems to have been characterized by a lack of decadence, with no new temple building and a return to a more rustic style of ceramic ware. The ruling classes seem to have been more concerned with extending their sphere of influence. Tiwanaku became the religious and political centre of an empire spreading as far north as southern Peru and as far south as northern Chile.

By AD1150, however, Tiwanaku had started to decline politically. It is thought that its power waned as the water levels in Lake Titikaka dropped and the population was forced to move. Another possible theory is that they were attacked by the reputedly warlike Kollas from the west. Whatever the theory for the decline, it is clear that Tiwanaku was the centre of a vast empire for more than 2,500 years and, in comparison, the Incas were but a blip in history.

TREK 10: ZONGO TO COROICO

This varied trek takes you through an alpine area of lakes and waterfalls, through high meadows and past traditional villages, to the famous pre-Hispanic Choro Trail, which linked the Altiplano and Tiwanaku with the subtropical coca-, vegetable- and fruit-producing areas of the Yungas. The vegetation change is remarkable, from high mountain scenery down through stunted shrubs to lush, vividly green forests of cedar, laurel, mahogany, walnut and jacaranda. There is also a profusion of brightly coloured lilies, bellflowers and impatiens (bizzy lizzies) until finally the trek descends to the heat and papaya trees of Chairo.

The first 3 days of this trek take you into a little-visited alpine area; you hike up beside paternoster strings of brilliant blue lakes and rushing waterfalls, down to high meadows, and past traditional thatched roofed stone villages, around the foot of the mighty Cerro Tikimani.

Laguna Viscachani to Sanja Pampa

From Laguna Viscachani, head up towards what appears to be an impassable valley headwall, zigzagging first to the right, but then to the left, and finally pick up a small path that leads up into the next hanging valley. A stunningly vivid green lake lies before you, with a relatively new dam to feed the hungry hydroelectric scheme that provides electricity for the ever-expanding La Paz and El Alto. Now keep to the right of the valley, cutting off the zigzags of the new road, and cross the pass.

There is an incredible view of the great fortress of Cerro Tikimani, a truly awesome and consequently seldom climbed mountain and, before you, the bright blue of Laguna Warawarani. Follow the path round the lake on the left, then head down the valley directly beneath Tikimani, cross the small aqueduct and continue descending to the tiny hamlet of Uma Palca. You can camp here, in an idyllic spot at the junction of two valleys, with a view still dominated by the dark buttresses and hanging seracs of Tikimani.

The path climbs steadily up through a series of three lakes and arrives at the high point after 3–4 hours. Take the path on the left side of the left-hand valley and ascend steeply to reach a small lake. Continue round the right-hand side of this lake, then cross and re-cross the stream to arrive at a second lake. Now make a rising traverse up the right side of this lake, following a trail that is rather eroded in places, and cross the pass. Cerro Mathilde rises up

TREK ESSENTIALS

LENGTH 5-7 days. 48km (30 miles) to Chairo; 65km (40 miles) to Yolosa, on the main road below Coroico. From Laguna Viscachani, just above Botijlaca, trek around the foot of Cerro Tikimani to join up with the Choro Trail at Challapampa. Continue to Chairo and then walk or taxi to Yolosa. (4-5 hours on foot, 1½-2 hours by taxi). From there, by road to Coroico.
ACCESS *To start* By private transport or truck to Botijlaca (get off at Laguna Viscachani). *On finish* By local bus (every hour) or private transport from Coroico back to La Paz, along 'the most dangerous road in the world'!
HIGHEST POINT Unnamed pass, 4510m (14797ft).
TREK STYLE Backpacking or burro/llama assisted.
RESTRICTIONS None.
FURTHER OPTIONS This could be combined with the Cordillera Real trek (trek 11), to give 19-20 days of continuous trekking.
MAPS Liam O'Brien 1: 135 000 Cordillera Real de los Andes
Bolivian IGM 1:50 000 Milluni 5945 II
Bolivian IGM 1:50 000 Unduavi 6045 III
Walter Guzman Cordova 1: 50 000 Los Caminos de los Incas

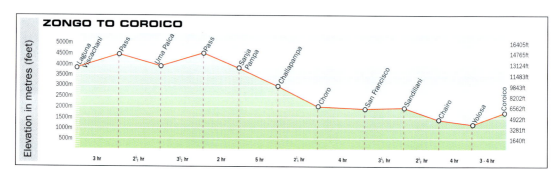

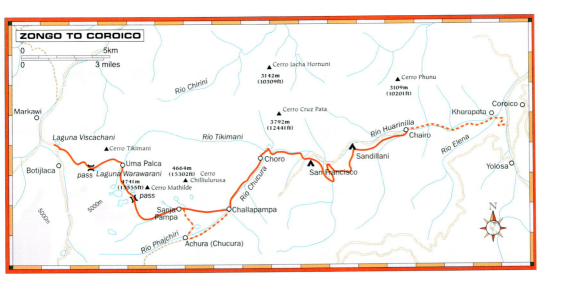

to your left. When you reach the valley floor, head downhill and find a suitable campsite.

The next day, follow the path on the left side of the valley, beside the stream, and 30 mins further downhill you come to the picturesque village of Sanja Pampa, with its traditional thatched roofs. What a location – in a fertile meadow, beside a babbling brook, at the foot of snowy mountains!

Sanja Pampa to the Choro Trail

From here, you have two options. The first is to cross the stream by the bridge and take the obvious rising path on the opposite hillside. This leads to a pass, then descends to a lake and the village of Achura (Chucura), where you can pick up the wide, much-travelled, Choro Trail.

Alternatively, you can spend another day off the beaten track by merely following the valley downhill. From Sanja Pampa, do not cross the bridge, but continue down on the left side of the river for another 15 mins. Cross here at a bridge. Keep on the right, picking your way through boulders and bushes. The path can be quite indistinct at times. You reach the first trees at about 3800m (12467ft). They are the chillka, said to have medic-inal properties. When you reach an area of bog, head towards the river and keep just above it until you pick up a path trending high above the river again, just as the broad Choro Trail comes into view in the distance.

Here, the vegetation becomes more dense and lush, with a proliferation of bushes and flowers. On turning into the main valley, first head uphill on the path, in order to cross the river. Then climb up to join the Choro Trail itself, the most well-known and frequented of all the pre-Hispanic paths in Bolivia. You are now more likely to encounter other trekkers for the first time.

Looking back to Tikimani from Sandillani.

One of the many hanging valley lakes on the way to Sanja Pampa.

The Choro Trail

Continue down the valley on a pre-Incan pavement to Challapampa, where there is a shop (selling *refrescos*, or fizzy drinks, and not much else) and a sloping campsite. If you camp here, cover up well: the mosquitoes are voracious. It is a beautiful place, though, and there is still a view of the mountains.

From here on, the trail mainly stays in the forest, climbing up and down, in and out of ravines. It is definitely not 'all downhill from here'. The next possible place to camp is about 2 hours away, where there are three houses and even a shop. Ten mins further on, you will come to the village of Choro itself, a rather ugly collection of corrugated iron-roofed houses by the river. Choro has acquired something of a bad reputation for theft.

Cross the river on a new suspension bridge, then ascend steeply for 2 hours, until the path contours round the hillside to San Francisco, where an old lady has created a pretty camping area, with a shop. She lives alone with her chickens and dogs, and has a wonderful vegetable patch and garden.

From here, the trail drops steeply down to the river, past a banana plantation and lemon grove, then re-ascends (also steeply) back up to the same height. Two more hours of ups and downs brings you to Sandillani, a veritable paradise, where Tamiji Hanamura, a Japanese man, has made an idyllic campground perched on the valley rim, with views back up the way you have come and to Tikimani. There are bananas, avocados, papaya, tomatoes (*tamarillos*), maracuya and yams, with sheep and chickens roaming around. Humming birds hover amongst the flowers. This is a place to spend some time, if you have it. Moreover, it is warm – positively hot after the mountains – and the fireflies glow at night. Tamiji Hanamura arrived here, armed with a machete, in 1960 and built himself a house, long before the Choro Trail had been developed for tourists. You have to sign his visitors' book and he is only too pleased to show you the collection of postcards and photos given to him over the years.

Sandillani to Chairo

From Sandillani, it is 2–3 hours down to Chairo, with its inevitable football pitch. Where there is a football pitch, however, there is also a shop, and this one is stocked from floor to ceiling. It also sells very welcome *refrescos*. This is also the road head, where it is possible to find a 'taxi' (for a price) to take you to Yolosa, where you can catch a bus up to Coroico. There is also a daily truck at 6am to Yolosa. You could always walk the 17km (11 miles) from Chairo to Yolosa if you do not want to pay the extortionate taxi fare, but it can feel quite a long way in the heat.

COCA

The coca leaf, known as the *hoja sagrada*, the sacred leaf, has been chewed in Bolivia since the time of the ancient Tiwanaku empire – a famous carving in the subterranean temple at Tiwanaku depicts a man's face with a swollen cheek, as if he were chewing coca. Interestingly enough, the Incas appear to have wanted to restrict the use of coca to their ruling elite; and the Spanish called it the *hoja del diablo*, the devil's leaf, because of its use in religious (Pachamama) ceremonies. However, on seeing its effect on the silver miners in Potosí (it numbed them to discomfort and dulled hunger pangs, turning them into a docile workforce), the Spanish were only too pleased to allow the miners to chew it. Moreover, some of the more enterprising Spaniards started plantations in the Yungas, in order to profit from its cultivation.

Coca leaf production became and remained big business throughout the following centuries. La Paz especially profited from the trade, as all coca passed through the city from the Yungas on its way to the silver mines in Potosí. As recently as 1940, due to the importance of coca cultivation to the economy, the government passed a decree declaring coca 'an article of prime necessity' and ordered its sale in all mining and railway companies.

In 1961, the United Nations Convention on Drugs (proscribing both cocaine and the coca leaf) was accepted by the Bolivian government, but a year later the government passed its own narcotics law, which did not include the leaf. Then, in 1988 the UN Vienna Convention recognized the 'traditional legal uses' of coca leaf in its natural state, and in the same year the Bolivian government allowed the continued cultivation of coca in 'traditional areas', although outlawing it everywhere else.

By 1967, the Chapare region, near Cochabamba, which produced a more bitter leaf better suited to the cocaine industry, had overtaken the Yungas as the prime coca growing area. This growth in production was due in part to governmental attempts to relocate people from the Altiplano to the lowlands; USAID even provided funds for a paved road. By the mid-1970s, when international demand for cocaine really took off, the Chapare was able to supply it. Migration to the Chapare was fuelled by the years of political instability from 1978 to 1982 (when there were seven military and two civilian governments) and the slump in the tin trade, which resulted in high inflation, massive unemployment, poverty and growth of debt. Coca cultivation for the cocaine trade provided, and still does provide, a major secure source of income.

Coca cultivation is still a hotly debated issue in Bolivia.

Coca production is, therefore, essentially an economic and development problem. Until poverty is alleviated and there is a viable alternative way of making a living for the *cocaleros* (those growing coca), it seems unlikely that people will stop growing it.

Increasing pressure from the US government has induced the Bolivian government over recent years to attempt to eradicate the illegal growing of coca. However, they have encountered massive opposition from the coca farmers. In October 2000, troops sent in to the Chapare region to clear the fields were met by road blockades, which resulted in food shortages in many cities, bringing the government to the negotiating table. The coca farmers demanded a comprehensive alternative economic strategy for their area and the right to produce coca for their own consumption. The government defused the situation by promising to find over US$80 million in resources for alternative development, but did not mention the cultivation of coca. Traditional coca production is, however, still to be allowed in the Yungas. At the time of writing, civil disturbances and road blockades over the growing of coca were still occurring.

It is an emotional issue; people's livelihoods are at stake. Bolivians complain that they are only supplying foreign demand; they do not use the finished product themselves. In addition, the government itself realizes that if all cocaine-related production stops, the country will lose a large percentage of its foreign earnings (some US$300 million to US$700 million). It is estimated that, at present, Bolivia still produces one-third of the world's coca leaves.

Meanwhile, most of the local Indian people chew coca leaves, which can be bought in the markets, and drink *maté de coca* (coca tea), which is available in every restaurant. Coca continues to have a significant religious, cultural and medicinal significance in Bolivian society.

TREK 11: CORDILLERA REAL

The Cordillera Real, or Royal Range, is the Andean backbone of Bolivia, running roughly southeast to northwest, separating the Altiplano, the high plateau that is home to the Aymara Indians to the west, from the subtropical Yungas to the east. The snow-covered peaks are said by the Aymara people to be home to the *achachilas*, the spirits of the ancestors. This is a high-altitude trek that takes you beneath five of Bolivia's eight 6000-m (19685-ft) peaks, from Illampu in the north to Huayna Potosí in the south, crossing at least one high pass every day.

In many ways doing this trek is like being in the middle of a geography text book, as you climb from one classic U-shaped valley up into the next, with its steep rocky sides, meandering river and high pasture. You'll also find one 'lost' valley after another, where the cattle are safe from any marauding rustlers and the thatched stone dwellings are straight out of *Rob Roy*.

Sorata to Estancia Utaña Pampa
Leaving Sorata is a bit complicated as there are so many paths, but basically head uphill and southeast out of Sorata to the aqueduct, which you need to follow rightwards for about 500m (1640ft). The trail then heads uphill, leftwards, away from the aqueduct. After another kilometre (1 mile), at the trail junction, do not cross the ridge immediately, but take the left fork, traverse round the ridge then cross it. Further on you will come to Quilambaya. If in doubt, keep asking for this village.

From Quilambaya, head north from behind the church, then follow the path up and over the ridge, contour east to a bridge across the Río Lakathiya and follow the path until you reach the village of Lakathiya itself. Its stone houses now have corrugated iron roofs, instead of the traditional thatch. About 100m (330ft) above the village is a large open meadow: an ideal campsite.

From the meadow, head uphill steadily for 3 hours to reach Abra Illampu, with its cairn and offerings to Pachamama. The view of Illampu from here is stunning. Descend through Quebrada

TREK ESSENTIALS

LENGTH 13–14 days. 150km (93miles). This is a north-to-south trek along the Cordillera Real, from Sorata to Huayna Potosí, crossing one high pass per day. From Sorata you trek to Chajolpaya and the Camino Calzada, then on to Hankolokhaya and the Wila Llojeta road; from there to Condoriri Base Camp, and on to Botijlaca.

ACCESS *To start* By bus to Sorata. An alternative start would be to hire a 4×4 from Sorata to take you up to the Paso Chuchu (between Sorata and Ancoma) at 4660m (15289ft) and walk down to your first night's campsite at the foot of Illampu. *At finish* By truck or private transport (which you should organize in advance) from Botijlaca back to La Paz.

HIGHEST POINT Paso Negruni, 5100m (16732ft).

TREK STYLE Backpacking or burro/llama assisted.

RESTRICTIONS None.

FURTHER OPTIONS Side trip to Pico Apacheta at 5363m (17596ft). Climbs to Condoriri (5648m/18531ft), Pequeño Alpamayo (5370m/17618ft), Huayana Potosí (6088m/19974ft).

MAPS Liam O'Brien 1:135 000 Cordillera Real de los Andes
DAV 1: 50 000 Cordillera Real Nord (Illampu)
Bolivian IGM 1:50 000 Sorata 5846 I
Bolivian IGM 1:50 000 Milluni 5945 II
Bolivian IGM 1:50 000 Penas 5945 III
Bolivian IGM 1:50 000 Zongo 5945 I
Bolivian IGM 1:50 000 Lago Khora Khota 5945 IV
Walter Guzman Cordova 1:50 000 Illampu-Ancohuma
Walter Guzman Cordova 1: 50 000 Condoriri-Negruni

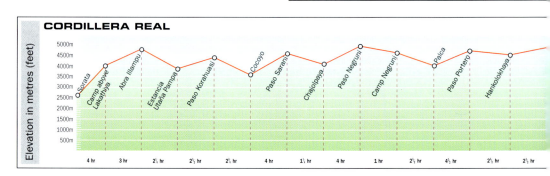

Illampu to the Sorata–Ancohuma road and camp at Estancia Utaña Pampa, just before the village of Ancohuma. (This is the first night's campsite, if you have taken a 4×4 from Sorata to Paso Chuchu.)

Estancia Utaña Pampa to Cocoyo

From Estancia Utaña Pampa, head up the valley towards Illampu, keeping on the left-hand side of the stream. Where the valley turns towards the right, head up the hillside to the left to pick up a path that leads past a string of small pools, used for freeze-drying potatoes (see p.78), to the Paso Korahuasi. From the pass, descend easily to reach a mirador overlooking a fine example of a glaciated flat-bottomed valley. The path then descends steeply through increasing amounts of vegetation – berberis, catoneaster and little firecrackers. Once on the valley floor, keep to the north of the river and follow it to the village of Cocoyo, where there are a couple of shops, a school and a football pitch. The best camping is 20 mins up the Sarani Valley, behind a huge boulder. In June the flowers are magnificent.

Cocoyo to Chajolpaya

The next day, head up the Sarani Valley to the Sarani Pass. Follow the path up the right-hand side of the valley then, just before the second set of houses, cross over to the left on a boulder bridge. Watch out for the houses; sometimes, they almost seem to merge into the hillside (they are made of the same stone, and their roofs are thatched with grass). You can almost walk past without noticing them. Then leave the valley floor and head up left, contouring above yet another perfect example of the effects of glaciation, a flat green meadow with a meandering river. The cows here live quite happily at 4000m (13123ft).

More large boulders make a good lunch spot beside the stream, and then it's another hour to the top of the pass. From there, descend to Chajolpaya and camp beside the river, with tremendous views of the Negruni Group, the Chajowara Group and La Calzada peeking over the top to the west. The Illampu Circuit heads west across the cordillera from here on the Camino Calzada.

Chajolpaya to Palca

From Chajolpaya ascend on a zigzag path next to the waterfall to the higher hanging valley. Head up the valley, keeping to the left through the boulder field (there *is* a path!). Then keep high above the valley floor and finally contour back to the river. The path then ascends through more boulders over small knolls to Paso Negruni, with the glaciated Negruni Chico on the left and Chajowara on the right. Descend to the valley floor, keep on the path to the right of the bog and camp above the lake.

The following day, you'll have earned time for relaxation after the exertion of several days of crossing high passes. It is a 2½-hour hike down-valley to good camping at Palca, a small farming community in a very fertile area. There are sheep as well as llamas, and *oca* (potatoes) drying in the sun. The trail leads down past the lake to two other brilliant blue-green lakes, where the locals catch trout. Then you drop down to the valley floor, with stunning views west to Chairoco, and continue down past small dwellings and fields. Keep going downstream, past Palca, to the next valley intersection, and camp near a modern building, whose purpose is rather unclear (perhaps it is a small church?).

Palca to Laguna Alka Khota

From the campsite, it is best to head slightly downstream and cross the river that descends from the secondary valley on a good bridge, before going up the valley itself. Then, you ascend into another hanging valley. There seems to be no obvious exit but, just when it looks as if you are heading for the headwall, the trail takes an improbable rising traverse leftwards, ascends a scree slope and you arrive at a magical tiny lake, set in a rocky cirque. Look back for a view of the spiky Tres Marias and the massive bulks of Chachacomani and Chairoco. It is an easy

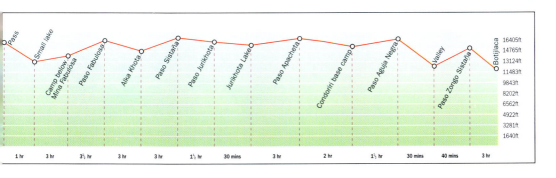

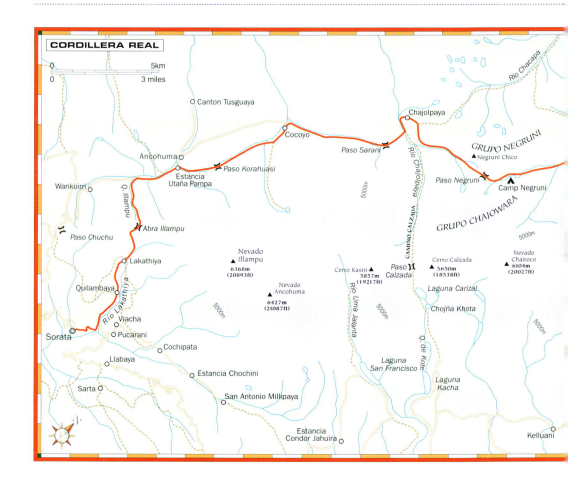

Descending Paso Negruni in the snow.

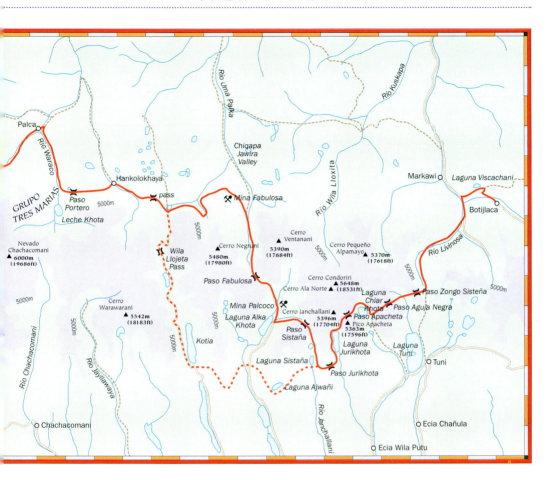

30 mins up to the Portero Pass and another 2½ hours down, accompanied by the calls of flocks of *tinamou* (Andean partridge), to the hamlet of Hankolokhaya and the mining road that crosses the Andes here. There is room for a couple of tents before you make the final descent into the valley, if you prefer to camp away from the road.

From Hankolokhaya, you can cross the range on the mining road, over the Wila Llojeta Pass to Kotia, and from there (via Lagunas Ajwañi and Sistaña) to Jurikhota Pass, and so down to Jurikhota Lake.

Alternatively, you may prefer the following, more interesting route. Hike for about an hour up the mining road west, until you are opposite a small hamlet, continue up the hillside south on a small, fairly indistinct path. This zigzags its way up to two passes for a first view of Huayna Potosí to the south, then descends steeply to a marshy area, which is best avoided on the right, and a small lake. Then, pick up another mining road, beneath a stunning array of rocky crenellated peaks, with views down to the Yungas, and the Mina Fabulosa – an old, formerly English-owned, tin mine, now run as a cooperative. The local inhabitants say they hope, eventually, to run the mine as a tourist attraction, but unfortunately, at present it does not live up to its name. In fact, the whole area appears to be one large rubbish heap. Luckily, it is possible to camp well below the mine, at the foot of some impressive rock fortresses.

From the campsite, head up the Chiqapa Jawira Valley, with its Andean geese and spectacular views into the cirque of mountains to the right. Spare a thought for the miners who had to transport the tin this way in all weathers. You will reach the Paso Fabulosa after some 3 hours. The panorama from the top is worth the hard slog. With Ventanani on your left and Negruni on your right, you look down into a mighty glaciated bowl, with tiny lakes in the bottom. Cerro Janchallani can be seen on the opposite side of the valley.

Drop down on scree and across snow to the lake below. Then ascend slightly to a brown lake, follow the devious path to the right, down a steep rocky gully and finally zigzag on scree terraces, trending right, to the

Coralling llamas at Jurikhota Lake, with Condoriri in the background.

valley below and the ruins of another old tin mine, the Mina Palcoco. From here, there are tremendous views of Condoriri and Janchallani. You can camp just below here, or continue on to Laguna Alka Khota, where there are often giant coots, and camp at the far end.

Laguna Alka Khota to Laguna Chiar Khota
From the west end of the lake, head up into the hanging valley to the south, then head towards the Sistaña Pass to the southwest. Climb a small mirador to the right for magnificent views of the arid brown Altiplano and the brilliant blue Lake Titikaka. Descend to a tiny jewel of a lake, a natural suntrap.

From here, descend slightly and continue along the trail, contouring high above Laguna Sistaña, to the Jurikhota Pass. A traverse east leaves your jaw agape as you take in the full splendour of Condoriri, with its condor's head and wings. It is arguably the most beautiful of Bolivia's mountains. Admire the view, then descend on near-perfect scree to camp beside Jurikhota Lake. There are no scree runs like this left in the UK!

Traverse round the left side of the lake, then ascend beside a stream to reach a small, usually frozen, lake directly beneath Condoriri's left wing. The route then ascends a rocky buttress. Gain a leftward slanting ramp and scramble upwards; there is a steeper section of some 5m (16½ft) to be negotiated near the top, but the rock is sound. You arrive in another hanging valley and ascend to the Apacheta Pass, with views down to Condoriri Base Camp.

It is worth making the 45-min ascent of Pico Apacheta, the rocky peak on the west of the pass. The views from here are stunning, with the whole length of the Cordillera Real laid out before you. You can see your starting point, Illampu, in the north Chairoco and Chachacomani en route, and a close up of Condoriri and Huayna Potosí, the finishing point, to the south. Look out for condors, too. Descend to the pass and head down to camp beside Laguna Chiar Khota, the black lake, where in the Base Camp, you will probably encounter the first Europeans you will have seen for some time. The camp is an impressive place, surrounded by glaciers and rocky peaks.

Laguna Chiar Khota to Botijlaca
There are only two more passes, the Paso Aguja Negra and the Paso Zongo Sistaña, both around 5000m (16400ft), before the final descent down the Liviñosa Valley to Botijlaca and the road. This day's trek takes you from the high snow-covered mountains down through green alpine meadows, herds of alpacas and flocks of *tinamou*, beneath rocky spires somewhat reminiscent of the Chamonix aiguilles, to the cultivated fields and lush vegetation of a much lower altitude.

Botijlaca is a thriving community, whose economy is based on the hydroelectric plant. Pick up your return transport here: either the jeep you have organized beforehand or, if you are prepared to wait, one of the electricity company's trucks.

PEAK: HUAYNA POTOSI

Huayna Potosí is Bolivia's most often climbed 6000-m (19685-ft) peak, mainly because of its ease of access.

It rears up as an impressive ice pyramid from the Altiplano. The normal route goes up from the Zongo Platform, where there is a dam, the holding tank for what must be one of the longest drops for any hydroelectric scheme in the world – from 4600m (15092ft) to 1480m (4856ft) in 33km (21 miles).

The starting point can be reached in less than 2 hours by 4×4 from La Paz, if you hire transport from one of the trekking agencies, or you can catch any bus up to the Plaza Ballivian in El Alto, from where trucks and minibuses leave regularly for Zongo.

There is a relatively new refuge at Laguna Zongo (tel: La Paz 323584). If you stay there, your route up to the obvious moraine lies across the dam wall. It then follows the aqueduct for 15 mins till you come to a well-trodden path that leads upwards (the old approach).

If arriving directly from La Paz, climbers now usually use the new approach, which starts from Paso Zongo, where there is a new hut and area for camping. From here, the path makes a rising traverse to the right to reach the moraine, where both paths merge. Next, follow the moraine to its top, then drop down and ascend a steep path on scree through boulders. Continue trending leftwards to reach the edge of the glacier (5200m/17060ft). The trekking agencies like to make their High Camp here, as they say it is less high and more comfortable (and it means they do not have to provide their staff with ice axe and crampons). It does, however, make for a much longer summit day. Either way, both High Camps are pretty squalid and you have to melt ice for water.

There is usually a big track up the glacier from here. Head straight up, then traverse rightwards. Where it steepens, go left and reach a wide open bowl, Campamento Argentino (5450m/17881ft). Camp to the right of the path, as crevasses open up to the left at the end of the season. Beware, too, of the wall below the seracs of the south summit.

The much-climbed route to the summit of Huayna Potosí.

From Campamento Argentino, head up the glacier rightwards and ascend a steep (40–50°) section to the ridge. Turn left and go up the exposed Polish Ridge. You then weave your way through and around a series of spectacular crevasses (usually on a well-trodden track) and traverse rightwards to below the summit face. Here you can either continue round to the right and ascend the airy ridge, or go straight up the face, a 250-m (820-ft) slope of 40–50°. The ridge route gives stunning views down the west face, but there are less opportunities to place protection. Conditions here also tend to become rather thin at the end of the season, nor is it a good place to be in high winds. Be aware that the summit of Huayna Potosí is quite exposed and is crowned by a strange snow mushroom. Allow 4–6 hours to get to the summit from Campamento Argentino. Descend by either the face or the ridge; this will take 2 hours to Campamento Argentino and a further 2 hours to the road.

CLIMB ESSENTIALS

SUMMIT Huayna Potosí 6088m (19974ft)
CAMPS Base Camp (Paso Zongo) 4600m (15092ft); High Camp (Campamento Argentino) 5450m (17881ft) or the edge of the glacier, 5400m (17717ft).
GRADE Alpine Grade PD

PEAK: CONDORIRI

An ascent of Condoriri is an experience not to be missed.

Condoriri, or, more properly, La Cabeza (the head) de Cóndor, has been variously called 'the Matterhorn of Bolivia' and 'Bolivia's most beautiful mountain'. Seen from afar, the mountain, with its outriders, the *alas oueste y este* (west and east wings) looks for all the world like a condor with its wings outstretched, as the name implies.

Although a mere 5648m (18531ft), it is one of the more interesting of the accessible mountains in Bolivia. Seen from below, the summit ridge looks unassailable, but there is a hidden gully that leads onto it, so avoiding the steeper lower section.

Base Camp is at Laguna Chiar Khota. If you have not trekked in on the Cordillera Real trek, you will need to arrange private transport from La Paz, as there are no buses to the nearest habitation of Estancia Tuni. Burros or llamas can be hired at Tuni. From there, head around the south end of Laguna Tuni, then go north, following a good path to Base Camp (3 hours). There are open-air, long-drop toilets, a tap with good water and camp guards, who charge a small fee per day to protect your belongings while you are on the mountain.

It is possible to make High Camp on a rock platform at the edge of the glacier, about 3 hours up from Base Camp, but most people just leave early.

From Base Camp, follow the path through the boulders, then head northwest up the moraine to the infamous scree couloir, which has to be ascended to reach the glacier and rock platforms of the High Camp. It is possible to avoid this by traversing further right and ascending a snow gully to the glacier.

Once on the glacier, traverse round the base of Condoriri until you reach a hidden snow gully (2 hours from High Camp) which leads onto the ridge at a notch. Follow the classic alpine snow ridge, with great exposure on both sides, through a series of rock steps to the final airy summit arête. Stunning!

Descend by the same route.

CLIMB ESSENTIALS

SUMMIT Condoriri, 5648m (18531ft)
CAMPS Base Camp (Laguna Chiar Khota) 4700m (15420ft); High Camp (rock platform on the edge of the glacier) 5100m (16732ft).
GRADE Alpine Grade AD+.

PEAK: PEQUENO ALPAMAYO

Pequeño Alpamayo, with its perfect summit pyramid of snow and steep final slope, can be climbed from Condoriri Base Camp). It is called Pequeño Alpamayo because it is said to be a smaller version of its eponymous Peruvian neighbour.

From Base Camp, head past the small lake to the moraine ridge, which you follow to just before the large boulder. The path then drops down to the glacier where, except after fresh snow, there is usually a well-established track. It wends its way round the obvious crevasses and ascends close to the left side. At the top, go right, to the summit of Tarija (5060m/16601ft), then descend on rock for 50m (164ft) to the snow below. Traverse the narrow snow ridge to the west-southwest ridge of Pequeño Alpamayo and head for the summit, taking care not to stray too near the edge, as the cornice can be huge. Descend by the same route.

Pequeño Alpamayo is a classic climb.

CLIMB ESSENTIALS

SUMMIT Pequeño Alpamayo, 5370m (17618ft)
CAMP Base Camp (Laguna Chiar Khota) 4700m (15420ft)
GRADE Alpine Grade AD

SORATA DIRECTORY

Sorata lies at 2670m (8760ft) towards the northern end of the Cordillera Real, at the foot of Illampu, a pretty little town set amidst lush vegetation in a rich agricultural valley. Once the thriving gateway to the rubber plantations and gold mines of the Alto Beni, it is now (since the building of roads between La Paz and the Yungas) a peaceful subtropical oasis. Its low altitude means that it is a great place to rest, recuperate or acclimatize.

REGIONAL TRANSPORT

La Paz to Sorata by bus: Transportes Larecaja and Flota Unifica da Sorata leave about 10 times every day from the Calle Manuel Bustillos, at the corner of Avenida Kollasuyo, two blocks above the Cementario, between 6am and 2pm. The journey takes 4 hours. There is a police checkpoint at Achacachi, so you will need your passport. It is wise to book in advance, especially on Fridays. Buses return to La Paz from Sorata's main square between 5am and 3.30pm.

ACCOMMODATION

Residencial Sorata, on the Plaza, tel: (08) 115044, fax: (08) 115218, email: resorata@mail.entelnet.bo. Full of character, but uncomfortable beds! A 'faded glory' colonial-style mansion, built around a flower-filled garden, complete with hummingbirds and the odd tame parrot. Friendly, with excellent home cooking.
Hotel Copacabana, approximately 10 mins down from the plaza on the way to San Pedro, tel/fax: (08) 115042, email: landhaus@khainata.com. Another popular spot.
Hotel El Paraiso, tel: (08) 115043. More upmarket.
Hostal Panchita, tel: (08) 364919. Has a courtyard. Reservations can be made in La Paz.

RESTAURANTS

There is now a surprisingly large selection of good restaurants in Sorata, mostly situated on the plaza:
Restaurante Altai, excellent vegetarian food.
Pizzeria Restaurante Italia, 'como en Italia'.
Restaurante Pizzeria Panchita, in the Hostal Panchita.
Spider Bar, down from the plaza. Good for an alternative evening.
Altai Oasis, a campsite and café, located down river from the town.
Cafe Illampu, very good home baking, located downriver from the town.

LOCAL ACTIVITIES

Guides and trekking equipment can be hired (and burros arranged) both at the Residencial Sorata and at the Hotel Copacabana.

QUINOA

Quinoa is a so-called supergrain that has been grown on the Altiplano for millenia. Known as the 'mother grain' by the Incas, it was regarded as sacred, but has only recently been discovered by nutritionists in the developed world. It has a higher protein content than other grains such as corn, barley and rice, although only slightly more than some wheats. It is high, too, in the amino-acid lysine, as well as in calcium, iron, phosphorous, Vitamin E and several of the B vitamins, and is rich in oil and fat.

Quinoa is not a true cereal grain, but technically a fruit of the Chenopodium family. An annual, it grows 1–2m (3–6ft) high and has seeds clustered at the end of the stalk. The plant and seeds can vary in colour from pale yellow, through orange, red and purple, to black. The seed itself is small and looks like a cross between a sesame seed and a millet seed.

Quinoa grows almost exclusively in the Andes, where the habitat is ideal – the plant thrives at 3000–4000m (10000–12000ft), survives on as little as 5cm (2in) of rainfall per year and is resistant to frost.

Every bit of quinoa can be used. By removing the bitter outer coating, called *saponin*, and boiling the seeds, it can be used as a grain. Typically, the seed is used in soups and stews. Toasted seeds can be ground and used as flour in baking breads. They can also be popped, like popcorn. The leaves, called *llipcha* in Quechua, can be eaten raw or boiled, like spinach. The leaves are also often used in puddings, syrups and tonics. The *saponin* has foaming properties and is used as a soap to clean hair and clothes, and to make frothier *chicha*. The stalks are used in the preparation of dyes, or dried as fuel.

In May 1997, quinoa became the subject of much controversy. Two agronomists from Colorado State University, Johnson and Ward, applied for and were granted American Patent No 5,304,718 for a Bolivian variety of quinoa known as Apelawa, after a village near Lake Titikaka where they had collected the seeds. The patent guaranteed the agronomists exclusive monopoly. Bolivians were horrified that North Americans were able to appropriate and patent a seed that had been growing in their country for thousands of years. Opposition from local farmers' groups and the Bolivian National Association of Quinoa Producers was so strong that the scientists dropped the patent. This was an important victory on the part of indigenous peoples throughout the world

Today Andean countries have realized the importance of quinoa, not only in terms of feeding their population but also in terms of their economies as a whole. Governments in Ecuador, Peru and Bolivia have pushed for an increase in quinoa production. The current value of the quinoa export market from Bolivia is roughly US$1 million per year.

Quinoa, the Inca's 'mother grain', still feeds the Andes today.

TREK 12: ILLAMPU CIRCUIT

This is another high-altitude trek in the northern section of the Cordillera Real. It features stunning views from all sides of the Illampu/Ancohuma massif, as it makes a complete circuit of the peaks, crossing the Andes beneath the scenic Cerro Calzada on a pre-Hispanic pavement, the Camino Calzada, which was once a main thoroughfare between the Altiplano and the subtropical Yungas. This is Andean scenery at its best, with four high passes, brilliant blue lakes, glaciated peaks, condors, viscachas and Andean geese. What's more, you start and finish in relaxing Sorata, where there are flowers, hummingbirds and where the air is warm and easy to breathe.

The first 3–4 days are the same as for the main Cordillera Real trek (see trek 11). From Sorata to Estancia Utaña Pampa, either walk via Lakathiya and Abra Illampu or travel by 4×4 to Paso Chuchu, then down, on to Cocoyo and as far as Chajolpaya.

Chajolpaya to Laguna Hualatani

From Chajolpaya, head up the northwest side of the Río Chajolpaya and reach a wide, paved path after 20 mins. This is the Camino Calzada, a pre-Hispanic road, which crosses the Andes and links the Altiplano with the Yungas. The trail leads up the valley, with tremendous views of La Calzada, a small, perfectly shaped, snow-covered pyramid peak on the left, and Kasiri on the right. Camping is possible just before the pass, 4½ hours up the Camino Calzada.

Cross the barren, broad Paso Calzada after 30 mins, then descend to the beautiful Lagunas Carizal and Chojña Khota. The path then crosses the Quebrada de Kote and ascends slightly on the eastern side. Drop down to the northern end of Laguna Kacha. From here, it is scenically more worthwhile to make a 1-hour climb up to a pass to the northwest for panoramic, breathtaking views of the Altiplano, Lake Titikaka, to the south, Ancohuma to the north, Cerro Kasiri to the northeast and Cerros Calzada, Chairoco and Chachacomani to the southeast. Then, descend to the eastern lakeshore of Laguna San Francisco and pick up the main trail round the north end of the lake. This turns southwest, then west, to reach a pile of stones (point 4867 on the DAV map), another brilliant mirador. Follow the old road down to the aqueduct, where a small path leads right. Cross a stream and at the next path junction turn right again (northwest) to Laguna Hualatani (unmarked on Liam O'Brien's map). The way is all downhill from here. The path crosses another aqueduct, then reaches an *apacheta* (cairn) and possible campsite.

TREK ESSENTIALS

LENGTH 5–7 days. 62 km (39 miles). All the way round Illampu and back to Sorata.
ACCESS By bus to/from Sorata, then 4×4 to/from Paso Chuchu, or trek to Estancia Utaña Pampa.
HIGHEST POINT Paso Calzada, 5045m (16552ft).
TREK STYLE Backpacking or burro/llama assisted.
RESTRICTIONS This is not a trek to attempt alone. Even as a group it is probably a good idea to hire a local guide as there have been reports in recent years of robberies on the Altiplano side of the Andes.
FURTHER OPTIONS Side trip to Laguna Subirana (from Estancia Utaña Pampa). Climb Illampu (6368m/20893ft).
MAPS DAV 1:50 000 Cordillera Real Nord (Illampu)
Liam O'Brien 1:135 000 Cordillera Real de los Andes
Bolivian IGM 1:50 000 Sorata 5846 I
Bolivian IGM 1:50 000 Warizata 5846 II 1:50 000

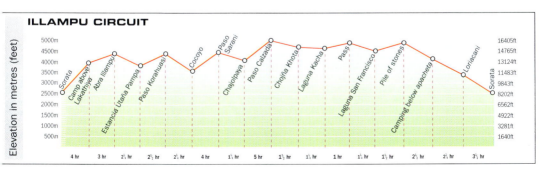

104 BOLIVIA

Illampu and Ancohuma, with Sorata in the foreground.

Laguna Hualatani to Sorata

Next, the trail crosses a new (mainly unused) road and reaches the dirt road just before Alto Lojena. Continue on to Millipaya. You can continue all the way to Sorata on this road (3–4 hours), but there are better views and less hairpin bends if you follow the road as far as the first hairpin and the Mina Mercedes, cross the river and ascend to Loriacani on the west side of the valley. From here, you get magnificent views of the western glaciers of Illampu and Ancohuma. Continue on down through Chihuani to meet the La Paz road where it crosses the Río San Cristobál. It is important to try to strike a middle line – not too high and not too low – when choosing from the variety of paths hereabouts to get you to this point. Use the river as a guide. Then it is a 1-hour walk to Sorata.

PEAK: ILLAMPU

The ascent of Ilampu is not for the inexperienced mountaineer.

Illampu is reputed to be the most technically difficult of Bolivia's 6000-m (19685-ft) peaks, as there is a steep (50–55°) headwall to be surmounted. Moreover, in dry seasons, late in the year, a huge bergschrund can develop, making it impossible to reach the summit.

Illampu is the most northerly peak of the Cordillera Real. It dominates the skyline from the Isla del Sol and as you drive across the Altiplano, past Lake Titikaka, towards Sorata. The view of the great snow-covered Illampu and Ancohuma peaks, framed by palm trees from Sorata's town square is not to be missed.

Aguas Calientes is Base Camp for an ascent of Illampu. This can be reached in 1 or 2 days, depending on how much money you want to spend.

You can hire a 4x4 to take you to Ancohuma, then hire burros from Estancia Utaña Pampa or Ancohuma to carry your equipment up the valley. Follow a path on the left, then cross to the right, to finally reach a camp below the *terminal moraine* (high point for the burros).

The 2-day trip is via Lakathiya up to the Paso Huila Khota (4886m/16030ft) and down to Aguas Calientes. Burros can be hired in Sorata to go as far as Lakathiya, from where porters can be hired to carry your gear to Base Camp.

From Aguas Calientes, head up towards the left, then drop down into the next valley. Go up the right-hand side through the maze of cairns, then descend slightly to the moraine, which you follow to the glacier. Keep on the right, wending your way through seracs and snowfields, until you reach the flat but crevassed area, which is the High Camp.

From here climb straight up the 300-m (984-ft) headwall, to reach the col between Illampu and Huayna Illampu in 3–4 hours. Follow the ridge up to the left and reach the summit after 3–5 hours. The final 80m (262ft) are very exposed, steep and subject to strong, gusty winds.

The views from the summit are superb: to the west the Altiplano and Lake Titikaka; to the east the verdant forested valleys of the Yungas; and to the south a view along the whole cordillera.

Descend by the same route. Make sure you set out early, as snow conditions become unstable in the afternoon when the sun hits the headwall.

CLIMB ESSENTIALS

SUMMIT Illampu, 6368m (20893ft)
CAMPS Base Camp (Aguas Calientes) 4600m (15092ft); High Camp (below NW face of Illampu) 5600m (18372ft).
GRADE Alpine Grade AD+

WHY HUMMINGBIRDS ARE SO SMALL

The Andes are home to 126 different species of hummingbirds, including the sparkling violet ear, sword-billed, shining sunbeam and hillstar. Some of these, such as the Andean hillstar, are found at altitudes of up to 4800m (15748ft).

Andean hummingbirds can lower their metabolism at night-time, when they go into a state of torpor or hibernation, with substantial drops in body temperature, which returns to a normal temperature in the morning. The Andean Hillstar drops its body temperature to 15°C (60°F) at night from 39.5°C (102°F) during the day and slows its heart down to approximately 35 beats per minute. Its nests are usually built on the eastern side of rock faces so as to catch the early morning sunlight.

Hummingbirds' wing beats can be as frequent as 80 beats per second, which enables them to hover and fly backwards. They feed every 12 minutes. Andean plants of the puna have adapted to allow the hummingbirds to pollinate them – they have evolved trumpet-shaped flowers with long stamens that dust the birds' heads as they are feeding. The nectar can be reached only by hummingbirds, with their long bills and tongues, but just so much is supplied before the bird must move to another plant. This facilitates the cross-pollination of many plants.

Myths and stories play a great part in Indian culture. Here is one as told by a friend.

Once upon a time, when stories began, condors were half-bird and half-man, so that when they were high up in the Andes, on their nests or circling on the thermals, they were birds, but when they came down to earth and landed they were humans. This particular condor was a very fine young bird so, of course, when he landed in the fields he changed into a very handsome young man.

In the fields was a young girl, tending her parents' sheep and, because she was pretty and he was handsome, she and the condor soon became friends. He would come down from the sky near where she was and turn into a young man. She thought he was from the next village. They got on well together – they played tag and running games and gave each other piggybacks. One day, after she had carried him for a while, he carried her, but all of a sudden, he took off and flew up to his nest in the high mountains, with her on his back. She screamed and pleaded to be taken back to her parents, whom she loved, but the condor was determined to keep her for himself.

After several years, she had begun to grow feathers and they had children who were half-condor, half-human, except for one, who was wholly condor. Back in the valley, the girl's parents were still mourning her loss. They had a beautiful garden, where all types of wondrous flowers grew, but they were

A hummingbird taking nectar.

having problems with a marauding hummingbird. He kept coming to steal the nectar from their flowers and squashing them, for at that time hummingbirds were the size of turkeys. They could, however, also fly high up into the mountains, and there the hummingbird had recognized their daughter, despite her feathers, with the condor. When he told her parents where she was, they wept, for they thought they would never see her again. But he said, 'I will try and rescue her for you, but only in exchange for all the nectar I can ever hope to want!' 'Of course', they cried.

So the hummingbird flew up to the condor's nest, waited for him to leave, then called the daughter. He told her he had come from her parents and she could go home with him, if she wished. She wept for joy, but asked what she should do with the young half condors, half humans. They decided that they had to kill them. The young one, who was wholly condor, managed, however, to hide under a rock. The hummingbird carried the daughter back down to her parents, who were overjoyed. They poured boiling water over her and plucked her feathers.

When the condor returned, he was beside himself to find his wife gone and his children murdered. The young condor told him what had happened. In a rage, the condor returned to the valley and found the hummingbird. He attacked him and chopped him into tiny pieces but, as he chopped, each piece rose up and flew away as a tiny hummingbird.

From that day, condors have never been able to change into human beings, and hummingbirds are so small that they can eat all the nectar they like, without squashing the flowers.

TREK 13: APOLOBAMBA

The Apolobamba region lies to the northwest of the Cordillera Real, curving its way into Peru. It is incredibly beautiful, with its glacier-covered mountains, alpine meadows with flocks of ibises, hanging valleys with meandering rivers, brilliant blue lakes and jagged rocky peaks. You are unlikely to see other trekkers in this region. It is a wild and remote area, where there are few villages, but much wildlife. What's more, there are still unclimbed peaks in the area. The local people do not speak Aymara, but Quechua, as in Peru.

Charazani to Jatunpampa

From Charazani, it is possible to hire a 4x4 to save you the 4-hour walk up to Curva; otherwise head down to the thermal baths, cross the river, then go steeply uphill to join the dirt road. Follow this for a short while, then take the path leading up to the distinctive white-towered church above. From here, either descend slightly to pick up the bigger trail or continue on to a path, which first contours left, then descends again. Both trails merge and cross the river at a bridge. Now head uphill to Curva, home of the Kollowaya medicine men. From Curva keep the cross (which you can see on the hillside to the north) on your left, head round the hillside and down to cross a stream. Then move up through walled fields, keeping the stream on your right, to meet up with the main path coming in from the left. Follow this up to the small village of Jatunpampa, above which is a good campsite.

Jatunpampa to Sunchuli

If you have negotiated transport from Charazani to Curva, you will probably want to continue upwards to La Piedra Grande, an excellent campsite in a pampas beside a huge rock (3 hours from Curva).

From La Piedra Grande it is only a 4-hour walk to the next campsite at Incacancha. The path ascends steeply to the pass on the east of Akamani. It is not as bad as it looks! On the other side, first head straight down, then contour left and drop down into the idyllic Incacancha Valley, with its buff-necked ibises, egrets, wild horses and viscachas. The Quechua name for Incacancha means 'where the condors land'. Look out for them in the early morning.

From Incacancha, cross the stream at the bridge, then ascend steeply up a zigzag path in a scree gully beside the waterfall to the first pass. From here it's another 30 mins to the second pass. Then traverse left, following the ridge around Akamani, past an almost camouflaged village, with incredible views back to Illampu and Ancohuma, to a couple of lakes. Stop at the second lake for a tremendous view of the bulk of Akamani, reflected in the water. This is also a good spot to see Andean geese, puna hawks and (if you're lucky) the rare diamant sandpiper plover.

TREK ESSENTIALS

LENGTH 10–11 days. 100km (328 miles). A south-to-north trek through the Cordillera Apolobamba on pre-Hispanic goldminers' trails, from Charazani to Pelechuco, around Chaupi Orco and over the border into Peru.
ACCESS *To start* By bus or private 4x4 to either Charazani or Pelechuco from La Paz. *At finish* Return either by private transport or by local bus from Suches and Antaquilla to La Paz.
HIGHEST POINT Paso Sunchuli, 5100m (16732ft) or peak just east of Sunchuli, 5150m (16896ft).
TREK STYLE Backpacking or burro assisted.
RESTRICTIONS None.
FURTHER OPTIONS You can return along the Río Pelechuco (1 day from Pelechuco). You can visit the Base Camp in the Nakara Valley (1 day from the meadow below the Paso Sanches junction), or you can visit the community of Puina from Rancho Huarantara (4 hours return).
MAPS National Imagery and Mapping Agency, Fairfax, VA, USA, and Bolivian IGM 1:100 000 Pelechuco, 3041 H632. This map is not very accurate.
Bolivian IGM Umanata 3040, 1:100 000
Bolivian IGM Sheet 3140, 1:100 000

THE MEDICINE MEN

Curva is home to the Kollowaya medicine men, an extraordinary group of Indians who are renowned from Patagonia to Ecuador for their healing skills. The Kollowaya travel throughout the Andes administering herbal remedies; they believe that all illness is a disease of the psyche, and therefore promote the need to treat the whole person, not merely the symptoms. The Kollowaya were the personal doctors of the Incan royalty, and although the Kollowaya probably descended from one or more Aymara tribe, they speak their own Quechuan dialect which may have been imposed on them while under Incan rule.

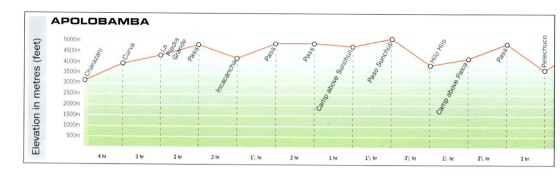

Continue for 30 mins to the now deserted Viscachani gold mine and pick up the old mining road across the pass. The devastation, caused by the still operational Sunchuli gold mine, is not a pretty sight, but avert your eyes skywards and take in the panorama of Cerros Sunchuli and Cuchillo. There are food shops in Sunchuli village, which is linked by road to Hilo Hilo and Ulla Ulla. From the pass, make a descending traverse leftwards on llama tracks to below Cuchillo and camp in a flat area just off the road.

Sunchuli to Pelechuco

From here, cross the Sunchuli Pass on the mining road – look out for the cairns, empty bottles of *alcohol potable* and scraps of material, where people have cha'lla'ed (blessed) their vehicles for a safe journey by sprinkling *alcohol potable* on them. From the pass it is possible to climb up some rather loose rock to a cairn at 5150m (16896ft) for stunning views of the mighty Cololo, the highest mountain in the southern Apolobamba. The 30-min descent is by a series of zigzags and a final scree run to the valley below. The abandoned gold mine at the bottom is again a place to avert your eyes. Cross the bog and follow the stream down to the village below, to join the dirt road to Hilo Hilo. Hilo Hilo is an unprepossessing place, although it does have a town square, three shops and several trucks (all covered over). As you leave you walk past old Hilo Hilo, which is very picturesque, with its thatched roofs blending into the surrounding brown landscape. But this part of town is largely abandoned.

From Hilo Hilo, do not take the path up to the left, which leads to Ulla Ulla, but continue through the village and walled fields, until the path becomes more pronounced again and leads up a valley. Follow this trail for about 1½ hours and camp in a pampas with herds of llamas for company.

The next day, follow the Río Atacuani uphill. It is yet another classic glaciated flat-bottomed valley and its river is home to crested ducks. At the head of the valley the mountain rises up before you, but there is a (somewhat unlikely) path. Ascend steeply, and when you are nearly at the top, look out for a little path leading to a rocky outcrop on your right. Follow this to what must be a man-made flat area, a *huaca*, or Tiwanaku ceremonial site. There is a breathtaking view down to the valley below.

Ascend to the pass, then descend to a wonderful meadow, with its own small stream, on the edge of a hanging valley. This is a real suntrap. Follow the path down to the small colonial town of Pelechuco, founded in 1560, where there are several shops, (all advertising that they will buy your gold!) three *alojamientos*, two of which have bars, a church, a telephone exchange and a town square in front of the church. There is even a medical clinic. It's a wild place on a Friday or Saturday night, when the workers from the neighbouring gold mine at Aguas Blancas come to town to spend their weekly earnings – and even wilder during fiesta week (starting 25 July), when they celebrate the founding of the town. Gold has been mined in the Apolobamba

Old Hilo Hilo.

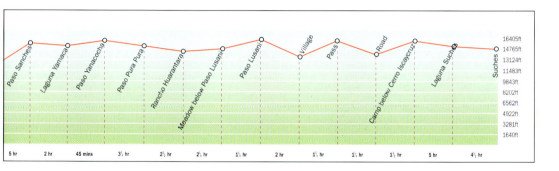

region since the time of the Incas, hence the pre-Hispanic pavement in southern Apolobamba. Today gold is mined either by large (usually foreign) companies or in small cooperatives, some very tiny.

Pelechuco to Lusani Pass

Head out of Pelechuco on the new dirt road, which was supposed to go all the way to Apolo but ends after about 1.5km (1 mile). Opposition to the road was so great (because Pelechuco is in the Ulla Ulla National Park and the semi-tropical forest beside the Pelechuco River is a protected area) that the road was literally stopped in its tracks. The forest is home to the rare and very shy *jukumari* (the Andean spectacled bear) and the torrent duck, amongst others.

Leave the road after 20 mins and take the old path uphill beside the Nakara River, passing through a mass of flowers – borage, blue penstemon, koa, lupins and, higher up, *puya raimondii*, which is the tallest flower spike in the world (indigenous only to Bolivia and Peru) and a favourite food of the spectacled bear. The trail leads steadily uphill, past several small, almost camouflaged, thatched-roofed settlements with their llamas, tilled fields, cairns to Pachamama and barking dogs. On reaching a broad meadow, a path leads up to the Paso Quera (known locally as the Paso Sanches) on the ridge to the right. It is quite a haul to the top, but the view of the mountains at the head of the Nakara Valley – Huascarani (Azucarani) and the Soral Group – is breathtaking. This is also condor territory. Drop down from the pass to a beautiful deep blue lake, with a backdrop of the most amazing rock scenery – a cross between Colorado and Stac Pollaidh. Follow the path past the ruined buildings at Yamaca (a possible campsite), then contour to the right, viscachas scurrying into the rocks as you approach, to Laguna Yamaca. There is a walled corral for a campsite above the lake. Watch out for the *cajaphora horrida* underneath the big boulder in the middle; it has brilliant orange flowers, but its leaves can give you a nasty sting.

At the lake, cross the bridge, then head up steeply on a path of broken slate to the Paso Yanacocha. Keep looking back, as there are great reflections of the Sorals in the lake, then more views of Pico Mirador and Huascarani from the top. Descend to another gem of a lake, then contour to the left, around a spur, with a village below. Move on to a second ridge and down into a wide valley. Follow the river uphill now to the Paso Pura Pura (west) and drop down to Laguna Soral, a stunning lake surrounded by steep jagged mountains. The best camping is at the southeast end, although you will need to share it with numerous Andean geese!

Continue around the west side of the lake, drop down to the platform above the vivid emerald Laguna Celeste, with views of Chaupi Orco and Soral Oeste. From there, descend to Rancho Huarantara. Now head up the beautiful Arroyo Huancasayani with its rushing waterfalls, herds of llamas and flocks of Andean geese. There is a perfect meadow for camping just before the Lusani Pass.

Lusani Pass to Lago Suches

It takes 1¼ hours up to the pass, which marks the border with Peru. The view from the top is magnificent: snow-capped peaks in all directions. Ahead is Señal Nevado Ananea Grande (5829m/19125ft), to the right Nevados Cunuyo and Losoccocha, and on the left Nevado Sorapata. The trail descends easily down to a small hamlet, then turns north to meet the main road back to the Bolivian border at Tansana. You, however, should head up the valley towards the southwest until below a pass. The rock wall looks impregnable, but it can be breached from the bottom left by an unlikely, rightwards trending, rocky ramp. Once at the top, descend to the small lake below, go over the next pass, then keep heading down until you reach the road. Follow this south, until you pick up the old road, which you then follow as a shortcut to a good campsite below Cerro Iscaycruz.

Continue following the new road, past a tiny lake with giant coots and ruddy ducks, for 2½ hours, to a

110 BOLIVIA

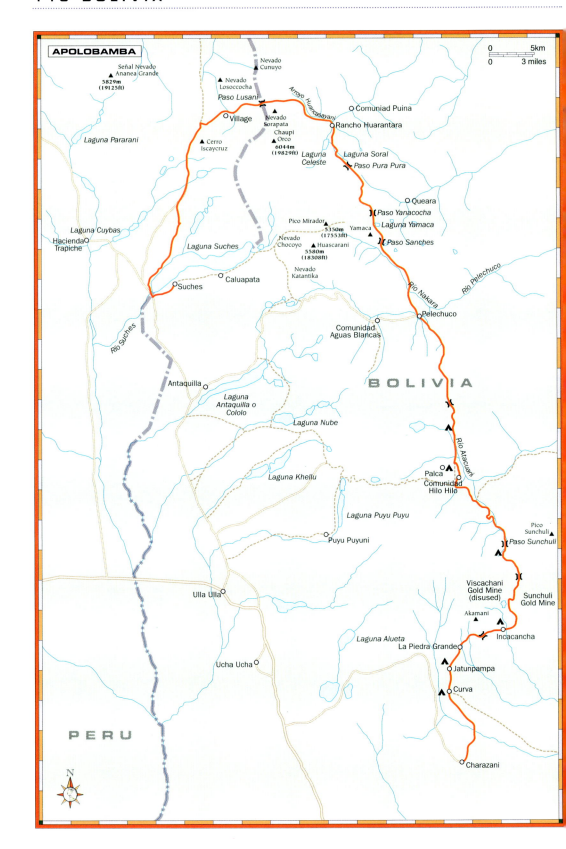

place where there is a tremendous view down to two bright blue lakes and the village of Trapiche. From here, you can either follow the dirt road all the way to the border at the western end of Laguna Suches or (after another 30 mins of road walking) head off cross country to the lake, then walk back along its northern shore. Either way, the road walking is not that interesting. Laguna Suches itself is stunning, with tremendous views of Nevados Katantika and Chocoyo.

If you have arranged private transport, it is probably best to be picked up as soon as you arrive at the road. Your driver would need a permit, but any trekking agency could organize that. Otherwise, you will need to find transport back from Suches village to Antaquilla, to link up with the Friday or Saturday bus back to La Paz.

If you have private transport, the open-air thermal baths near Antaquilla are definitely worth a visit. They are situated in the middle of nowhere, surrounded only by vicuñas, against a backdrop of the whole of the Apolobamba Range.

Descending to Laguna Suches at the end of the trek, with Nevado Katantika in the background.

APOLOBAMBA DIRECTORY

The Cordillera Apolobamba stretches for some 80km (50 miles), from Charazani at the southern end to the Peruvian border in the north. Treks can be started either from Charazani and walked in a south to north direction, or from Pelechuco and walked from north to south.

CHARAZANI
Charazani, the biggest village in the Apolobamba region, is the administrative centre of the Bautista Sauvedra province. There are a few small shops and a medical post, but no telephone. There are also thermal baths situated 10 mins walk below the main square.

REGIONAL TRANSPORT
Charazani to La Paz by bus: daily services leave at 6am from Calle Reyes Córdoba and take 10 hours. The bus sometimes continues on to Curva (a further 1½ hours) to pick up passengers for the return trip to La Paz. The return bus to La Paz departs daily at 7am.
Charazani to La Paz by 4x4: 6½ hours to Charazani, and 8 hours to Curva.

ACCOMMODATION IN CHARAZANI
There are several very basic *alojamientos* in Charazani, often serving trout as the main meal:
Hotel Charazani
Hotel Kallawaya
Hotel Akamani

LOCAL ACTIVITIES
Burros can be hired from Curva or Canisaya. Santos is reliable.

PELECHUCO
Pelechuco, a colonial village founded in 1560, boasts many fine buildings, several small shops (where you can sell your gold!), a medical post, telephone, electricity and a water tap in the main square. The main economic activity in the area is gold mining, based on a large gold mine at Aguas Blancas, further up the valley. There are, however, many small mines in the surrounding hills, which are usually the property of two to three people.

REGIONAL TRANSPORT
La Paz to Pelechuco by bus: a weekly bus leaves on Wednesdays at 8am from the corner of Calle Reyes Cardona and Avenida Kollasuyo, three blocks from the Cementario. The journey takes 14–24 hours. The return bus leaves for La Paz on Fridays and Saturdays at 7am. It is best to check these times before you set off on trek.
La Paz to Pelechuco by 4x4: 10 hours.

ACCOMMODATION IN PELECHUCO
There are three very basic *alojamientos* in Pelechuco:
Rumillajita (the most well equipped)
Pensión Mexico
Chujlla Wasi

LOCAL ACTIVITIES
Pelechuco fiesta is held every year around 25 July for about a week, to celebrate the founding of the town.
Burros can be hired from Alcides Imana or from Reynaldo Vásquez.

5
PERU

Peru is not only the land of the Incas and Chavín cultures and home to the magnificent ancient city of Machu Picchu, it also contains some of the most stunning and dramatic mountains in South America, the highest serviceable railway in the world and some of the most marvellous festivals on the planet.

Most of these attractions can be experienced by pulling on your hiking boots and going on a trek. From the paths of the Inca Trail to the isolated routes of the Huayhuash, Peru always has a warm welcome to offer.

A traditional shepherd's home in Quebrada Shallap (trek 18).

The Land

Peru is divided into three regions: narrow coastal desert and extensive lowland tropical rainforest, which are separated by the high ranges of the Andes. The southeast winds that blow across the continent make coastal Peru one of the driest regions of the world, while the influence of the cold Humboldt current keeps the land cooler than it would otherwise be at that latitude. Many of the rivers from the Andes flow to the coast, providing water for the coastal communities.

In Peru, the Andes are 150km (93 miles) wide at their narrowest, in the north, widening to 300km (186 miles) wide in the south. The high range of the Cordillera Occidental forms the continental watershed where several rivers drain southwest to the Pacific, while the Amazon and its tributaries drain into the Atlantic in the east. The less continuous Cordillera Oriental forms the interior side of the Andes. Snow-clad peaks, high plateaux and deep canyons are some of the most common geographical features of the Peruvian Andes.

We start our Peruvian odyssey in the Cuzco area with a visit to the remote Auzungate circuit, followed by the Cordillera Vilcabamba, and finally the world famous and most popular trek in South America: the Inca Trail. Moving north, we visit the more remote Cordillera Huayhuash and Cordillera Blanca.

Politics

Incan civilization was flourishing, its empire extending from northern Ecuador to central Chile, when the Spanish arrived in Peru in 1531. Debilitated by civil war, however, the Incas stood little chance when Pizarro and his army attacked. The Spanish conquered the imperial city of Cuzco within just two years and consolidated control in Lima by 1534. The Incas offered little resistance to their conquerors during this period. Exposed for the first time to European ailments such as smallpox, whooping cough and bubonic plague, the native population plummeted from 32 million to 5 million within 30 years.

Although Spanish rule was occasionally disturbed by uprisings against the government, it was not until José de San Martín and Simón Bolívar fronted the independence movement that there was any serious threat. San Martín liberated Peru in 1821. Peru's first years as an independent republic were difficult, but the political situation stabilized when Ramón Castilla ascended to the presidency. Castilla approved a moderate constitution, which ended slavery, established an educa-

Zigzagging trails cut into the hillside lead tour buses full of tourists up to the popular historic site of Machu Picchu.

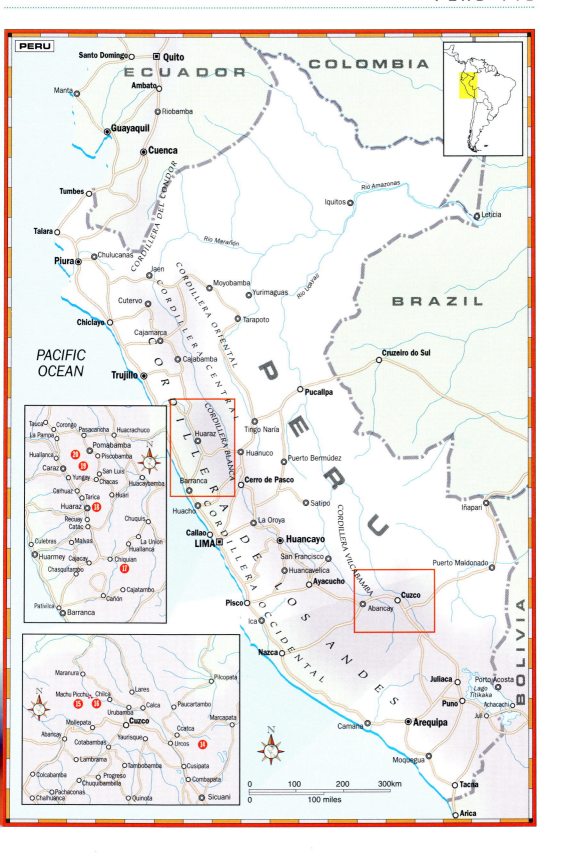

tion system and promoted the extraction of guano – nitrates produced from seabird droppings and used as fertilizer in North America and Europe.

The export of guano brought an enormous flow of revenue to the state, temporarily pulling Peru out of its post-independence stagnation. However, crisis struck when the guano deposits were depleted. Peru's financial problems were compounded when it was dragged into the costly War of the Pacific in 1879 – the country was forced to declare bankruptcy in 1889.

An international plan was soon hatched to bail Peru out of its financial straits. The Peruvian Corporation was formed in London and assumed the US$50 million national debt in return for control of the national economy. Foreign companies took over Peru's rail lines and many of its ports, and exploited its rubber resources and the remains of the guano deposits. Though cash was flowing into the country, none of it found its way to the peasants, and the first half of the twentieth century saw several Indian rebellions and the rise of the first labour movement.

The stock market crashed in 1929, and a military coup shortly followed. Thus began a long period in which military coups repeatedly interrupted civilian government. However, since 1980, when General Francisco Morales Bermudez Cerruti voluntarily handed power over to the once-deposed and now newly elected President Belaunde Terry, Peru has had civilian governments.

Belaunde Terry's administration, like that of his successor, Alan Garcia, was riddled with problems. Economic woes left over from the military government persisted and were worsened by the 'El Niño' weather phenomenon. Furthermore, rural terrorism by Sendero Luminosa (SL) and the Tupac Amaru Revolutionary Movement (MRTA) was on the rise.

Deeply troubled by these issues, voters elected relatively unknown Alberto Fujimori in 1990. Fujimori implemented drastic economic reform – including privatization of numerous state-owned companies, creation of an investment-friendly climate and sound management of the economy – which saw inflation nosedive. Fujimori also took the hard line on national terrorism, reducing such activities to little more than the occasional car bomb.

The run-up to Peru's presidential election of 2000 was marked by Fujimori's constitutionally questionable decision to seek a third term and subsequent tainted victory. When a bribery scandal broke shortly after the election, Fujimori was forced to call a new election in which he would not run. A caretaker government conducted the 2001 election in which Alejandro Todo, Peru's first freely elected leader of native Indian descent, prevailed.

AIRLINES

International Airlines
KLM, Av Pardo 05, Piso 6, Miraflores, tel: (51 1) 242 1240/1241
American, Juan de Arona 830, Piso 15, San Isidro, tel: (51 1) 442 8555/475 6161
Continental, Victor Andres, Belaunde 147, via Principal 110, Of 101-102, tel: (51 1) 221 4340/222 7080
Iberia, Av Camino Real 390, Piso 9, San Isidro, Torre Central del Centro Camino Real, tel: (51 1) 421 4616/421 4622
Avianca, Av Paz, Soldan 225, San Isidro, tel: (51 1) 221 7822/7530

Domestic Airlines
Aerocontiente, Av Francisco Marsias 544, San Isidro, tel: (51 1) 442 6456/451 8280
LanPeru, Av Jose Pardo 269, Miraflores, tel: (51 1) 446 6995
TANS, Av Arequipa 5200, Miraflores, tel: (51 1) 241 8519
AviaAndina, Edif Central Piso 8, Elias Aguirre 110, Esq Av Pardo Cdra 5, Miraflores, tel: (51 1) 242 4242
Taca Peru, Av Commandte Espinar 331, Miraflores, tel: (51 1) 213 7000
Aerocondor, Juan de Arona 781, San Isidro, Lima, tel: (51 1) 442 5215

ARRIVING IN PERU
Most people arrive in Peru by air to Lima, the capital city. Flying in on a clear day, or travelling into the centre by taxi, they must wonder what on earth they've come to. With its crazy traffic, slums and unfinished houses, it looks more like a war zone than a capital city. However, once you've taken time to recover from the flight and culture shock, you can discover some superb colonial Spanish architecture in the centre and small fishing areas on the outskirts of town. If you're staying in one of the suburbs (such as Miraflores) there are all kinds of modern restaurants and bars to try. The museums in the city are fascinating and the San Francisco Cathedral and Plaza D'Armas are also well worth visiting.

TRAVELLING TO PERU
By Air
There is a US$25 departure tax payable on all international fights.

BUS COMPANIES

Cruz del Sur, Av Prado, San Isidro, tel: (51 1) 423 1570/424 1005 or Central Lima on Quilca 531. Excellent service nationwide, especially good for Huaráz or Cuzco. Fares are almost double those of any other service, but the quality is excellent. Services are non-stop with meals served on board.
Ormeno Expresso Ancash, Av Prado, San Isidro, or Carlos Zavala, 177, tel: (51 1) 427 5679/428 6453. Good nationwide service, particularly in the Huaráz area.
Rodrigues, Roosevelt 354, tel: (511) 428 0506. Services to Huaráz. Beware of luggage theft.
Movil, Abancay 947, tel: (511) 427 5369. Services to Huaráz.
Transfysa, Montevideo 724, tel: (511) 428 4510. Direct service from Lima to Chiquian.

EMBASSIES

Canada, Frederico Geredes 130, Miraflores, tel: (51 1) 444 4015
UK, Natalio Sanchez 125, 11th floor, tel: (51 1) 433 4738
USA, Grimaldo del Solar 346, Miraflores, tel: (51 1) 444 3621
Spain, Jorge Basadre 498, San Isidro, tel: (51 1) 4705600
New Zealand, Natalio Sanchez 125, 11th floor, tel: (51 1) 433 4738

Visas
Most travellers to Peru can stay in the country for up to 90 days without a visa. All nationalities need a tourist or embarkation card, however, which is issued either at the country's borders or on the plane before landing in Lima. Tourist cards are valid for between 60 and 90 days and can be extended for 60 days through local immigration officials. Overstaying without proper authorization is a serious matter; visitors will be denied permission to leave the country and can be held in detention until a fine is paid.

For your own safety and freedom of movement, a copy of your tourist card and passport should be kept on your person at all times.

Customs/Immigration
Peruvian law strictly prohibits the export of antiques and artefacts from pre-colonial civilizations. It is also illegal to remove certain flora and fauna items, such as live birds or animals or handicrafts made from insects, feathers or other natural products.

Money
The Nuevo Sol (S) is Peru's unit of currency, but US$ are widely accepted throughout the country. Break up large notes whenever possible as it can difficult to obtain small change, particularly in remote towns.

Money can be changed at banks, hotels or *casas de cambio* – which can be found in most towns and usually offer the best rates of exchange.

TRANSPORT
By Taxi
Make sure you agree a price for all journeys before you start and use only offical taxis at night (usually yellow). Radio cars can be called by most hotels. Alfonso Perez Vela's taxi service is excellent for travel to all areas of Lima and for airport transfers (tel: [51 1] 4663561/9081377 or contact Hostal La Castellana). Alfonso knows all the city tours and can provide great advice on places to eat and visit.

By *Collectivo*
Private cars or minibuses with the routes listed on the front window are the best way to get around the city cheaply and efficiently.

ACCOMMODATION
Hostal La Castellana, 222 Grimaldo del Solar, Miraflores, tel: (51 1) 444 3530. Excellent small hotel in quiet district of Miraflores.
Hostal Roma, 326 Jiron Ica, tel: (51 1) 277576. Small budget hotel. Very handy for visits to the Plaza d'Armas area.
Hostal Espana, Calle Azangaro, tel: (51 1) 285546. Budget hotel near San Francisco Cathedral. Cheap and cheerful, but often noisy.
Hostal San Martin, Av Nicolas Perola 739, tel: (51 1)

Tricycle transport in Peru.

236465. Mid-range hotel.
Albergue Anderson, Las Garzas 230, San Isidro, tel: (51 1) 441 6607, email: manderson@latinmail.com.
Residencial el Castillo, Diez Canseco 580, Miraflores, tel: (51 1) 469501. Small hotel, mid-range, in a quiet district.
Pension Yolande, Escobar Domingo Elias 230, Miraflores, tel: (51 1) 457565. Very friendly family-run *pension* where you can store gear, etc. Small rooms.

Restaurants
L'eau Vive, Ucayali.
La Rosa Nautica, Espigon y Costaq Verde, Miraflores, tel: (51 1) 445 0149.
Las Tejas, Av Diez de Canseco, Miraflores.
Costa Verde, Playa Barranquito, Barranco, tel: (51 1) 477 2424.
La Campagnola, Henry Revett 175, Miraflores, tel: (51 1) 444 3357.
Mango, Av Canaval y Moreyra 312, San Isidro, tel: (51 1) 241 3239.
Bircher Benners, 487 Diez Canseco, Miraflores, tel: (51 1) 444250. Vegetarian.

COMMUNICATIONS
Peru's country code is 51, and the city code for Lima is 1. Although it is possible to make local calls at most corner shops and restaurants, you will need to place international calls at Teléfonica del Peru offices, which are located in all towns. Another option is to purchase phone cards – available at corner shops, pharmacies or cigarette stands – for use in outdoor phone kiosks. Peru has good internet connections, with internet cafes in even the smallest towns. The country's best internet service provider is Red Cientifica Peruana (RCP).

The Peruvian postal service is fairly efficient. Outbound letters to Europe and the United States take between 10 days and three weeks to reach their destination; incoming letters from Europe and the US will generally reach you within two weeks. You can have mail sent to you poste restante, care of any main post office.

TIME DIFFERENCE
Peru is 5 hours behind Greenwich Mean Time.

ELECTRICITY
220 volt/60 cycles AC is the standard electric current, except in Arequipa where it is 220 volt/50 cycles.

SECURITY
Although Peru is relatively safe, its cities have a growing reputation for street crime. Theft is the biggest problem, with pickpockets targeting crowded areas such as street markets, bus and train stations and airports. Armed mugging also occurs, so travellers should remain vigilant at night and when withdrawing money from bank ATMs. Travellers should use only registered taxis and must never accept offers of transportation or guide services from individuals seeking clients on the street.

If you are assaulted, you should file a report with the tourist police as soon as possible. The telephone numbers for the tourist police in Lima are (51 1) 225 8698 and 225 8699 and their main office is located at Jr. de la Union 1048, one block from Plaza San Martín. Travellers are also encouraged to use the Tourist Protection Service (tel. [51 1] 224 7888), whose operators are available 24 hours a day and can handle calls in English.

PISCO SOUR

Pisco Sour is the traditional national drink of Peru. It is served at weddings, birthdays and all special events, often along with roasted *cuy* (guinea pig, see p.131). In the hill villages, *pisco* may be substituted for *aguarte* – a very potent local hooch, usually distilled from potatoes, but occasionally from barley.
Ingredients:
A bottle of *pisco*
2 egg whites
3 tablespoons sugar
10 lemons
Angostura bitters
Method:
Liquify all the ingredients and serve in small glasses with crushed ice.

USEFUL ADDRESSES

South American Explorers Club, Av Portugal 146, tel: (51 1) 250142. Clubhouse with information on all of South America. You are allowed one visit to check out the club, and then you must become a member. Membership allows you access to the library.
Direccion General de Immigraciones, Paseo de la Republica 585. Open: Mon-Fri, 9.30am-1pm. You must visit here if you wish to extend your visa or if you lose your passport and need to have a new entrance card issued.
Banco de Credito, Jiron Lampa 499.
Clinica Anglo American, Calle Salazar, San Isidro, tel: (51 1) 403570.
Clinica International, Calle Washington 1475, Central tel: (511) 288060.

TREK 14: CORDILLERA AUZUNGATE

Cordillera Auzungate, one of the more remote mountain ranges in southern Peru, offers a wonderful view of the life of the people living on the puna, with their herds of llama and staple diet of freeze-dried potatoes and llama meat. Their way of life has changed little, and they are renowned for their brightly coloured shawls and hats.

TREK ESSENTIALS

LENGTH 5-10 days. 80-110km (50-68 miles). From Tinqui, trek to Upis, and on to Janpaucacocha, and up and down again to Jampa and Tinqui, taking in lakes on the way.
ACCESS To start Bus/truck to Tinqui (6-8 hours from Cuzco). Buses go from the Coliseum in Cuzco to Urcos, then take a local truck or bus heading to Puerto Maldonado. On finish Bus/truck from Tinqui to Puerto Uncos, and then bus to Cuzco.
HIGHEST POINT Palomani/Huaranyo Punco Passes, 5100m (16732ft).
TREK STYLE Burros and arrieros recommended
RESTRICTIONS None.
FURTHER OPTIONS Auzungate is the highest peak in southern Peru and it can be linked with a traverse of the Cordillera Vilcanota and Cordillera Carabaya starting in Corani, a village near Puno. Side trip to Laguna Sibinacocha. Climb: Paco (5500m/18045ft). Extensions: The trek can be extended by trekking from Laguna Sibinacocha (6-7 days) to Macusani. Alternatively, you could trek from Raqchi after visiting the Incan temple of Viracocha and trek to Pitumarca or to Tinqui.
MAP Peruvian IGM 1:100 000 Ocongate

You will pass hot springs, stunning glacial lakes and glaciers that extend right down to the passes. This trek, which crosses a number of passes over 4500m (14764ft), is recommended only for the fit and well acclimatized. The trails are rough and stony, with a myriad of colours in the rocks. On arrival in Tinqui, it is possible to stay in local accommodation, or camp on the edge of town. You must also provide accommodation and food for the arriero. Horses and guides can be hired at Tinqui.

Tinqui to Janpaucacocha

To start the trek, follow the trail that leaves town in a southeasterly direction towards Upis. It is an old track that is very distinct and difficult to lose, and right from the start, there are stunning views of the Auzungate Range. It is possible to camp in Upis at 4500m (14764ft) by some hot springs.

From Upis, the trail heads towards Janpaucacocha crossing the Arapa area with its many corrals and small adobe homesteads, which have enormous herds of llamas and alpacas. Soon, you'll cross your first pass on a trail that gradually ascends to the Arapa Pass at 4750m (15584ft), then traverses the southern slopes of Auzungate, passing some small glacial lakes linked by waterfalls. The route finally descends to Janpaucacocha (4600m/15092ft), and one of the most amazing campsites you could imagine, with superb views of Sorimani, Tacusiri and the Inka Peaks. A wonderful feeling of remoteness will envelop you.

Janpaucacocha to Jampa

After a cold night, you'll be on a trail that ascends, very gradually, to Apaneta Pass at 4900m (16076ft). A short, steep descent for an hour brings you to the shores of Laguna Auzungatecocha, from where the trail ascends again to the Palomani Pass at 5100m (16732ft). At the pass there are some absolutely mind-blowing views of the Cordillera Vilcanota to the southwest, the Sorimani and Inka Ranges to the northwest, and the peaks of the Santa Catalina Range. If you have the energy, it is

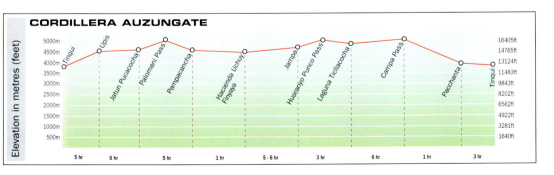

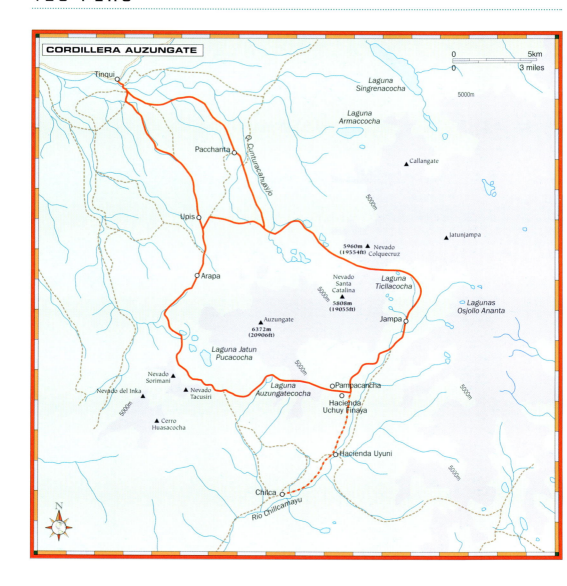

PACHAMAMA

The indigenous population has worshipped Pachamama, or Mother Earth, since pre-Hispanic times. Today, the land is still considered to be sacred. Locals regularly make offerings to Pachamama, who they believe is alive, especially before digging their land. Although the rituals vary from place to place, alcohol is always present.

The Rituals:
T'inka: Before drinking alcohol from a glass, you must first drop some to the earth, in an offering to Pachamama. This is done both indoors and outdoors!
Challa: Alcohol is scattered with the fingers onto a house, animal or vehicle (including buses), to bless them.
Chura: Alcohol is thrown from a glass to the spirits of the snow peaks (Apus). Alcohol is also thrown in a full circle around the person holding the glass.

well worth the extra effort to ascend Cerro Lomo (1 hour), a hill directly off the pass. Another descent over steep scree takes you to the meadows of Pampacancha, a beautiful area for camping. If you are short of time, continue to the Hacienda Uchuy Finaya at 4500m (14764ft).

The trail now heads in a northeasterly direction to enter the Quebrada Yanamayo, an area of stunning colours. There are peaks of 5000–5400m (16404–17717ft) in the area for ascent, and it is worth spending an extra day in the area for exploration. An excellent side trip is the ascent of Paco (5500m/18045ft), which involves an easy scramble over rough scree slopes. There are stunning views of Laguna Sibinacocha.

After a day either relaxing or exploring, head northeast into the Quebrada Jampamayo, a valley with many viscachas, a cross between a rabbit and a squirrel which whistles like a marmot. These small animals belong to the same family as chinchillas. You eventually arrive at the small community of Jampa. You may be able to buy some freeze-dried potatoes, but you will probably find they are an acquired taste! The Incas used to tell the time by how long it took to cook a pan of potatoes.

Jampa to Tinqui

The route to Laguna Sibinacocha from Jampa crosses the Huaranyo Punco Pass at 5100m (16732ft), passes Lagunas Osjollo and Ananta and descends to Quebrada Huampunimayo, where it is possible to camp by the lake. At its northern end, Laguna Sibinacocha has an amazing variety of birdlife, with Andean gulls, coots, geese and herons. From the lake you can either continue the circuit trail or head for Pitumarca (a small town 2–3 days away) via the Río Cullcamayo route which crosses two passes of 4900m (16076ft) and travels through various settlements, until it arrives at Pitumarca, from where you can return to Cuzco.

From Laguna Sibinacocha, follow the trail to Pacchaspata, passing the tiny Laguna Ticllacocha, where it is possible to camp at 4800m (15748ft). Heading northeast from the lake, the trail climbs to the final pass, Campa, at 5000m (16404ft), where there are superb views of Nevado Colquecruz, the Cayangate Group and the Santa Catalina Range. At the pass, there are several *apachetas* (cairns).

Snow-capped peaks and azure lakes are typical of the Cordillera Auzungate.

Descend from the pass to the Quebrada Cunturacahuayjo, where the best place to camp is around the hot springs of Pacchanta (3950m/12959ft) – a great place for a soak and to wash away the dust of the trail. From here, the trail heads back across rolling plains to Tinqui (3800m/12467ft) – and your first chance in a while of a beer or soft drink.

Alternative options

If you wish, the trek can be extended from Laguna Sibinacocha, with its superb birdlife. Head through an area of lakes towards the Cordillera Vilcanota, crossing a number of passes and traversing the Vilcanota icecap to arrive in Macusani (not far from Corani). This takes 6–7 days and crosses very rugged terrain, with sculptured rock formations of all colours and high mineral content. There are a number of vicuñas in this area. The trail traverses the Cordillera Carabaya across the Altiplano, and it is

CUZCO AND THE SACRED VALLEY

According to Incan legend, Cuzco (3400m/11155ft) is the spot where Manco Capac, son of the sun, plunged his golden staff into the earth and proclaimed it the navel of the universe. The Incas founded the city around AD 1100, but previous civilizations are known to have occupied the area as early as 900 BC.

Cuzco was the religious and administrative centre for the Incan empire known as *Tawantinsuyo*, meaning the four quarters of the earth. It was built in the shape of a puma, with the Río Tullumayo forming its spine, Sacsayhuamán the head and the main city centre the body. Today, it is a stunning city with superb examples of Incan stonework and Spanish colonial architecture.

The Spanish marched into Cuzco in 1532 and began to tear down the temples and use the stone to build new churches, cathedrals and military posts. There were several rebellions over the years, as well as a tremendous earthquake in 1650, which further destroyed remaining Incan structures – although the Incan buildings fared much better than the Spanish ones.

Despite the Spanish destruction, Cuzco today contains an intriguing mixture of the Inca and the Spanish. Magnificent Incan stone walls can still be seen in a number of places in the valley and in Cuzco itself they often form the foundations for the monasteries, churches and convents that make the city a World Heritage site. The city now has a population of 300,000 and is still growing. As the gateway to the Sacred Valley and Machu Picchu, Cuzco is the New York of South America.

Sacsayhuamán was built from huge, interlocking stone blocks.

best to take a local guide and burros for this section; this can be arranged in Cuzco or Puno ahead of time.

An alternative trek, but in the same area, goes from Raqchi (after visiting the Incan temple of Viracocha) to Pitumarca or Tinqui. This is a superb trek and, although very difficult – requiring excellent physical condition – it is worth the effort. From Viracocha, climb the trail that heads northeast from the ruins, crossing some scree, and follow the trail past some houses and a few trees, heading in a northerly direction and staying on the right hand side of the gorge until you reach a pass at the top of the valley. Descend on a zigzag trail over scree slopes to arrive in Paucaros, where it is possible to camp, or continue to the Río Salca (5–6 hours). Follow the river until you find a crossing place (using a flying fox – a wire box to carry people, attached to a wire strung across the water – to cross the river) and continue to Salloca village, where you should ask for the trail to Salca Valley. It is possible to camp at the head of this stunning valley.

From here, pass through the village of Pulpera to enter the Palcoyo Valley. The trail ascends to arrive at the tiny village of Palcoyo, then continues up the valley to Chulloca, where you can camp. If you want to press on, follow the trail that heads to the left just before the village, passing some corrals and climbing steeply to cross the pass (4900m/16076ft) at the end of the valley. Descend on the trail that heads northeast by crossing some scree slopes, and continue to the next pass (also 4900m/16076ft), which has tremendous views of the Auzungate Range. Descend to the Río Pitumarca and, if heading to Pitumarca, follow the trail in the valley that heads west. If you are going to Tinqui, continue west in the valley until you reach the bridge at Uchullucllo. Cross it, then follow the trail to Quebrada Chillcamayo until you reach Chilca. Then, follow the trail heading northeast to Uyuni and into the Quebrada Jampamayo, until you get to the village of Jampa, where you can join the main Auzungate circuit.

TREK 15: CORDILLERA VILCABAMBA

Trekking in the Cordillera Vilcabamba offers everything from subtropical valleys to high mountains, with the added attraction of Incan ruins and the chance to see traditional lifestyles that have changed little over the centuries. The Vilcabamba area is still very remote, with some of the most amazing varieties of vegetation and environments in Peru. With its mystical cloud forests and high alpine valleys, it is easy to understand why the Incas built fortified strongholds in the area, and why they escaped here from the Spanish conquistadors once Cuzco had fallen.

The drive to Huancacalle from Cuzco takes approximately 8–10 hours. Towards the end of the journey, the road crosses a pass, the Abrada de Malaga, with views of Mount Veronica (5700m/18701ft),

Local horseman in the meadows near Huancacalle.

TREK ESSENTIALS

LENGTH 12-16 days. 120km (74.6 miles). From Huancacalle trek to Quebrada Mayuyoc, and then onto Yanama and Collpampa. The trek then continues Huayracmachay and Pampa Cahuana before joining the world-famous Inca Trail.
ACCESS *To start* Bus from Cuzco to Huancacalle. *At finish* Continue on to the Inca Trail and finish as for trek 16.
HIGHEST POINT Incachiriasca Pass, 4830m (15846ft).
TREK STYLE Guide and burros recommended as the trail is often faint and confusing and there are no reliable maps. Local guide services cost US$5 per day.
RESTRICTIONS None. No park fee payable unless you join the Inca Trail.
FURTHER OPTIONS Link with the Inca Trail by either joining at km88 or taking the train from km88 to km104 and then hiking up to Winya.
MAPS IGN 1:100 000 Machupicchu

then descends through a spectacular cloud forest before ascending to Huancacalle at an altitude of 2900m (9514ft).

It is possible to camp at Huancacalle, or you may find a room in a local house. Alternatively, you can stay at the Hotel Six Pac Manco. If you arrive in time, it is worth making a side trip up to the ruins of Nusta Hispaña or Yurac Rumi, which are about an hour from Huancacalle. These ruins include a large white rock with carvings and knobs, which was once the holy shrine of Vilcabamba.

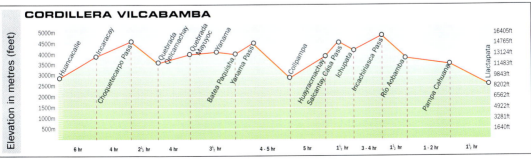

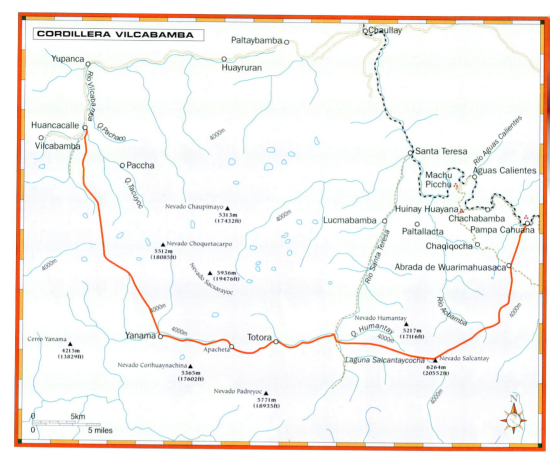

Another side trip possibility is to go to Vitcos or Rosaspata, which stand on a bluff above the Vilcabamba River and comprise a large fortress, with a square, where (it is said) Manco Capac, one of the last surviving Incan warriors after the conquest of Cuzco, was murdered by his Spanish guests. There are also the remains of a complex of buildings on a knoll above the square, and some agricultural terracing on the eastern flanks of the hill above the city. This lies about an hour above Huancacalle. You could also go to Los Andenes, which has a fine system of terraces and ancient rock shrines, located just beyond Vitcos.

Huancacalle to Yanama

From Huancacalle, it is a long walk up the Quebrada Colpa to reach the meadows of Incaracay at 3800m (12467ft).

You are now on the way to the first pass, with the trail ascending to the Choquetacarpo Pass at 4500m (14764ft) then descending gradually to the Quebrada Qelcamachay and the entrance to a superb gorge at 3650m (11975ft). From here, the trail descends a short distance before heading up steeply, crossing a ridge, to enter the Quebrada Mayuyoc, with views of Yanama Peak. You can camp by the river in the valley.

From here, an indistinct trail leads to the waterfall at Paccha, where friendly local shepherds will tell you all about local life, if you take the time to visit them. The trail then traverses the hillside before descending to the Yanama Valley, where the river must be crossed frequently as you travel along the valley. From here, the trail passes through the tiny settlement of Yanama where it may be possible to buy some basic supplies, and then ascends to Batea Paquisha at 4000m (13123ft) and a possible camping area (situated below the Yanama Pass).

Yanama to Pampa Cahuana

The trail ascends gradually to the Yanama Pass (4520m/14829ft), with brilliant views of Humantay, Salcantay and Veronica to the south and Panta Pumascillo to the north. Descend through cloud forest with bamboo vegetation, orchids and many hummingbirds to the river, then continue to the tiny settlement of Collpampa at 2800m (9186ft), where there are some refreshing hot springs – well worth the visit before setting up camp in a beautiful meadow on the outskirts of the settlement.

Back on the trail the next day, you will pass through cloud forest. Be careful to enter the correct valley – you are heading for Huayracmachay (3850m/12631ft), locally known as 'Eye of the Wind', which is situated below the beautiful Salcantay and Humantay mountains. Here, you'll find a meadow with great camping.

The following morning, ascend through alpine meadows to Salcantay Casa Pass at 4515m (14813ft) then descend to Salcantay Pampas and Ichupata, situated below Salcantay Glacier at 4390m (14403ft). A long (frequently cold and windy) ascent over a switch-backing trail leads to the Incachiriasca Pass at 4830m (15846ft), a narrow notch in the ridge before a descent to meadows on the far side, where you enter the Río Aobamba Valley. You will pass the small ruins of Palcay along the way, before arriving in Acobamba and Pampa Cahuana, where it is possible to camp.

THE LANGUAGE OF KNOTS

The Incas used knots and different coloured yarns or *quipus* to record all events in their empire, such as crop results and the cycles used for different agricultural crops. This in turn enabled accurate predictions of the amounts of food needed by each community. The experts who read the *quipus* were called *quipucamayocs*. There was also a supernumeracy officer, or *tucuyrioc,* who would act as a law officer, recording any transgressions with certain types of knots. This information was woven into fabrics, and, along with the use of different colours, it was possible to record a history of events.

On the Inca Trail

The trail now follows the Inca Trail (trek 16) as far as Llactapata at 2600m (8530ft), where you can camp beside the ruins. It is possible to catch the train to Chachabamba from Llactapata and walk up to Huinay Huayana and the famous Incan ruins of Machu Picchu (walk takes 4 to 5 hours). From the ruins, descend to Aguas Calientes from where you can catch the train to Cuzco.

Vicuñas, relatives of llamas, live in the mountainous Andes. They can be difficult to spot in the landscape, due to their muted colouring.

TREK 16: THE INCA TRAIL

The Inca Trail is undoubtedly the most popular trek in South America, and due to this popularity it is not the trek to do if you want a wilderness experience. However, there is some breathtaking scenery, as well as a series of fascinating Incan sites to explore on the way to Machu Picchu, the famous 'Lost City of the Incas'. The trek involves walking from one ruin to the next, often on intricately cut stone staircases, amidst thick cloud forest.

Chilca to Huayllabamba

The shortest trek on the Inca Trail takes 4 days and starts at Chilca. From here, the trail descends to cross the Río Cuischaca and then ascends gradually up the left bank for approximately 5 hours before re-crossing the river to arrive at the ruins of Llactapata. Below the village, close to the river, is the *pulpituyoc,* an enormous carved rock. The trail enters a side valley and continues shadowing the Río Cuischaca, climbing to the village of Huayllabamba (2950m/9678ft), situated at the junction of the Río Llullucha, where it is possible to camp.

Huayllabamba to Río Pacamayo

The trail continues in a northwesterly direction up the south bank of the river, climbing steeply towards Llulluchapampa (3650m/11975ft) where there is camping. Here, you may see white-tailed deer and the rare *taruca,* a small deer with spiky antlers.

The next day, the trail climbs steeply to the Abrada de Wuarimahuasaca or Dead Woman's Pass at 4200m (13780ft), where there are traces of ancient steps at the head of the pass. There are several places to camp in the cloud forest below the pass. The trail passes a series of waterfalls to arrive at the Río Pacamayo, where the camping is particularly good.

Río Pacamayo to Phuyupatamarca

The trail crosses the river and climbs steeply, often on stone steps, to eventually arrive at Runturakay (5km/3 miles from Río Pacamayo) where there are

TREK ESSENTIALS

LENGTH 4-6-day trek, depending on start point. 44km (27½ miles). Starting from Chilca, the first night of the trek will be spent at Huayllabamba before moving on to Llulluchapampa and then the Río Pacamayo. Take in the ruins of Phuyupatamarca before finally reaching Machu Picchu.

ACCESS *At start* Possible to start at km88, which is accessible by train. It is also possible to start from Chilca, which is accessible by train, bus or river raft from Cuzco. *On finish* Take the train from Aguas Calientes.

HIGHEST POINT Wuarimahuasaca, 4200m (13780ft).

TREK STYLE You must go through an agency, with a registered guide.

RESTRICTIONS Park fees payable and set camping only, see below. This trek requires a permit. There are only designated campsites, and only a set number of people are allowed per group and per camp. Open fires are forbidden on this route, and all litter must be carried out and returned to Cuzco.

FURTHER OPTIONS None.

MAP Lima 2000 1:50 000 Camino Inka

some ruins and stunning views of the Pacamayo Valley below.

Climbing to the Abrada de Runturakay Pass, the trail bypasses two small lakes to arrive at 4000m (13123ft) and superb views of the Cordillera Vilcabamba. Descending from the pass on an Incan highway, the trail heads towards a spur where the fortress-like ruins of Sayacmarka (3800m/12467ft) overlook the valley below. Follow the

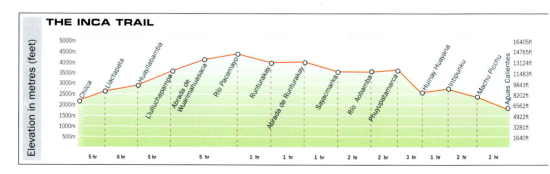

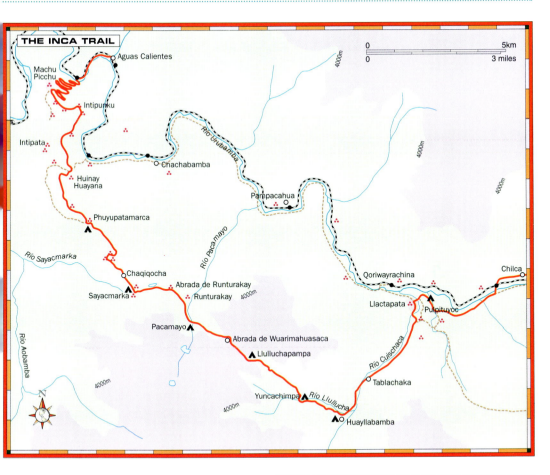

steep trail that climbs up to the ruins via flights of steps that hang above a cliff.

The trail then descends to the valley floor and the Río Aobamba only to climb again, albeit gradually, through cloud forest. The trail is comprised of superbly cut white granite stones, some almost 2m (6½ft) wide, and ascends to the final pass, with more breathtaking vistas of the Urubamba Valley.

The trail crosses a causeway and Incan tunnel system 20m (65ft) long before arriving at the beautiful ruins of Phuyupatamarca (or 'Town above the Clouds') at 3650m (11975ft). The ruins include some ceremonial baths. Camp here.

Phuyupatamarca to Machu Picchu
A short traverse, followed by a long steep descent, brings the trail to the ruins called Huinay Huayana (Forever Young). There is a hotel here – with a shower! Perched above the Urubamba Gorge, you'll enjoy great views of Mount Veronica. The ruins are about 5 mins off the main trail, around the hillside to the south. The trail then contours round the hillside through cloud forest, on a narrow exposed trail, to arrive at a steep stone staircase that leads to Intipunku (Gate of the Sun). From here, there are superb views of Machu Picchu and the tall peaks of Huayna Picchu. Descend to Machu Picchu over a stone trail to arrive at the city. After visiting the ruins you can descend to Aguas Calientes to catch the train back to Cuzco.

HUAYNA PICCHU & THE TEMPLE OF THE MOON

Huayna Picchu is the huge granite peak that overlooks Machu Picchu. There is a very steep path, the original Incan staircase, that takes you to the top. You pass through ancient terraces, which are thought to have been ornamental gardens.

The Temple of the Moon is situated about halfway down the north face. There is an Incan pathway leading to it that leaves the main trail about a third of the way up Huayna Picchu. The stonework of the ruins is some of the best in the whole area, and the view from the top of Huayna Picchu is superb and well worth the effort.

MACHU PICCHU

The extensive Incan ruins of Machu Picchu were first discovered by North American historian Hiram Bingham in 1911.

The sacred city of the Incas, which dates from AD1430, is tucked away in a saddle between two peaks of the Andes. It consists of a series of walled terraces, temples, roofless stone houses, huge ceremonial rocks, courtyards, stairways and plazas laid out in harmony with the contours of the land with superb views of the surrounding area, yet well hidden from marauders. The city is particularly difficult to spot from the Río Urubamba below, which may explain why it was never discovered by the Spanish. However, it is also possible that the Incas had abandoned Machu Picchu before the conquistadors arrived.

The high proportion of female skeletons at Machu Picchu suggests that it may have been a religious sanctuary provided for the Incas' chosen women, however it is unlikely that we will ever be certain of its true purpose. Its location and contents certainly indicate a ceremonial or religious purpose, but also a defensive one.

The Funerary Rock and House of the Caretaker are of particular interest. You enter the ruins by the House of the Caretaker, which flanks the agricultural sector (an enormous area of terracing thought to have enabled the city to be self-sufficient) and pass a moat and a number of waterfalls or fountains to a main fountain and the Temple of the Sun. The Temple of the Sun is a round tapering tower with excellent stonework thought to have been used as an astronomical observatory.

From the Temple of the Sun you can see the Funerary Rock, a curiously shaped rock thought to be a place for lying in state or an area for drying bodies in the sun for mummification. Above this area is an old quarry and another staircase that leads to the Temple of the Three Windows, which has trapezoidal windows. After this there is the Principal Temple and Sacristy. Ascending a small mound you arrive at Intihuatana, or the Hitching Post of the Sun, below which are a number of buildings and plazas. To the east and main entrance is the Temple of the Condor, and to the east of this is a cave, Intimachay, which is thought to have been something of an observatory for marking the December Solstice.

Tickets for Machu Picchu can only be purchased at the park. The ruins open at 7am and close at 5pm. Camping in the ruins is not permitted.

CUZCO DIRECTORY

Cuzco is a well-established tourist centre, being the main starting point for travellers wanting to embark on the well-trodden Inca Trail. Although still an important market town for many of the farming communities that surround the city, Cuzco's main source of income is most definitely tourism and consequently cafes, bars and hotels abound, providing the city with a buzzing atmosphere.

REGIONAL FLIGHTS
The easiest way to reach Cuzco is to fly from Lima. See box on page 116 for contact details of Peru's national airlines. Several tour operators offer special deals at certain times of the year.

REGIONAL TRANSPORT
Taxis:
Be sure to use only licensed taxis with real plates and documents as there have been a number of taxi robberies in Cuzco over the past few years. Always agree a price beforehand. Travel advice produced by the South American Explorers Club (www.samexplo.org) explains what to look for.
Buses:
Microbuses depart for the Sacred Valley every 20 mins from Calle Intiqhawarina, near Av Tullumayu. Local buses also run to Pisac, Ollyantaytombo, Tinqui, Huancacalle, Pitumarca and Viracocha.
Trains:
Trains for Machu Picchu leave from San Pedro station on Cascarpo, near the Santa Clara market. Local train tickets should be bought the day before travel.
Backpacker Express train tickets can be bought the day before travel. It is not possible to reserve seats in advance. Autowagan and Inka Class tickets can be bought up to 5 days in advance and are only available for round trip travel. There is only one line and cheaper tickets tend to sell out fast. Some tour agencies sell tickets, but they tend to charge higher prices. At Aguas Calientes you can buy tickets for the local train or the Backpackers Express the day before travel at 2pm.
One-way Autowagon/Inka Class tickets are available on a limited basis, especially during high season. It is possible to make a 1-day trip to Machu Picchu from Cuzco (7-8 hours there and back).

ACCOMMODATION IN CUZCO
El Dorado Inn, Av Sol 395, tel: (51 84) 233132, email: paula96@telser.com.pe.
El Balcon Tambo, Montero 222, tel: (51 84) 236738, email: balcon@peru.itete.com.pe. Free airport pickup. Great views of Cuzco; breakfast included; hot water.
Monasterio del Cuzco, Calle Palacio 136, Plazoleta Nazarenas, tel: (51 44) 241777. A very expensive but stunningly beautiful, renovated monastery.
Ninos Hotel, Calle Meloq 442, tel: (51 84) 231424, email: ninos@correro.dnet.com.pe. Very comfortable café lounge near Plaza D'Armas; all profits used in aid projects to help Cuzco's street children.
Kusi Runa, Calle del Medio 134, tel: (51 84) 241254. Prices include American breakfast. Clean and friendly; hot water; TV.
Hostal Corihuas I, Calle Suecia 561, tel: (51 84) 232233, email: corihuasi@amauta.rcp.net.pe. Price includes breakfast.
Hostal Suecia, Calle Suecia 332, tel: (51 84) 233282. Basic shared bathrooms; central; safe storage facilities.

ACCOMMODATION IN MACHU PICCHU
Aguas Calientes Hotels:
Gringo Bills, Calle Raymi, tel: (51 84) 211046, email: gringobills@yahoo.com. Group rates available. Good choice for budget travellers.
Hostal la Cabana, Av Pachacutc M20/L3, tel: (51 84) 211048. Prices include continental breakfast. Excellent and very friendly. Group rates available.
Machu Pichu Pueblo, Linea Feria km110, Cuzco, Quillabamba, tel: (51 84) 211038, email: reserves@inkaterra.com.pe.

LOCAL ACTIVITIES
Numerous Incan sites can be visited from Cuzco on foot, including Sacsayhuamán and Tambomachay.
Trekking:
Using the cheapest companies is not recommended, as they often pay their guides and porters poorly and take little if any interest in environmental issues and conservation. Reputable companies ensure that their porters are not carrying too much and check that the pace and route of the trek is suitable for clients, too.
Peruvian Andean Treks, Av Pardo 705, tel: (51 84) 225701, fax: (51-84) 238911, email: atlima@lullitec.com.pe or postmaster@patcusco.com.pe. Contact Tom Hendrickson. An excellent company, well organized, and with an environmental approach to trekking as well as a sympathetic approach to porters.
Inca Explorers, Calle Suecia 339, tel: (51 84) 243736, email: inqusa@qenqo.rcp.net.pe.
TrekAndes, Av Benavides 212, of 1203, Miraflores, email: trekandes@mail.cosapidata.com.pe.
Tambo Treks, contact Andreas and Rachel or Pablo Segovia, tel: (51 84) 237718/441950, email: tambotrx@qenqo.rcp.net.pe. Excellent service and guides for treks in the Vilcabamba, Inca Trail and Auzungate areas.
Auzungate Treks, Hotel Luzurna, Calle Bajo 205.
Guides for Auzungate:
Teofilo Villagro Yupa, contact by radio phone: 6477, call sign Alpha Omega.
Cayitano Crispin, Mi Cabana Simple (*hospedaje*), Tinqui.
South American Explorers Club, 930 Av Del Sol. Postal Address: Apartado 500, Cuzco, tel: (51 84) 223102, email: saec@wayna.rcp.net.pe. Open: Mon-Sat, 09.30-17.00; May-Sept, Sun, 09.30-13.00; Oct-April 09.30-17.00. The office can recommend guides to various areas. Worth checking out.

USEFUL WEBSITES
www.stevenson34.freeserve.co.uk: a journal of two travellers.
www.seanet.com/~dg/index.htm: information on how to organize a trek.
www.incas.org: Incan culture and textiles.
www.geocities.com/Yosemite/George/3147/inti-raimi.htm: Inti rami festival site.
www.mpichu.org: promotes awareness of the proposed cable car and further hotel plans for Machu Picchu.

TREK 17: CORDILLERA HUAYHUASH

The Cordillera Huayhuash measures only 35km (22 miles) from end to end, but within this area lies some of the most dramatic mountain scenery found anywhere on earth. Stunning peaks with their knife-edged ridges, vertical walls of snow, ice and rock flutings are set amidst a series of turquoise glacial lakes; and, so far, the area sees relatively few trekking groups.

The stunning high-level Huayhuash circuit offers one of the world's finest treks. It is a difficult trek, though, with more than 6000m (19685ft) of climbing and crossing eight passes of 4600–5000m (15092–16404ft). Llamac, Pocpa and Huyallapa are sizeable villages where basic supplies can be bought.

Chiquian to Pocpa

Drive to Chiquian by either local bus or private transport. It is suggested that you organize *arrieros* and burros in Chiquian, where there are some basic hostels. The trail starts in the northeast corner of town, on the way to the cemetery, descends to the Río Quero and crosses the river at Quisipata, where it is possible to camp in the fields south of the village. Make sure you ask permission and pay the small pasture fee if you have burros.

The next day, the trail descends to the bridge at Cora (2700m/8858ft) where it joins the Río Llamac. The trail then ascends through dry, desert-like vegetation with numerous cacti. On the way to Llamac you will often be accompanied by green parakeets, which fly noisily overhead. About an hour after Llamac, the trail crosses the Río Llamac and climbs to the beautiful village of Pocpa, with its 600-strong population, terracotta tiled roofs, cobbled streets and tiny church. Camp in the school grounds.

Pocpa to Laguna Carhuacocha

From Popca, the trail heads east and enters the Quebrada Rondoy. It follows the new road, which was constructed to ease access to the Mina Luisa – a small, Japanese-operated mine that opened a few years ago. After passing the mine, follow a path across meadows that were once filled with many different kinds of waterfowl. Unfortunately, the mine has re-routed the water supply and the birds have all but disappeared. Camp can be set up in the corrals of Qortelhuian (4100m/13451ft), at the base of the Cacanpunta Pass.

Ascending in zigzags, the trail continues to the pass (4700m/15420ft), with stunning views of the southern Cordillera Blanca's peaks as well as the peaks of the Cordillera Raura. You will probably encounter condors showing off their amazing flying skills, closely followed by caracaras (smaller birds of prey). As you enter the mountains, the feeling of leaving the villages and people behind is strong.

> ### TREK ESSENTIALS
>
> **LENGTH** 12-14 days. 165-180km (103-112 miles). From Chiquian, trek to Quisipata, Pocpa, Janca, and Punta Cuyoc. The homeward straight includes Huyallapa and Quebrada Hacris before finishing at Chiquian.
> **ACCESS** *To start* By bus from Huaráz to Chiquian (see Huaráz Directory, p.145) *On finish* By bus from Chiquian to Huaráz.
> **HIGHEST POINT** Punta Cuyoc, 5000m (16404ft).
> **TREK STYLE** Burros and an *arriero* are highly recommended.
> **RESTRICTIONS** None.
> **FURTHER OPTIONS** Trek into Cordillera Raura; climb Diablo Mundo.
> **MAP** South American Explorers Club 1:80 000 Cordillera Huayhuash

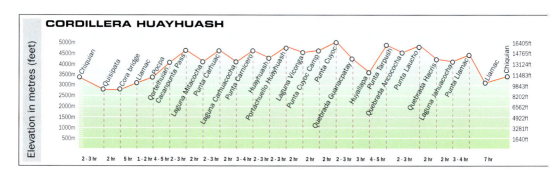

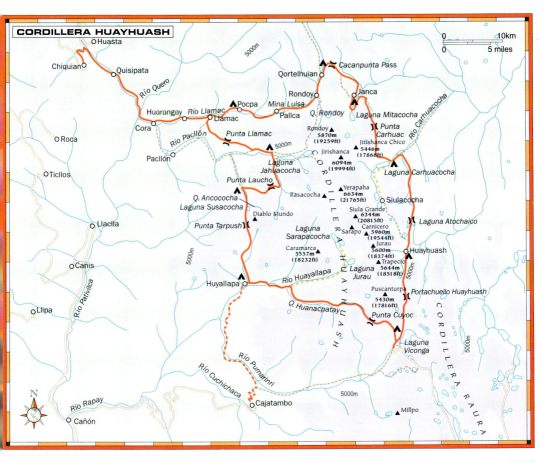

CUY (GUINEA PIGS)

Cuy have been domesticated in Peru for many years for home consumption; some archaeologists' diggings have found *cuy* skeletons dating back to 2500BC. *Cuy* are clean and very easy to raise, eating mainly household scraps, and most rural houses have large numbers running around. *Cuy* is a particularly popular dish at fiestas and weddings.

A steep descent is followed by a traverse to the settlement of Janca. It is possible to camp in the corrals or continue to the shores of Laguna Mitacocha (4200m/13780ft), set beneath the peaks of Rondoy, Mitacocha and Jirishanca. A short scramble up to the lake that nestles below Jirishanca Chico's icy ramparts is well worth the effort – keep a look out for viscachas. The trail now heads south, climbing gradually to the Punta Carhuac (4650m/15256ft) which offers stunning views of Jirishanca. A steep descent brings you to Laguna Carhuacocha (4200m/13780ft) and one of the most stunning campsites in South America.

The camp at Laguna Mitacocha, Cordillera Huayhuash.

PEAK: DIABLO MUNDO

Access is from the corrals below Punta Tarpush. From here, follow a vague trail up the valley to the base of the glacier's moraines. Be careful as you ascend these very loose moraines to reach a large rock face. Try and overcome this on the left via a gulley, to reach a snow ramp. Follow this ramp to the ridge, avoiding some crevasses. The ridge continues to the summit.

As you descend from the summit, look for a small gully off to the right and follow this down to the steep screes below and to the valley. You can return to camp down the valley.

Note that glacial changes have seriously affected this route over the past few years and it is no longer easy. Care is required, particularly in getting onto the ridge itself. Allow 5–6 hours for the ascent and 3 hours for the descent.

Diablo Mundo is also known as Diablo Mudo.

CLIMB ESSENTIALS

SUMMIT Diablo Mundo 5223m (17137ft)
PRINCIPAL CAMP Base Camp 4500m (14765ft)
GRADE Alpine Grade AD

This is a rewarding place to taking a rest and exploration day, visiting Siulacocha, set below Siula Grande, of Joe Simpson's *Touching the Void* fame. (Joe Simpson climbed a new route on the west face of Siula Grande and then, while descending, had a fall which led to an epic fight for survival.) Just soak up the atmosphere of this amazing array of peaks and lakes – and wonder how the incredible snow mushrooms and ice flutings hang so tenaciously to the faces of the peaks. Particular care should be taken around dogs in this area… carry a big stick!

Laguna Carhuacocha to Punta Cuyoc Camp
From Laguna Carhuacocha, the trail descends, heading east to cross the Río Carhuacocha on its southern bank by two small houses before entering a narrow valley to the south, where you climb steeply for an hour to enter the main valley. You now enter a boggy meadow and have to pick your way across what often seem to be floating islands of springy grass and herbs that gently sink beneath your feet before springing back. After the boggy area, you will pick up a track that ascends gradually to Laguna Atochaico and eventually the Punta Carnicero (4600m/15092ft) with tremendous views over to the peaks of Carnicero, Trapiceo and the south side of Siula Grande. Vicuñas can be seen on the ascent to the pass, so watch out carefully for these rare and shy cousins of the llamas.

From the pass, the trail crosses a series of ditches dug into the ground (which provide the locals with a form of charcoal) and then descends gently, bypassing two small lakes to arrive at the small settlement of Huayhuash in the Huayhuash itself. The two tiny houses are home to some very friendly families and, if you like, they will cook up some potatoes for you at a very reasonable price.

From here, the trail ascends to Portachuello Huayhuash (4750m/15584ft) with its stunning vistas of the Raura peaks. The valley below is home to numerous alpacas (relatives of the llama and vicuña families), which can be seen grazing on its steep slopes. The trail descends to Laguna Viconga (4500m/14764ft), where it is possible to exit the Huayhuash to the town of Cajatambo, 25km (16 miles) away.

The trail continues, crossing a ridge to the west of Laguna Viconga, and then ascends in a northwesterly direction towards some meadows below Punta Cuyoc (4600m/15092ft), which offer superb, albeit cold, camping. The view again is awe inspiring – a backdrop of the Raura peaks to the southeast and the superb hanging glaciers of Puscanturpa (also known as Leon Dormido) to the north.

Punta Cuyoc Camp to Huyallapa

You are now heading to the highest pass of the trek. The trail zigzags through a series of meadows, skirting a small lake, where you enter some rock ramparts with a tiny waterfall that tumbles gently down one of the rock faces. After some scree slopes you eventually plod to Punta Cuyoc (5000m/16404ft), set below the hanging glaciers of Puscanturpa. The view from here is breathtaking, with a panorama of the Raura peaks, Siula Grande, Yerapaha, Jurau and some of the lesser-known peaks of the Huayhuash.

You're on the west side of the Andes, and the vegetation is sparser here. Dropping on a steep and often slippery path, the trail descends past wind-sculpted rock towers to enter the Quebrada Huanacpatay. (It is possible here to do a side trip to Lagunas Jurau and Sarapacocha.) Now, you are on the trail to Huyallapa – and the chance of a beer. The valley is long and drops slowly initially (before a short ascent to a view point overlooking the valley and Huyallapa) before descending very steeply in a series of zigzags, passing below a beautiful waterfall and then through scrubby farmland to arrive at the small village of Huyallapa (3600m/11811ft). It is possible to buy basic supplies here, and to exit the circuit to Cajatambo, 30km (19 miles) away.

Huyallapa to Chiquian

The trail now heads north, climbing steeply over a number of landslides (caused by severe weather in 1998–99), passing through terraced fields reminiscent of Nepal, and finally entering high alpine meadows – home to a number of shepherds. It is possible to camp in some meadows on the west side of the pass, near some corrals and close to the home of some of the oldest shepherds. Alternatively, continue to the Punta Tarpush Pass (4800m/15748ft), with stunning views towards the peaks of the southern Blanca. Descend past Laguna Susacocha (watch out for Andean coots with their big red feet, and Andean geese) to camp in some corrals (4500m/14764ft) below Diablo Mundo (5223m/17137ft).

There is a short descent to enter Quebrada Ancococha below Punta Laucho (the pass is at 4850m/15912ft), where the trail ascends steeply over a boggy meadow before traversing some slabs and climbing multicoloured scree slopes to the pass. From here, it is worth the extra effort of climbing the small hill to the north of the pass for its unparalleled views of the Huayhuash Range and the southern peaks of the Blanca, with Huascaran's summit in the far north.

The trail drops very steeply to enter Quebrada Hacris, where it heads north to descend beside a waterfall. Just past the waterfall is another viewpoint with one of the most unbelievable vistas in the world: the lake surrounded by reed beds and a backdrop of some of the planet's most amazing peaks. A further descent eventually brings you to Laguna Jahuacocha (4100m/13451ft).

You will want to spend a day here for exploration and visits to Laguna Solteracocha (situated below Jirishanca), Yerapaha Base Camp and the ridge above Rasacocha. Alternatively, relax and simply enjoy one of the most amazing views in the world. The lake offers great bird-watching – glossy necked ibises, herons, geese, teals, condors and caracaras.

You are on the home stretch now, so take the trail heading west then north to climb gradually to Punta Llamac (4500m/14764ft). A steep descent on scree) brings you to the village of Llamac and the main trail to Chiquian. It's best to camp in Llamac and complete the trek the next day, getting an early start for the 'sting in the tale' – the final, heartbreaking climb from the Ríos Llamac and Quero junction to Chiquian – before the sun hits the trail.

MINING

With its centuries-old mining heritage, Peru is building on its strength as a mineral-rich country. Mining is the nation's premier industry, yielding 11 per cent of the GDP and 45 per cent of its export – with a plan to double this over the next seven years.

Although, traditionally, mining was the concern of families and communities, nowadays much of Peru's mining is controlled by foreign investors, who have provided the government with billions of dollars. The huge mining company Antamina has control of the copper and gold mining in the Huaráz area. the company is currently developing a method of carrying mining slurry to the coast that it hopes will replace traditional truck haulage through the Huascarán National Park.

Local residents expect to be employed by the mining companies. Antamina has consequently established training centres for locals, including Quechan speakers, as well as health and educational programmes for workers.

Unfortunately, this concern for the local community is not shared by other mining companies in Peru. In 1999, there was an underground explosion at the Mina Luisa in the Huayhuash area that contaminated the Río Llamac, causing serious problems for the local residents of Llamac, Pocpa and Palca.

TREK 18: CORDILLERA BLANCA TRANQUILO

This trek in the Quilcaywanka, Cayesh, Shallap and Rajucolta Valleys offers superb views, with scenery ranging from ice-filled lakes and waterfalls to colourful domes and towers. Despite its close proximity to Huaráz, the area does not see many visitors. The sunset on Huantsan (The King of the Blanca) at 6395m (20981ft), above Laguna Rajucolta, is an unforgettable sight. There are also wonderful views of the Central Cordillera peaks.

Start by driving to Pitec, or take local transport as far as Llupa and then walk to Pitec (3800m/12467ft). There are several places to camp, or you could sleep on the floor of the very basic refuge (no food for sale, but plenty of soft drinks). It is possible to make a side trip up to Laguna Churup (4600m/15092ft) from here, and this will help with acclimatization.

Pitec to Laguna Culliacocha
From Pitec, follow the road to its end, just before the *portada* (gateway). If taking burros, you must remember to organize a key from the gatekeeper in Llupa to gain entrance to the valley. At the *portada*, the trail continues up the north (left) side of the valley to enter some meadows, before reaching a junction with a side valley coming in from the north (the junction of the Quilcaywanka and Cayesh Valleys). There are excellent camping places around here, as well as the first views of Chinchey. From here, you can visit Laguna Tullparaju by following the trail on the left side of the canyon.

If you feel like the extra effort, continue on to Laguna Culliacocha (4650m/15256ft) by going directly up the valley to a small clearing. Cross the stream to the left of the old INGEMENT Hut (Instituto Geologico Minero y Metelurgico – a government-run agency responsible for lowering the lakes for safety reasons in the event of earthquakes). Follow a steepening zigzag path that will bring you to some old ruined buildings. From here, it is a short walk to the lake.

Laguna Culliacocha to Quebrada Rajucolta
At the junction of the Quilcaywanka and Cayesh Valleys, look for a bridge and cross this to enter the Cayesh Valley. Cross a number of swampy meadows where it will be hard to keep your feet dry, eventually arriving at a small lake with tremendous views of Cayesh. There are plenty of places to camp.

From here you will find a disused trail that starts on the right moraine wall of the valley. Look for a faint trail in the scrubby trees and follow it up an apparently impassable rock wall. Just a short scramble takes you above this rock band and onto an ancient track that has been built on the edge of the glacier. You can follow this to 5000m (16404ft) before climbing equipment is required. Descend the same way and continue back down the valley to the *portada* at the entrance to the valley.

A short walk past the *portada*, look for a bridge across the river. This will take you to the obvious trail to Quebrada Shallap, passing a couple of small set

> **TREK ESSENTIALS**
>
> **LENGTH** 5-day trek. 75km (45 miles). From Llupa, trek to Pitec, Laguna Culliacocha, Quebradas Cayesh, Shallap and Rajucolta, before finishing at Unchus.
> **ACCESS** *To start* From Llupa take a local truck or private car to Pitec. *On finish* Take truck from Unchus to Huaráz.
> **HIGHEST POINT** Laguna Culliacocha, 4650m (15256ft).
> **RESTRICTIONS** If taking burros, you must remember to organize a key from the gatekeeper in Llupa to gain entrance to the valley.
> **FURTHER OPTIONS** Ascent of Huamasaraju.
> **MAPS** Información Turistíca Kuntur/Felipe Diaz 1:100 000 Cordilleras Blanca & Huayhuash
> Alpine Clubs of Canada and America Cordillera Blanca, Map)
> DAV 1:100 000 Cordillera Blanca

TREK 18: CORDILLERA BLANCA TRANQUILO

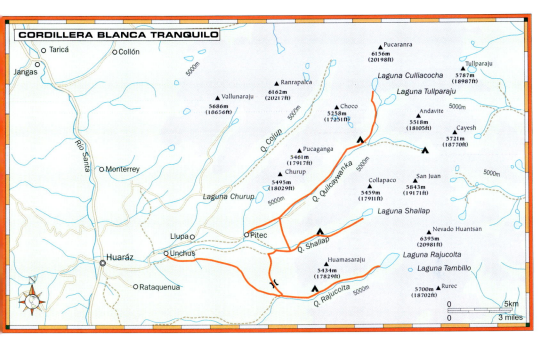

tlements. Be careful of the dogs! Follow the trail to the Shallap *portada*; a short walk past the gate brings you to a beautiful camping area. An excellent trail leads to Laguna Shallap at the end of the valley. Returning to the Shallap *portada*, follow the trail back a short distance to a small bridge and cross this to the south bank. Pick up a vague trail that traverses the hillside – its vagueness will have you guessing as to whether you are on the correct path. Once you pass a reforestation plantation and a group of houses, you can relax, as you will be on the right trail.

From the houses, the trail climbs to a small col with superb views back to the peaks of Churup and Ranrapalca. Descend to a group of corrals on the valley floor, below the Rurec and Cashan Peaks. Here, you need to watch out for a trail heading east, traversing the hillside above the valley floor, in order to avoid the enormous areas of marshy ground. Follow this trail until you reach the *portada* for Quebrada Rajucolta. Just inside the gate is superb camping.

Quebrada Rajucolta to Unchus

It is a few hours walk up to the Laguna Tambillo from here. The trail switches from one side of the valley to the other, crossing an old landslide. It is a very marshy area; just keep looking for the best way. Sunsets on Nevado Huantsan are absolutely stunning from anywhere in the valley. Return to the corrals that you passed on the descent from Shallap. Look for a trail going west. Cross the river and climb on steep zigzags to a pass (4400m/

Local shepherds in the Cordillera Blanca.

14436ft) with stunning views of the peaks to the north. Especially impressive are Ranrapalca's icy ramparts. Pass a group of shepherds' huts where the trail crosses marshy land. Keep west and then descend to pick up an old trail to Unchus.

PEAK: HUAMASARAJU

Access is from Pitec. Trek to the small settlement of Janca. Follow the trail ascending to the col. There is a vague trail off to the left about three-quarters of the way to the col which goes to Rajucolta. Take this and follow it steeply up to some high lakes situated below the peak. Passing the lakes by their eastern shores, head to the moraine wall at the base of the glacier, climb some slabs and loose rocks, and then head up the glacier towards the summit, passing any crevasses on the right. The summit is narrow and exposed.

Descend via the same route. Allow 2–3 days for this climb.

An ascent of Huamasaraju can be a lengthy expedition.

CLIMB ESSENTIALS

SUMMIT Huamasaraju 5434m (17829ft)
PRINCIPAL CAMPS Base Camp 4800m (15750ft); High Camp 4790m (15715ft).
GRADE Alpine Grade PD

PEAK: PISCO

Pisco is one of the most popular climbs in the Cordillera Blanca. However, it should not be underestimated, as there are several very serious crevasses on the southwest ridge. Access is from the Llanganuco Valley and Pisco Base Camp (4000m/13123ft), at the base of Quebrada Demanda. Follow a steep path up on a series of zigzags and continue over a moraine crest to arrive at Moraine Camp (or go to the refuge at 4700m/15420ft). Ascend the huge moraine wall above camp and descend its loose wall. Cross the moraine via a well-marked route and ascend to another camp by a small lake at 4900m (16076ft). Climb a series of slabs to the glacier. Follow directly upwards, keeping slightly left, close to the slopes of Huandoy, to the col at 5350m (17552ft) and climb the north side of the southwest ridge passing a few large crevasses. Descend via the same route. Allow 2–3 days for this climb.

Pisco is one of the Cordillera Blanca's most popular summits.

CLIMB ESSENTIALS

SUMMIT Pisco (Southwest Ridge) 5752m (18872ft)
CAMPS Base Camp 4000m (13123ft); Refuge or Moraine Camp 4700m (15420ft).
GRADE Alpine Grade PD

TREK 19: CORDILLERA BLANCA

The Cordillera Blanca is the highest mountain chain outside the Himalaya, and is very long and narrow – 185km (115 miles) long and 20km (12 miles) wide. It has 22 peaks over 6000m (19685ft) and 35 over 5500m (18045ft). To the west lies the Cordillera Negra, a snowless range of peaks that rise to 5200m (17060ft). Between the two ranges lie the Río Santa or Callejon de Huayallas, and the towns of Huaráz and Caraz. The Cordillera Blanca is easily accessible via a series of U-shaped valleys and several unglaciated passes.

The Llanganuco to Cashapampa trek is one of the most popular treks in South America. It passes beneath a number of peaks over 5800m (19029ft) including Huascarán Sur and Norte, Chopicalqui, Chacaraju, Pisco, Alpamayo and the imposing Talliraju. There are two ascents. The one from the Punta Union (4750m/15584ft) is quite long, with some mind-blowing viewpoints; the other is to the Portachuello de Llanganuco, with its stunning views of the Huandoys Huascarán and Chopicalqui.

At Colcabamba and Cashapampa it is possible to lodge with locals and sample the food and drink of the region. Fit, acclimatized trekkers should have no problem backpacking the circuit, but burros and *arrieros* can be hired at either Llanganuco or Cashapampa (if hired at Llanganuco, you must give your *arrieros* an extra day to arrive from Huasahua, the village below the park gates. If you start in Llanganuco there is 1400m (4593ft) less climbing involved.

TREK ESSENTIALS

LENGTH 5-7-day trek. 65–80km (40–50 miles). From Llanganuco, trek to Pisco Base Camp, Colcabamba, Quebrada Paria, Morococha Lakes and on to Cashapampa.
ACCESS *To start* Drive to Yungay from Huaráz, and then bus/*collectivo* to Llanganuco from Huaráz. *To finish* Bus/*collectivo* from Cashapampa to Caraz (early morning).
HIGHEST POINT Portachuello de Llanganuco, 4750m (15584ft)
TREK STYLE Backpack or burros and *arrieros*.
RESTRICTIONS Park fee US$25 per person.
FURTHER OPTIONS Ascents of Pisco and Chopicalqui. Join Alpamayo Circuit at Alto de Puccara Pass trail junction at Tuctubamba below Morococha Lakes and continue to Pomabamba.
MAPS Infomación Turistíca Kuntur/Felipe Daz 1:100 000 Cordilleras Blanca & Huayhuash; Alpine Clubs of Canada and America Cordillera Blanca, Map 3; DAV 1:100 000 Cordillera Blanca

Llanganuco to Colcabamba

The road to Llanganuco from Huaráz passes the headquarters of the Parque Nacional Huascarán where you must pay an entry fee. From here, the road ascends and enters a spectacular canyon with huge granite walls on either side. It is best to alight at Yurac Corral. Camp here, or continue to Pisco Base Camp, known as Cebollo Pampa.

The trail to Pisco and its refuge follows a steep zigzag path for approximately 3 hours. From the Base Camp area follow the trail up to Cave Camp, and you'll find the refuge at 4700m (15420ft).

A side trip will take you into the Quebrada Yanapacha; follow the trail to the lakes situated above the very obvious waterfall. From the meadows it is possible to cross the stream and follow an old INGEMENT camp trail to Laguna 69 (4650m/15256ft), a jewel set below Chacaraju.

From Base Camp or from Yurac Corral, the trail to Colcabamba shadows the road that crosses the Portachuello de Llanganuco at 4750m (15584ft). Follow the zigzag path that crosses the road just below the old road-workers' camp of Huasahua.

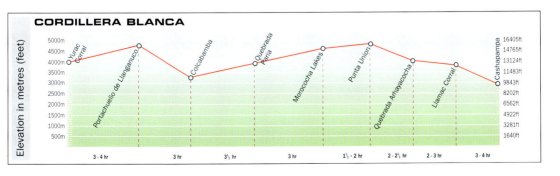

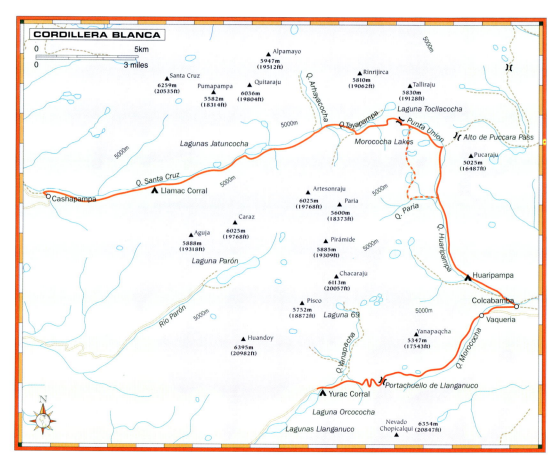

Continue following the steepening trail through some quenal trees and finally out and up, traversing below a rocky peak to the south, directly below Chopicalqui (6310m/20847ft).

At the Llanganuco Pass, follow the old donkey trail that heads away from the road and bypasses some small lakes. The trail arrives on the road just above Vaqueria (3700m/12139ft), a tiny and often uninhabited village. About 1km (½ mile) below Vaqueria, the trail branches to the left and descends towards some houses where it meets another trail. Take the right-hand fork to Colcabamba (3300m/10827ft), where the old Hacienda Callanges offers accommodation, food and basic supplies.

Side trips to Yanama or Pasaje de Yanajacu, situated below Contrahierbas, are possible from here.

Colcabamba to Punta Union

The main trail from Colcabamba heads in a north-westerly direction from the village up the Quebrada Huaripampa, following the right-hand side of the valley. The trail passes a number of settlements before skirting a swampy area and passing a small lake on the east side. It then follows a vague track though some quenal forest to arrive eventually at an excellent campsite opposite the entrance to the Quebrada Paria (3850m/12631ft). This valley makes a delightful side trip and there are superb camping areas at its end beneath the rock walls that bar the exit of the valley.

CHAVIN DE HUANTAR

This small town on the eastern side of the Cordillera Blanca is home to some amazing ruins. The Chavín culture is thought to date from 1300–400BC, with the remaining ruins built around 500BC. The sculptures and carvings often display feline forms, along with condors, snakes and enormous stone heads with fierce-looking engravings. There are seven underground chambers with incredible stonework and a huge sacrificial stone in the centre of the complex.

The trip from Huaráz takes a full day by bus. You can trek here from Olleros on the west side of the range in two or three days; and this makes an excellent acclimatization trip.

From here there are two choices. You can continue to follow the main trail up Quebrada Huaripampa towards the Morococha Lakes. This trail passes through ichu grass and then passes below a distinctive granite tower on the east wall of the valley. Crossing the stream, you hit a trail junction; the right path heads for the Alto de Puccara Pass (4600m/15092ft). The trail to the left ascends to the lakes, steeply at first for 500m (1640ft), and then in a northerly direction towards Nevado Talliraju. Gradually a series of switchbacks leads to meadows with good camping places by the lower Morococha Lakes – or you can continue to the upper lake at 4600m (15092ft). From the camp, it is possible to ascend the ridge that runs directly south from the pass; there is a vague trail with a short section of scrambling to the ridge at 4850m (15912ft).

The other, more difficult but thoroughly rewarding, way of reaching Punta Union from Quebrada Paria is by following the vague, rough trail that ascends beside the waterfall near the entrance to the *quebrada*. The trail heads in a northwesterly direction to the lower Laguna Tocllacocha (4359m/14301ft). It skirts the lake on its eastern shore, then a short steep ascent brings you to the upper Laguna Tocllacocha (4500m/14764ft). The trail now traverses the hillside to arrive at upper Morococha.

Punta Union to Cashapampa

From the upper Laguna Morococha (below the Punta Union) the trail heads towards Nevado Talliraju climbing on a zigzag track to the pass where you can look out for the Rima rima flowers (Peru's national flower) clinging to the rock faces. From the pass, a trail descends across a series of granite slabs into the upper Santa Cruz Valley. It crosses the stream in a big meadow and follows the north bank to drop into Quebrada Tayapampa, then descends to the junction with Quebrada Arhayacocha, where there is a small quenal forest. The walk up the Arhayacocha Valley is the main access route to Alpamayo and Quitaraju.

The main trail continues down valley, skirting a swampy area on the south side and passing Lagunas Jatunacocha Grande and Chico. Keep on the trail that skirts the lakes or you could end up in the bog. Descend to Llamac Corral (3800m/12467ft) and through quenal forest to enter a stunning canyon full of beautiful waterfalls. The trail crosses a number of landslides before reaching the *portada* and, finally, Cashapampa (2900m/9514ft).

PEAK: CHOPICALQUI

A stunning peak, Chopicalqui is one of the highest peaks in the Blanca. Access is from the Llanganuco Lakes. Stop by a hairpin bend on the road to the Portachuello de Llanganuco and go to Base Camp in a small meadow at 4200m (13780ft). From here, follow the trail from camp to the moraine and then follow the crest of the moraine across the rubble-covered glacier. The trail is in good shape. Cross some loose boulders to arrive at Moraine Camp at 4900m (16075ft). Go up the glacier, keeping left of a rock rib, and then move right, bypassing several very large crevasses. Cross a small basin, and climb a steeper slope to the High Camp area at 5600m (18372ft). Find a route round some large crevasses and climb a steeper slope to gain the ridge crest. Then cross a very big crevasse to the extreme left, pass some seracs, then follow a narrow and exposed ridge crest to the summit. Descend via the same route.

The southwest ridge of Chopicalqui.

CLIMB ESSENTIALS

SUMMIT Chopicalqui (Southwest Ridge) 6354m (20847ft)
PRINCIPAL CAMPS Base Camp 4200m (13780ft); Moraine Camp 4900m (16075ft); High Camp 5600m (18372ft).
GRADE Alpine Grade AD

TREK 20: ALPAMAYO CIRCUIT

This is one of the most stunning treks in the Cordillera Blanca, with amazing ruins, traditional villages, azure lakes and a mind-blowing array of snow-capped peaks. Mountain highlights include Alpamayo, often described as one of the most beautiful mountains in the world. The trek goes through a wide variety of habitats with a wonderful array of plant life, and you may see rare spectacled bears and pumas in the remote valleys north of Alpamayo.

TREK ESSENTIALS

LENGTH 12-14-day trek. 150km (93 miles). A circular route round Alpamayo, through local villages and across high passes.
ACCESS *To start* Collectivo to Cashapampa via Caraz from Huaráz. *On finish* Collectivo to Huaráz from Cashapampa.
HIGHEST POINT Paso Los Cedros, 4900m (16075ft).
TREK STYLE *Arrieros* and burros recommended (can be hired from Caraz).
RESTRICTIONS Park fee of US$25 per person.
FURTHER OPTIONS Ascents of Alpamayo, Pisco and Huascarán Sur.
MAPS Infomación Turistíca Kuntur/Felipe Daz 1:100 000 Cordilleras Blanca & Huayhuash; Alpine Clubs of America and Canada Cordillera Blanca, Map 3; DAV 1:100 000 Cordillera Blanca

A traditional home in the Cordillera Blanca.

Cashapampa to Quebrada Arhayacocha Junction

From Cashapampa, take the trail that enters the Quebrada Santa Cruz and follow this to Llamac Corral at 3800m (12467ft). The trail is long, steep and hot and follows the right bank of the river, traversing old landslides as it gains height on a series of zigzags. The path levels out at around 3800m (12467ft), where it enters some pastures with corrals that make for excellent campsites. Follow the trail up to Lagunas Jatunacocha Chico and Grande (3900m/12795ft), passing them on their south sides. These lakes used to be the home of large flocks of geese and ducks. In 1996, however, there was an enormous landslide, and the run-off of sediment and granite changed the plant life to such an extent that the birds no longer had a reliable food supply. Continue up to the junction with Quebrada Arhayacocha (3950m/12959ft), the valley normally used for access to Alpamayo. There are good campsites set amongst quenal (polylepsis) trees, with abundant epiphytes and bird life, and from where it is worth visiting the Base Camp for Alpamayo and Quitaraju. Or continue up the Santa Cruz Valley to another meadow, set below a rock wall on the southern aspect of the valley.

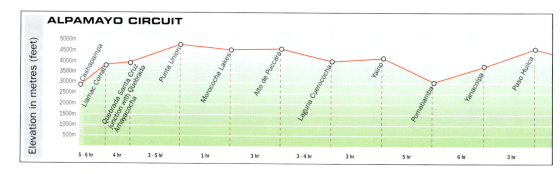

Quebrada Arhayacocha Junction to Yaino

It is now a long and steep ascent to Punta Union (4750m/15584ft), walking over a series of slabs that have seen donkeys carrying loads for centuries. This used to be one of the main trade routes across the mountains from east to west until road access to Portachuello de Llanganuco was opened up in the late 1970s. The view from the pass is tremendous, with a superb panorama of peaks including Talliraju, Huascarán Sur and Norte, and Chopicalqui. Descend to camp at the lower Morococha Lake at 4500m (14764ft) or continue down to the trail junction with the Huaripampa Valley and camp in the meadows below Alto de Puccara.

It is a steep ascent to the Alto de Puccara Pass (4600m/15092ft) on a zigzag track. Then, a long and initially steep descent into the *quebrada* leads to Laguna Cuerocorcha (4000m/13123ft). You can follow the trail heading directly east that traverses above the Río Cullupampa to the ruins of Yaino, the Machu Picchu of the Blanca mountains. Situated on a ridge at 4200m (13780ft) with an all-encompassing view of the cordillera, the fort-like ruins are very impressive. They contain a variety of structures that may have been homes, grain storage shelters and guard posts (set out on a number of terraces).

Yaino to Laguna Safuna Baja

The trail now heads northeast, descending steeply to Pomabamba (3050m/10007ft), a small, friendly town on the east side of the Cordillera Blanca famous for its week-long festival in June, with its particularly impressive *Dia del Campesino* (24 June), one of Peru's major annual festivals. The local Indians dress up in outfits that depict everything from the Devil to Pachamama. There are numerous events, from horse races and music competitions to bull fights Peruvian style.

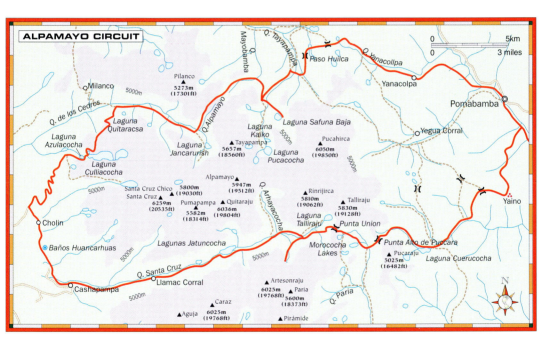

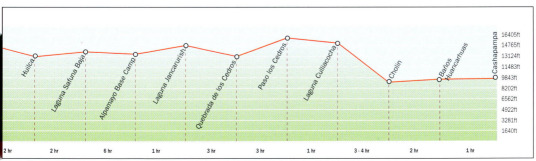

PEAK: ALPAMAYO

A climber prepares for an ascent of Alpamayo.

This is a steep, fluted, wedge-shaped peak. Access is from the Santa Cruz Valley, via Cashapampa at 2900m (9514ft), and then the Quebrada Arhayacocha to Base Camp.

Ascend to Moraine Camp at 4900m (16076ft) and from here to the Alpamayo–Quitaraju Col at 5300m (17388ft), which is gained by a snow ramp which has sections of 45° (3–5 hours). The popular Ferrari route ascends one of the runnels on the southwest face. From the Col Camp, cross easy snow slopes and climb to the bergschrund. Cross the snow bridge and follow the flutings up right at an angle of 45–60° to reach the lowest point of the summit ridge. Descend the same way.

Please note that the ascent to the col has been particularly dangerous in the past few years, with some very large seracs hanging over the snow ramp. In 1999, a group was avalanched by seracs on the ascent to the col.

CLIMB ESSENTIALS

ROUTE Ferrari (Southwest face)
SUMMIT Alpamayo 5947m (19512ft)
PRINCIPAL CAMPS Base Camp 4200m (13780ft); Moraine Camp 4900m (16076ft); Col Camp (High Camp) 5300m (17388ft).
GRADE Alpine Grade AD.

Descending the rough trail that makes up much of the Alpamayo Circuit.

This is also a good place to restock (supplies include bread), and you can sample local food from one of the basic restaurants. If you are lucky enough to arrive at festival time you will be invited to join in the general singing and dancing and will probably be asked to imbibe *aguarte,* the local fire water brewed specially for the occasion, which is likely to blow your head off.

The trail leaves the town following the Río Shiulla before entering a valley where it climbs steeply up a rocky trail, eventually arriving in the small and beautiful village of Yanacolpa (3700m/12139ft; 12km/7½ miles from Pomabamba) with the myriad colours of the houses' small flower gardens. The trail crosses the river and enters the Quebrada Yanacolpa, crossing the stream many times and passing several small lakes. It climbs past a swampy area (where you'll be lucky to keep dry feet) and through a meadow, to arrive at two small lakes with excellent camping at 4200m (13780ft).

You start in the morning with a climb to the Yanacolpa Pass (4600m/15092ft) and descend on the west side of the pass across a further intervening ridge to arrive at Huilca (4000m/13123ft). If camping here, take care of your gear, as there have been a few cases of equipment disappearing from tents.

You then follow the rough road to enter the Quebrada Tayapampa and take the trail through the meadows to Laguna Safuna Baja (4250m/13944ft), situated below the stunning, multi-peaked Pucahirca. You will find suitable camping by the lake. (With an extra day, you can follow the trail to Quebrada Tayapampa, Laguna Kaiko and Pucacocha and, for a little extra effort, you can reach the tiny Laguna Quitaracsa, situated directly below Alpamayo.)

This is one of the most remote and quiet valleys in the Blanca and you will probably share the valley with a few caracaras (the smaller birds that are frequently mistaken for condors when seen in flight), an occasional condor and the wind.

Laguna Safuna Baja to Laguna Jancarurish

The trail from Safuna now climbs the ridge northwest of Quebrada Tayapampa and ascends to a cirque at the head of Quebrada Mayobamba, crossing an intervening ridge at 4600m (15092ft). The trail is very steep and rocky (take care in bad weather), reaching the Gara Gara Pass at 4850m (15912ft), where it descends very steeply to enter the Quebrada Alpamayo below. Laguna Jancarurish, a small, turquoise lake set in barren surroundings, is seen below the cliffs leading to the Alpamayo–Quitaraju Col and it is possible to camp in a large flat area below the lake by crossing a marshy area. The view from the camp is

The entrance to the Santa Cruz Valley.

magnificent and it is worth planning an extra day here to explore the hanging valley to the west of Laguna Jancarurish and to visit Santa Cruz Base Camp.

Laguna Jancarurish to Laguna Azulacocha

Follow the trail down the valley, passing some ruins thought to be old Incan *tambos,* Incan staging posts for the mail runners (who used to run 50-km/31-mile stages at a time). The *tambos* were staffed with locals who could prepare food and drink for the runners on their journeys across the country. You will have to cross the stream several times to arrive at the Los Cedros Valley where more ruins are situated at 4000m (13123ft). You are on the last lap now. There's an ascent to the Los Cedros Pass, climbing a series of ridges via zigzags to arrive at the first pass (4830m/15846ft), with splendid views of the Milanco and Pilanco Peaks. This is followed by a descent to some meadows, before reascending to the main pass at 4900m (16076ft) where you have tremendous views of Champará to the north – the most outlying peak in the Blanca Range and the start of the Cordillera Rosco. A steep descent, initially across some granite slabs, leads to another magnificent viewpoint with Santa Cruz and Santa Cruz Chico lying above Laguna Culliacocha. A series of switchbacks takes you to Laguna Azulacocha (4650m/15256ft) which is situated to the north of the outlet tunnel of Laguna Culliacocha (4650m/15256ft). This is by far the best place to camp with yet another amazing view.

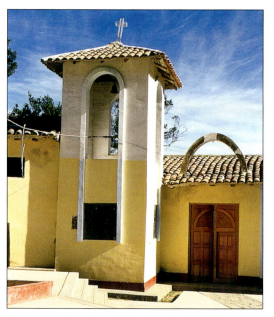

Cashapampa's church is architecturally typical of Latin America.

Laguna Azulacocha to Cashapampa

You have a great walk across some granite slabs before the big descent of the day. Start down on a series of switchbacks to a meadow where it is possible to camp, should your knees be rebelling – or if you just fancy another night out in the wilderness. The trail heads west and south, descending steeply to cross a series of landslides to arrive at an area of ancient Incan terracing, situated on a ridge with great views out over the Cordillera Negra. From here, you can descend to the settlement of Huallanca and, if you're lucky, catch transport back to Caraz. Alternatively, follow the trail south to Cholin (2850m/9350ft), 20km (12 miles) from Huallanca. There is very little water above Cholin. Make sure you ask for permission to camp at the small houses here but be careful of the dogs. The last day's walk from Cholin is an easy walk across rolling hillsides to Cashapampa, passing two small settlements. At the Banos Huancarhuas, you may wish to sample the waters of the new hot pools before the final short steep climb to Cashapampa.

PEAK: HUASCARAN SUR

The enormous peaks of Huascarán dominate the Cordillera Blanca, and the south peak is the highest in Peru. Although technically fairly straightforward, it pays to be vigilant when passing through the icefall to reach the *garganta* or col, as the dangers here have been increasing over the past few years.

Access is from Musho via Mancos, where it is possible to hire burros to take your equipment to Base Camp (3–5 hours). From here, follow the rock groove by the stream and then follow the cairns up and right over slabs to reach the Moraine Camp. There are some sections of fairly stiff scrambling over the slabs and a short rope may be useful. Continue to follow the slabs to gain the glacier at 5000m (16400ft) and follow easy-angled slopes to Camp One.

Follow the route through the icefall and cross a large crevasse near the top. Head left, passing below an area of seracs. Camp can be made at the *garganta* at 5980m (19620ft). From here, head northeast to a steep snow slope at 40° and follow this, crossing another very large crevasse which is sometimes impassable. Follow a series of seemingly never ending snow slopes to the top. Descend by the same route.

The sun creates a golden glow on the enormous mountain of Huascarán Sur.

CLIMB ESSENTIALS

SUMMIT Huascarán Sur 6786m (22264ft)
PRINCIPAL CAMPS Base Camp 4150m (13615ft); Moraine Camp 4800m (15740ft); Camp One 5300m (17390ft); Camp Two 5980m (19620ft).
GRADE Alpine Grade PD

HUARAZ DIRECTORY

Huaráz (3028m/9934ft) is often referred to as the Chamonix of South America. It is the base for treks and climbs into the Cordillera Blanca and Huayhuash Ranges, and an excellent place for buying supplies, getting acclimatized and organizing guides, burros and *arrieros*. Huaráz is the commercial and cultural capital of the Ancash department of Peru.

REGIONAL TRANSPORT
Buses and *collectivos* run between villages; ask locals for times and prices. You can also hire taxis and pickup trucks.
Huaráz to Lima:
Cruz del Sur, Av Lucar y Torre 585 y Julian de Morales, tel: (51 44) 722491. Leaves at 10am and 10pm.
Ancash Ormeno, Raimondi 825, tel: (51 44) 721102. Leaves at 10am and 9.30pm.
Rodrigues, Av Tarapaca 226, tel: (51 44) 721353. Leaves at 9.30am.
Movil Tours, Av Raimondi 730, tel: (51 44) 722555. Leaves at 10am and 9pm.
Huaráz to Chiquian:
Rapido, Jr Figueredo 2162. Leaves at 2pm.
Chiquian Tours Leaves from behind the market.
Huaráz to Caraz:
Numerous *collectivos* run between Huaráz and Caraz daily (from early morning to 9pm). They leave from the bridge area about every 15 mins, and stop at all the villages on the way.
Huaráz to Vicos, Llanganuco, Chavin, Colcabamba:
Check with your hotel or ask at the Casa de Guias for details on where to catch the bus as this changes every year.
Huaráz to Llupa:
Local pickup.

ACCOMMODATION IN HUARAZ
Hostal Colomba, tel: (51 44) 721501, email: Colomba@mail.cosapidata.com.pe. Contact: Lucho or Sylvana Maguina. Excellent. Superb gardens. Quiet and well run. Upper to mid-range.
Hostal Edwards, Av Bolognesi 121, tel: (51 44) 722692, email: edwarsinn@terra.com.pe. Excellent source of information on trekking and climbing.
Casa de Guias, Parque Genebra 28-G, tel: (51 44) 721811. Situated next to the Guides school. Dormitory accommodation. Very clean and a good place to meet people.
Hostal Colonia, Río Quillcay, Malecon sur Jiron Huandoy 103, tel: (51 44) 721325, email: colonia@latinmail.com. Well run with a nice garden. Close to the market. Good source of information for trekking and climbing.
Sierra Nevada, Lucar y Torre 538, tel: (51 44) 721203, email: sclc@qnet.com.pe.
Casa Hospadeje, Jiron José de Sucre. Run by a friendly couple with mountaineering experience. The owners often wait for clients at the bus station.

LOCAL ACTIVITIES
Trekking Guides and Arrieros:
Val Pitkethly, 133 Rundle Crescent, Canmore, Alberta T1W2L6, Canada or 8 Trinity Park, Ripon, HG4 2ER, England, email: valpk@hotmail.com.
Melkie Bedon, Prologacion Cajarmarca y Pasaje Ranrapalca No 6, tel: (51 44) 727731. Can organize cooks, porters, burros and *arrieros* for the Huayhuash and Blanca.
Natavidad Bedon, Jiron Thomas Ayllon y Espinar 220, Chiquian. Excellent and extremely experienced guide/*arriero* for the Huayhuash.
Casa de Guias, contact Hugo Sifuntes or Jose Chacon, tel: (51 44) 721811, fax: (51 44) 722306, email: agmp@net.telematic.com.pe, www.clientes.telematic.com.pe/agmp. Lists of recommended guides. Good source of information on all aspects of trekking and climbing in the area.
Raphael Figueroa, Edwards Inn. tel: (51 44) 722692, email: edwardsinn@yahoo.com. UIAGM fully qualified guide. Excellent.
Alfredo Quintana Figueroa, Mountclimb, Jiron Mariscal Avelino Caceres 421, tel: (51 44) 726060, email:mountclimb@yahoo.com. Excellent guide who runs a very good equipment shop.
Arrieros and Cooks:
Please note that you should provide your *arriero* with a tent and food for his trip. If you are not doing a circuit trek, you should also pay something towards his homeward journey.
Manuel Serafin Santiago, Llupa. Contact through the Casa de Guias or in Llupa. Excellent cook/*arriero* with experience of all the valleys in the Cordillera Blanca. He has worked as a porter for 25 years and has an excellent knowledge of the popular peaks.
Herrmann Sanchez Rapry, contact via the Casa de Guias or by the Collón village local radio phone. Excellent *arriero* and cook for the Ishinka Valley. Can also work as a porter or cook for other mountains in the Blanca.
Equipment Rental:
Equipment for trekking or climbing can be rented from numerous shops in Huaráz but remember to check all hire items carefully.
Mountclimb, Jr Mariscal Avelino Caceres 421, tel: (51 44) 726060. Excellent.

ACCOMMODATION IN CHIQUIAN
Hostal Nogales, tel: (51 44) 747121 or (51 44) 1460807, email: hotel_nogales_chiquian@yahoo.com.pe. Nice rooms; a little noisy as it is located near the town square, where the buses depart for Huaráz and Lima. Hot showers. Breakfast available.
Hostal San Miguel Jr, Comercio 233. A nice old hotel with garden.

TRAVEL AGENCIES
Sport Yerapaha (run by the Bedon family) in Chiquian and Huaráz, tel: (51 44) 727731.
Ceasar Sifuntes Trek Peru, Av Centenario 687.
Independencia, tel: (51 44) 722789.
Colonia Adventures, tel: (51 44) 721325.

RESCUE
Casa de Guias, tel: (51 44) 721811.
Policia National del Peru, tel: (51 44) 793333, fax: (51 44) 793292, email: usam@pmp.gob.pe.

6
ECUADOR

Perched high in the Cordillera Real of the Andes between the Amazon and the Pacific Ocean, Ecuador is one of the smallest countries in South America, yet it contains an astonishing variety of physical extremes, with towering mountains, immense tracts of green – from cloud forest to thick luxuriant jungle – ice, water, fire and small areas of cultivation.

It is in Ecuador that the equator crosses the continent, and it is here that the Spanish conquistador Pizarro murdered the Incan king Atahualpa. Fifty per cent of Ecuador's population is Indian. Their lives are generally ruled by the sun, moon and the climate, and most still speak the native language of Quechua.

The mountains of Ecuador are divided into two separate ranges and are dominated by thirty volcanoes, the Lords of the Andes; these brooding giants are a source of mystery to the Indians who live in their shadows.

Outstanding natural beauty defines the landscape of Ecuador's high paramo.

The population of Ecuador is 12 million, with a mix of indigenous, *mestizo* and European peoples, almost 50 per cent of whom live in the Andean sierra.

Politics

Following their success in Peru, the Spanish arrived in Ecuador in 1532. Though Quito, Ecuador's capital city, held out for some time, the region was ultimately defeated. The years following the Spanish victory were marked both by the decimation of the native population by European ailments and dissension amongst the Spanish colonists.

The Spanish crown maintained direct control over Ecuador until 1822, when independence forces under Antonio Sucre liberated the country. Ecuador at first joined Simón Bolívar's Republic of Gran Colombia, but later split off to form a separate republic in 1830.

Farmers will often be the only people you meet on a trek; they lead a harsh and lonely existence.

Ecuador's first 30 years as an independent republic were rent by disputes between the conservative landowners of the country's interior and the more liberal business community of the coastal plains. In 1860, conservative Garcio Moreno ruthlessly re-established order, going on to lead the country for 15 years with the support of the Catholic Church, until he was finally assassinated in 1875.

A period of stable government under liberal, anticlerical administrations followed. At the same time, skyrocketing worldwide demand for cocoa brought foreign money into Ecuador and tied the country's economy to commodity exports.

The end of the cocoa boom at the beginning of the 20th century produced renewed political instability and a military coup in 1925. Populist politics and a disastrous war with Peru marked the 1930s and early 1940s. Though a brief recovery in the agricultural commodities market restored political peace and prosperity for a few years, recession plunged Ecuador back into populist politics and domestic military interventions until 1972.

Democratic government was restored in 1979, but by 1982 Ecuador faced chronic economic crisis. In 1984, León Febres Cordero became president. He introduced free-market economic policies and pursued close relations with the United States, but he was unable to check the economy's downward spiral.

In 1988, Rodrigo Borja Cevallos won the presidency. He, too, was undermined by Ecuador's economic woes, and was replaced by a three-person coalition led by Sixto Durán Ballén in 1992. Durán Ballén introduced several free-market economic reforms and cut public spending, provoking popular unrest. His popularity was further eroded by a border skirmish with Peru in 1995, and he was easily defeated in the 1996 presidential election by Abdala Bucaram.

Bucaram's short term in office drew criticism for corruption, and he was ousted in 1997 on grounds of insanity. Fabián Alarcón became acting president, overseeing the 1998 election in which Jamil Mahuad won by a narrow margin. Mahuad's announcement in 2000 that he would 'dollarize' Ecuador's economy – in a desperate bid to stop the decline of the country's currency – met with a firestorm of protest. The unrest culminated a few weeks later, when demonstrators entered the National Assembly building and declared a three-person junta in charge of the country. Mahuad was forced to flee Ecuador, and vice president Gustavo Noboa took over the presidency.

CLIMATE

The climate is quite variable, and different regions have their own subclimates. There are two seasons, the wet and the dry, with mid-November to early February being the best period for climbing and trekking. It is possible to go into the mountains during July and August, although there can be high winds during these months, which vary depending upon your location in the mountains. There has been a change in the weather pattern over the past few years and Ecuador has been in a relative drought, contributing to the recession of glaciers.

THE LAND

Ecuador has an amazing variety of habitats. Despite being situated in the tropics, it has relatively arctic-like tundra due to the altitude – which greatly influences the vegetation. The highland vegetation starts at 3200–4700m (10499–15420ft) and is known as the paramo. Weather on the paramo is generally cold and wet, with frequent rain and sometimes snow, and the flora of the area has adapted accordingly.

The extreme topography of the country also provides an insight into Ecuador's persistent poverty. The core of its indigenous population lives in an environment where agriculture is almost impossible – a land of sharp angles, high altitude and poor soil. Most farming is done on the steep mountainsides, while a few cows usually graze in the fertile lands that lie between the mountains. This is the result of a loophole in the land reform acts of the country. Ecuador's ruling families agreed to part with some of their enormous land holdings, but they kept most of the land that was not steep, agreeing that it would be put to agricultural use – hence the small number of cattle seen grazing in flat areas whilst most of the local Indians work ground up to 70°.

The Andes are at their narrowest in Ecuador, and they form two major cordilleras that run north–south and are 40–60km (25–37 miles) apart. Unlike most mountain ranges, they are not a series of crests, but are separated by valleys as extensive as the mountains themselves, so you alternate between being high enough to look down on the clouds, and being surrounded by peaks. The central valley is only about 400km (249 miles) long, and most of the country's major towns lie within this fertile valley.

Local people in the Chimborazo area (trek 22).

ARRIVING IN ECUADOR

Quito (2850m/9350ft) is the capital city of Ecuador – a beautiful city with stunning views of the valley of the volcanoes from the Panacillo or Breadloaf, a small hill that overlooks the city, with a statue of Jesus outstretching his arms.

Quito is also the most important city of the Central Valley. The old city is full of cobbled streets and red-tiled colonial buildings, with many monasteries and churches. It is a world heritage site. The new city is expanding rapidly, and many travellers use the city as a base for the rest of Ecuador.

By Air

KLM, American Airlines, Lufthansa, Iberia and Saeta all operate in and out of Quito.

Visas

You must have a passport that is valid for at least six months. On arrival, you will be given a T3 tourist card, which you must keep, as this is required to exit the country. You are allowed a maximum of 90

EMBASSIES

Australia, Calle San Roque and Av Francisco de Orellanada Guayquil, tel: (5932) 298823
Canada, 6 de Dicembre 2816 and Jr Orton, tel: (5932) 543214
UK, Gonzales Suarez 111 12 de Octobre, tel: (5932) 560670
USA, Patria and 12 de Octobre, tel: (5932) 562890

USEFUL WEBSITES

www.lonelyplanet.com.au/dest/sam/ecu.htm
www.qni.com/~mj

TREKKING AGENCIES

South American Explorers Club, Jorge Washington 311 y Leonidas Plaza, tel: (5932) 225228, email: quitoclub@saexplorers.org, www.saexplorers.org. The club house is open Mon-Fri, 9.30am-5.00pm. You can visit for free once and then you have to pay to join. Offers an excellent reference source for trekking and climbing reports, recommended guides, etc.
Camillo y Marjellino Andrade of CAMPUS, Box 17-12-45, Quito, tel/fax: (5932) 970 6045, email: campus@pi.pro.ec. This is the best agency in Quito for organizing treks and climbs. It specializes in the Papallacta Cotopaxi and Chimborazo Circuit treks and in climbs of all the volcanoes in Ecuador.
Safari, Calama 380 y Juan Leon Mera, tel: (5932) 223 1381, email: admin@safariec.ecx.ec.
Freddy Ramirez of Sierra Nevada Tours, Pinto 637 y Cordero, Quito, tel: (5932) 554936, email: marlopez@pi.pro.ec.
Pamir, Juan Leon Mera 721 y Ventimilla, tel: (5932) 220892. Owner is Hugo Torres, a long-time climber and guide.
Guias de Montana, Ivan Rojas, who can be contacted through Campo Abierto, a climbing and trekking gear shop on Baquedano 355, Juan Leon Mera, tel: (5932) 524422.

Local market at Latacunga below Cotopaxi.

days stay on initial arrival, but this can be extended at the immigration office on Av Amazonas 2639 in Quito. You should carry a copy of your passport and tourist card with you at all times.

Time Difference
Ecuador is 5 hours behind Greenwich Mean Time.

Money
As of July 2001, Ecuador's monetary unit is the US dollar ($). The paper sucre is no longer in circulation.

The easiest and quickest way to change money is at a *casa de cambio*. The street changers are fine for changing small amounts of cash, but be aware and count your cash carefully before handing over your dollars. Make sure you know the offical exchange rate. The best rate for cash and travellers cheques is to be found in the larger cities and towns. It is possible to have money wired to you from your bank at home, and it is also possible to withdraw money on Visa. Note that the charges that Ecuadorian businesses pay to credit card companies are relatively high and that these are usually passed on to the card holder. Credit and ATM cards are useful for obtaining cash from machines, but this is usually only possible in large towns and cities.

TRANSPORT
By Bus:
It is very easy and cheap to travel by bus in Ecuador. The Bus Station Terminal is at Terrestre Av Cumada (buy your ticket in advance).

By Road:
It is possible to hire taxis, which generally run on meters, and rent cars. Travellers should use only registered taxis and must never accept offers of transportation or guide services from individuals seeking clients on the street.

By Air:
There is an excellent national air service. Air Tame and San Saeta offer daily flights to various cities.

By Rail:
The train from Quito to Riobamba runs on Saturdays and travels along the Avenue of the Volcanoes, which includes some of Ecuador's finest scenery (8 hours). The train returns on Saturday evenings.

ACCOMMODATION
Hostal Embassador, President y Wilson 441, tel: (5932) 561990. Quiet, well-run, mid-range hotel.
Hostal Ebano, Av Amazonas 3009, y Rumipampa, tel: (5932) 450466. Very good.
Hostal Vienna, International Flores 600, tel: (5932) 213605. Good service and helpful.
Hostal Charles Darwin, Colina 304, tel: (5932) 592384.
La Casa de Elisa Isabella, La Catolica 1559, tel: (5932) 226602. Excellent budget accommodation with use of a kitchen. Helpful advice given about tours and cultural events.

Hostal Sierra Nevada, Pinto 637 y Cordero, tel: (5932) 224717, email: marlopez@pi.pro.ec. Close to embassies, banks, restaurants, museums, etc. Provides good advice and information about the best transport and guides for trekking and climbing.
Residencial Marcella, Los Rios y Castro. Family-run.
The Magic Bean, Foch 681 y Juan Leon Mera, tel: (5932) 566181.

COMMUNICATIONS
Ecuador's country code is 593, and the city code for Quito is 2. Public telephones are difficult to find in Ecuador. Many small stores will let you make local calls for a fee, but you must place long-distance calls at your hotel or at the IETEL telecommunications buildings, which can be found in every town. Internet service is available in most large cities, including Quito, Guayaquil and Cuenca.

The Ecuadorean postal service is reasonably efficient. Outbound letters to Europe and the United States take a few weeks to reach their destination; incoming letters will generally reach you within one to three weeks. You can have mail sent to you poste restante, care of any main post office.

ELECTRICITY
110 volt/60 cycles AC is the standard electric current throughout Ecuador.

SECURITY
Since a national state of emergency was declared in 2000, Ecuador's security situation has progressively worsened. Most of the unrest is in opposition to the government's handling of the economy. Travellers should avoid areas where demonstrations are in progress and keep informed by following the local news and consulting hotel personnel and tour guides.

Ecuador's northeastern border with Colombia should also be avoided, as Colombian rebel groups and contraband are increasingly crossing the San Miguel River due to an escalating civil war. Law enforcement officials are having difficulty containing drug trafficking, armed insurgency and organized crime – including theft, extortion and kidnapping – in this region.

Travellers should be vigilant in Ecuador's cities, which are experiencing a dramatic rise in street crime. Theft is the biggest problem, with pickpockets targeting crowded areas such as street markets, bus and train stations and airports.

You should report any crime to the police within 48 hours. Police headquarters in Quito are located at Cuenca y Mideros in the Old City.

Ingapirca area (trek 21).

TREK 21: EL CAMINO DEL INCA

The Incas built a series of roads that stretched more than 4000km (2486 miles), from Ecuador to Chile. These roads acted as a superb communications network throughout their vast empire, providing a transport and postal system, a means to travel and much more. Although much of the roadway has been lost, it is still possible to travel sections of it today. In Ecuador, El Camino del Inca offers a short trek that provides a fascinating insight into rural Andean life, along with some incredible Incan ruins at Ingapirca.

Achupallas to Laguna Las Tres Cruces

From Achupallas, take the trail that leaves from the Plaza and follow the track that leads south to enter the Río Cadrul valley. Cross the river after 40 mins to enter the Quebrada Gadrui. Stay on the east bank until you reach Cerro Mapahuiña (4365m/14321ft) and a flat-topped hill on the east side of Cerro Callana Pucará. Head for the well-defined notch and pass through a hole in the rock. Descend and re-cross Río Cadrul, then follow the ascending trail on the opposite side. The Incan road parallels the road on the west side of the Quebrada Gadrui. There are some ruins just before you reach Laguna Las Tres Cruces, where there are good camping places above the lake at 3900m (12795ft).

Local child on market day in Alausí.

TREK ESSENTIALS

LENGTH 2-3-day trek. 45km (28 miles). Trek from Achupallas to Laguna Las Tres Cruces, Laguna Culebrillas and to Ingapirca.
ACCESS *To start* Drive to Alausí, south of Quito, or take the train ride called the Devil's Nose – an exciting journey where you can sit on the train's roof for a bird's eye view of the western Andes. From Alausí, take local or private transport to Achupallas, 12km (7½miles) away. *On finish* From Ingapirca take a bus to El Tambo and then on to Cañar. From Cañar, it is easy to get a bus back to Quito or travel on to Cuenca.
HIGHEST POINT Paso Tres Cruces, 4350m (14272ft).
TREK STYLE Backpack/burros and an *arriero*.
RESTRICTIONS None.
FURTHER OPTIONS Extra time trekking in the wild lakeland area near Quillo Loma.
MAPS Ecuadorean IGM 1:50 000 Cañar; International Travel Maps/Kevin Healey 1: 1 000 000 Ecuador.

Laguna Las Tres Cruces to Laguna Culebrillas

Continue southwest on the trail, which crosses a pass. You will need to use your compass and the map here if the weather is bad. From the pass, follow the upper trail, which travels along the ridge of Cuchilla Tres Cruces with superb views down to the valley, Espindola and the lake district to the east.

Follow the trail to Quillo Loma, where it descends along a rocky path to enter the valley below. Join the distinct Incan road that runs in a straight line across the valley floor. You will pass an old abandoned

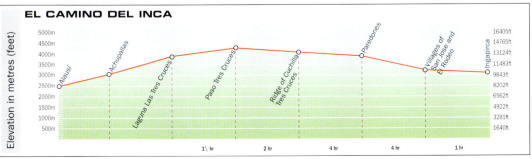

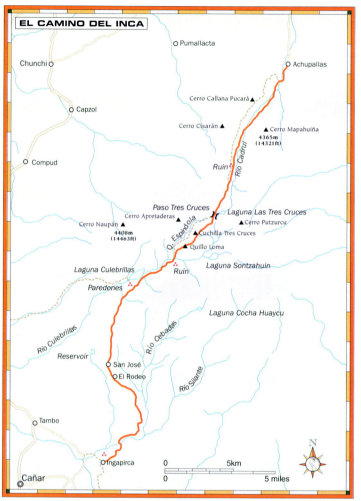

house here and another lake. Cross the river by an old Incan bridge and follow the trail to Laguna Culebrillas and the ruins of Paredones, situated on a bluff above the lake. Superb camping is available here. This region is excellent for spotting Andean teal and gulls, as well as short-eared owls.

Laguna Culebrillas to Ingapirca
Follow the trail leading southwest from Paredones on the Incan road. The trail passes through sections of bog, so be prepared for wet and muddy feet. After passing a section with huge boulders and a newly built reservoir, the trail becomes vague and passes through some very marshy land. Head for the villages of San José and El Rodeo.

The area here is heavily farmed, with many houses, and it is easy to follow the road to Ingapirca (3160m/10367ft). The village of Ingapirca offers accommodation and basic supplies. From here, it is possible to get public transport to Cañar and on to Cuenca.

Farming in the Ingapirca area.

INGAPIRCA

Ingapirca is Ecuador's most important Incan archaeological site. Meaning 'wall of the Inca', it was built by that great civilization in the 15th century on a strategic rocky promontory at 3160m (10367ft). However, prior to that date, the site had been used by the local Cañari people.

As with so many Incan ruins, it is impossible to know the exact use of this site, although it is thought by many to have been a temple to Inti (the sun), the Incas' most supreme deity, as the main building on the site is the Adoratorio, the sun temple. There are also numerous smaller buildings and an open plaza area.

The Adoratorio was the most solidy constructed building in the complex and, as such, is the best preserved. It is a fine example of typical Incan construction methods – tightly interlocking stones, with trapezoidal doorways and niches.

PARQUE NACIONAL CAJAS

This is one of the best-managed reserves in the country, which has a lot to do with the local Cuencano pride in the area. Situated only 29km (18 miles) from Cuenca, Las Cajas is the weekend retreat for many locals, particularly fishermen, a few hikers and birdwatchers. There are buses to the reserve which leave from the San Francisco market area of the city. The journey to the reserve takes 2 hours, and you can ask to be dropped at the information centre at Laguna Toreadora, where you must pay a US$10 entrance fee. There is a refuge here with bunk beds, or you can camp. Camping is free throughout the park. The trails in the park are relatively well signposted and you can cross the park, which consists mostly of paramo vegetation and lakes, in 2 days. Combined with a trek to El Camino del Inca, this makes for a fascinating trip to the area of Cuenca.

CUENCA DIRECTORY

Cuenca, the capital of the southern highlands, was once the home of the Cañari Indians, who were exceptionally skilled jewellers, weavers and ceramic artists. The Incas conquered the Cañaris and built several major complexes in the area, such as Ingapirca. The Spanish conquistadors refounded Cuenca in 1557 and there are several remnants of this colonial era around Cuenca. The Parque Nacional Cajas close to Cuenca is an excellent area for exploration and hiking.

REGIONAL TRANSPORT FROM CUENCA
By Air:
Air Tame – 3 flights per day from Quito.

By Bus:
To Quito (10 hours).
To Alausí (4 hours).
To Las Cajas (2 hours).
To Ingapirca (direct, 3 hours).

By Taxi:
To Las Cajas (1 hour).

ACCOMMODATION
Hotel Oro Verde, Av Ordonez Lazo, tel: (593) 783 1200, fax: (593) 832849. Luxurious.
Hotel Crespo, Larga 7-93 y Cordero, tel: (593) 782 7857. Mid-range hotel. Friendly owners.
Cabana Yanuncay, Calle Canton Gualaleco, tel: (593) 788 3716. Small cabin in a beautiful setting.
Hostal Chordeleg, Gran Colombia y Torres, tel: (593) 782 4611. Pleasant and well-run.
Hotel Inca Royal, Torres 8-40, tel: (593) 782 3636. Nice and quiet.
Hotel Villa Rosa, 12-22 Gran Colombia, tel: (593) 783 7944. Reasonably priced and quiet.

LOCAL ACTIVITIES
Trekking Guides:
Ecotrek, Calle Larga 7-108, tel: (593) 842531, fax: (593) 843202.
Edwardo, Quito Cordero 20-56, tel: (593) 823018, fax: (593) 835387.
Humberto, Chico Cabanas, Yanuncay, tel: (593) 883716, fax: (593) 819681.

Trekking to Ingapirca.

TREK 22: CHIMBORAZO CIRCUIT

This trek is one of the most scenic in the Ecuadorean Andes, with the huge massif of Chimborazo, an extinct volcano and the highest peak in Ecuador (6310m/20702ft), dominating the area. Chimborazo is the point on the earth's surface that is farthest from the earth's centre, due to the equatorial bulge. The trek passes through an amazing variety of landscapes, with llamas, vicuñas and many birds, including condors. The only human habitations you are likely to see are tiny shepherds' houses in wild locations, with only the wind and the mist for company. You need to be well acclimatized before setting out on this high, remote trek.

Pogyos to Lomo Piedra Negra
The trek starts from Pogyos, a tiny collection of buildings situated on the old Ambato to Guaranda road. You'll be able to arrange burros here if you decide to take them. As the circuit is not popular, make sure that your *arriero* has done the route before. Head out of Pogyos on a dirt track (initially) to Laguna Colorado, heading in an easterly direction and crossing sandy paramo; camp at the lake at 4100m (13451ft).

Leaving this camp, you enter a remote area where you will see a vicuña reserve and shepherds bundled up in colourful shawls looking after their flocks. You head east towards Carihuairazo as the trail ascends, crossing a plain that reaches 4000m (13123ft), then descends to the Abraspungo Valley, which lies between Chimborazo and Carihuairazo. You can set up camp near the base of Carihuairazo at 4200m (13780ft).

It would be well worth spending a day in this area to explore the high Andean lakes and tarns, but be prepared to spend time negotiating the numerous bogs. Continuing on the trek, you head southwest around the western slopes of Carihuairazo, following the trail that lies near Lomo Piedra Negra, mainly on cow and sheep paths, with the occasional cairn to mark the way.

An interesting side trip is to the valleys that lie around Carihuairazo. Alternatively, if you are planning to climb Carihuairazo, look for a trail that heads east and you'll enter the Quebrada Tigre Saltana, followed by Quebrada Auaican, where it is possible to camp (and where the Base Camps for the Moche Peak of Carihuairazo are located). You can also scramble to the top of Cerro Piedra Negra for great views of the peaks of Chimborazo, Tungarajua and El Altar.

Lomo Piedra Negra to Totoras
From your camp at Lomo Piedra Negra, you'll be heading east over the paramo and some intervening ridges to shadow the eastern slopes of Chimb-

TREK ESSENTIALS
LENGTH 4-6-day trek depending on where you start. 70km (42 miles). From Pogyos, trek to Laguna Colorado, Carihuairazo, Lomo Piedra Negra, Chimborazo, Totoras, Refugio Edward Whymper and back to Pogyos.
ACCESS *To start* Go to Riobamba and Guaranda then take a local bus to Pogyos. *On finish* Take a local bus to Guaranda from Pogyos.
HIGHEST POINT Refugio Edward Whymper, 5000m (16404ft).
TREK STYLE Backpack or hire llamas in Pogyos.
RESTRICTIONS US$10 park fee and US$5 to enter the vicuña reserve at Laguna Colorado.
FURTHER OPTIONS Climb Chimborazo.
MAPS Ecuadorean IGM 1: 50 000 Chimborazo. While some maps indicate that the trail crosses glaciers, recent glacial recession means that these sections are now on scree and rock.

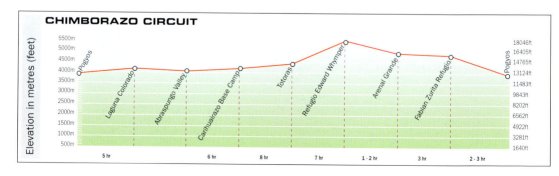

TREK 22: CHIMBORAZO CIRCUIT

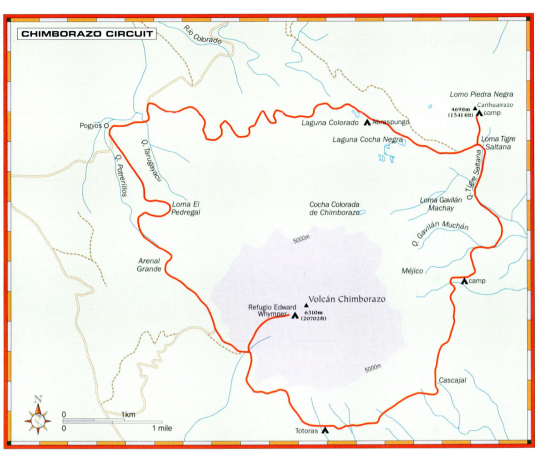

Refugio Edward Whymper sits at 5000m (16404ft), below Chimborazo.

orazo with its stunning glaciers. Traversing these slopes, you'll pass the trail from Refugio Urbina, which climbers use for ascending the Sun Ridge route on Chimborazo. There is an absolutely stunning camping area near the terminal moraine at the foot of Chimborazo, which gives you great views out over the paramo, including the peaks of El Altar, if you're lucky with the weather.

From this camp, keep heading west, eventually arriving in Chuquipogyo, where the trail swings south above the Riobamba Valley to Totoras and another place to camp. (Note that from the refuge you can descend to follow a trail that leads to Estancia Urbinas, which contains a small *posada* (rest house) set in a stunningly scenic area, about 8km/5 miles above Mocha, where you can catch transport to Quito.)

Totoras to Refugio Whymper

Finally, the trail heads in a southwesterly direction to the Refugio Edward Whymper (5000m/ 16404ft) at the foot of the Thielman Glacier. This is the base for the normal route of ascent on Chimborazo. The refuge was wiped out in 1992, when an enormous section of ice detached itself from the Whymper face, and it seems rather strange that the new refuge has been built in exactly the same spot as the previous one. It's worth climbing

PEAK: CHIMBORAZO

Mount Chimborazo (6310m/20702ft) is the highest peak in Ecuador and was long thought to be the highest peak in the world. The local Quechua Indians believed its perpetual mountain mists to be Nekous Wakan or 'True Souls', which after death are transformed into clouds that travel on an eternal journey.

Chimborazo was first climbed by Edward Whymper and the Carrels in 1880 after their ascent of Cotopaxi. Their ascent caused a storm of protest, for several reasons. First, Whymper wasn't Ecuadorean; but more importantly, the locals believed there was hidden treasure buried on the summit and that the only reason anyone would want to go to the trouble of climbing a mountain would be to search for gold. The locals were also worried that this ascent could upset the local gods of the mountain, especially if the treasure was removed. Whymper climbed Chimborazo again later in 1880, with David Beltran and Francisco Campana (two Ecuadoreans), to prove both that it was possible to climb the peak without upsetting the gods and that he had previously done so.

To climb Chimborazo, take a taxi from Ambato

The mighty peak of Chimborazo is, surprisingly, one of the easier Andean mountains.

or Riobamba to the parking area below the lower refuge. From here, it is a short walk to the upper Refugio Edward Whymper (5000m/16404ft). Basic food supplies are available here. From the refuge, follow the track that leads up towards the scree slope to the left of the glacier. Be careful and keep an eye out for rockfalls as you traverse the slope. Follow this slope to a very prominent snow ramp, El Corredor, which is situated below a rocky outcrop called the castle. From here, ascend in a northwesterly direction towards the Ventimilla summit, passing the crevasses near this summit on the right. The glacier is usually marked with footsteps and often wands. From here, it is a long slog across a big basin to the main summit. Return the same way.

The ascent takes 9–10 hours, the descent 4–5 hours. Make sure you get an early start as the snow from Ventimilla to the main summit becomes very soft by early afternoon. Ask the refuge warden for the latest route information, as the glacier here changes rapidly every year.

CLIMB ESSENTIALS

SUMMIT Chimborazo 6310m (20702ft)
CAMP Refugio Edward Whymper 5000m (16404ft)
GRADE Alpine Grade PD

---

up to the impressive Whympers Needles, which appear like sails from an ethereal ship, for their views of the mountains and valleys below. El Altar is particularly impressive.

On the last day, follow the trail across the Arenal Grande sand pit, a high-altitude desert with stunning coloured rocks and sand which encompasses the west and north slopes of Chimborazo. You'll pass the Fabian Zurita refuge, a now dilapidated building but still in use. Look out for the red walls (*murallas rojas*) which you will see above the refuge on the once popular old route of Chimborazo. From here it's a steady downhill walk over the sandy paramo until you reach Pogyos.

TREK 23: PAPALLACTA TO COTOPAXI

One of the best trips in Ecuador takes you through incredible paramo scenery and past the peaks of Sincholagua, Antisana and Cotopaxi. The vegetation of the area is wild and strange, quite likely different from anything you will have seen before. Don't be surprised to find yourself crawling through tunnels of dense foliage and root systems, especially at the Antisana end of the trek! In terms of animal life, feral horses and condors are often seen en route. The area seems to have its own climate pattern, so be prepared for any type of weather.

Drive to Papallacta, situated in the eastern cordillera of the Andes. The road passes through a series of crazy-shaped fields and rough pastureland that resembles a patchwork quilt. Accommodation can be found in Papallacta, or it is possible to camp on the edge of town. There are hot springs about 3km (2 miles) from the village, and it is well worth taking the time for a nice refreshing soak before starting the trek. On a clear day, you can lie back and relax as you gaze across to Antisana.

If you stay in Papallacta, ask the locals if they still have the pet tapir – a rare animal that resembles a hairless wild pig with a one-toed hoof. You are unlikely to see one in the wild as they normally inhabit the very dense cloud forest.

Papallacta to Laguna Volcán

If you arrive early enough, it is possible to trek to Laguna Volcán (also known as Tumaguina) at 3750m (12303ft) and camp. Follow the track heading west and bypass Laguna Papallacta, staying close to the Río Tambo. Near the hill known as El Tambo, look out for a path heading southeast. This frequently muddy trail goes through an enormous quenal and quiswar forest before descending to the lake. You'll find an amazing variety of plant life, including orchids, tucked away amongst the volcanic rocks.

A trip to the lava field above the lake is worthwhile. Alternatively, you can do a circuit round the lake. If you head into the forest here, you may be lucky and see an extremely rare Andean pudu (a very small antelope).

Laguna Volcán to Laguna Santa Lucia

Select your route with care when leaving the lake. To avoid the frustrations of walking in often impenetrable forest, follow the exit stream from the lake until its confluence with three rivers.

Ascend the hill on the south to reach Quebrada Sunfohuayacu, passing through very thick vegetation. Bamboo, moss- and lichen-festooned trees and ferns as tall as a man are all fighting for root space, along with the quenal forest. The sounds of

TREK ESSENTIALS

LENGTH 5-7-day trek. 70-80km (50 miles). From Papallacta, trek to Laguna Volcán, Laguna Santa Lucia, Cullirama River, Sincholagua, finishing at Lago Limpiopungo

ACCESS *To start* Take a local bus from Quito to Papallacta or private transport. *On finish* Take a private pick-up or taxi from Lago Limpiopongo to Lasso or Latacunga, and then local bus to Quito. Or return to the park entrance and try to hitch a ride to Latacunga with a climbing trip returning from Cotopaxi.

HIGHEST POINT Antisana Base Camp, 4800m (15748ft).

TREK STYLE Burros and *arrieros* recommended, otherwise it is a difficult backpack.

RESTRICTIONS US$10 for Cotopaxi park and US$10 for Reserva Ecologica Antisana.

FURTHER OPTIONS Ascents of Cotopaxi and Ruminahui.

MAPS Ecuadorean IGM 1: 50 000 Sincholagua. Ecuadorean IGM 1: 50 000 Pintag

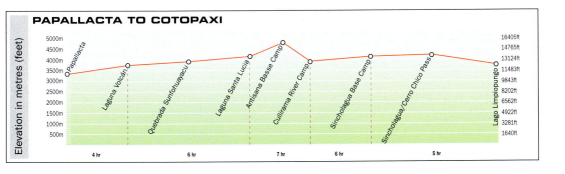

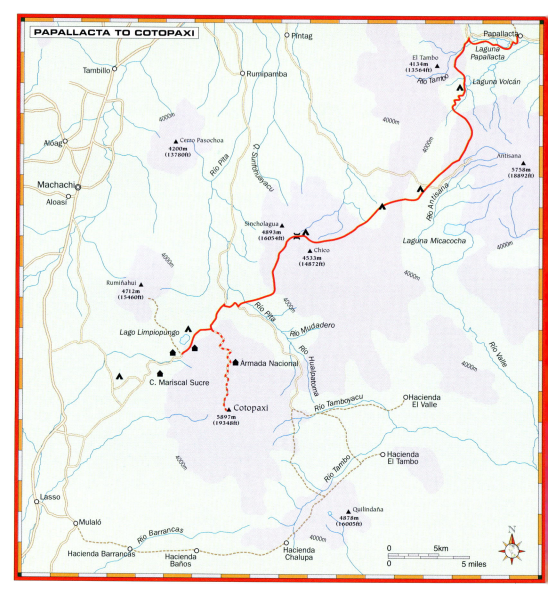

numerous birds can often be heard. Pipits, thrushes, swallows and hummingbirds, such as the Andean hillstar, are common in this area. The trail passes through some impressive tunnels of vegetation before emerging at 4000m (13123ft) on the paramo. The small hill ahead is called Cerro Lomo Chosalago Grande.

You must follow the trail across some boggy ground towards Antisana. Continuing across the paramo, feral horses can sometimes be seen. Camp can be made by Laguna Santa Lucia (4250m/13944ft) near the base of Cerro Lomo Chosalago. Look out for chuquiragua, a tall plant resembling a thistle with orange flowers and stems and dense spiky leaves. The locals make an infusion of the leaves and drink it to treat coughs and liver problems.

If the weather is good, it is worth ascending the *cerro* (hill) for excellent views of Antisana. It is also possible to ascend to the Antisana Base Camp (4800m/15748ft) by following a trail across the paramo and up along a number of moraine ridges to the glacier's base.

Laguna Santa Lucia to Cullirama River

The next day, you have a long walk towards Volcano Sincholagua. Travelling over the paramo, you will pass close to Hacienda El Hato, a well-established sheep farm. The trail is vague and crosses a huge rolling plain. If you are lucky, you may see buzzard eagles. From a distance, these birds are often mistaken for condors.

Keep in the general direction of Sincholagua. You will cross an area of tussock, spongy grasses or *almohandes*, which make for entertaining walking as you leap from one tussock to another trying to keep your balance and avoiding the marshy ground between them. Cross a valley towards a couple of streams until you reach a camping area not far from the Cullirama River (3850m/12631ft).

Fishing for trout on one of the many rivers that runs near Lago Limpiopungo.

Cullirama River to Lago Limpiopungo
The trail then climbs a small hill and keeps heading in the general direction of Sincholagua. Not far from the mountain's base you will see a small quenal forest and some enormous boulders. In the

PEAK: COTOPAXI

The ascent of Cotopaxi (5897m/19348ft) is not technically difficult but it does require crampons, an ice axe, a rope and knowledge of glacier travel. The best time for climbing is mid-November to mid-January. It is possible to hire a truck in Latacunga or in Lasso (no local buses go to the peak), both a short distance below the park entrance. Drive to the car park below the climbers' refuge. From here, it is a 45-min walk to the José Ribas Refugio at 4800m (15748ft).

From the refuge, ascend the scree slopes until you reach the glacier at 5100m (16732ft). Watch for crevasses. Head up the trail – it is generally well marked, due to the popularity of the climb. Keep to the right of the big rock face of Yanascha. From here, the snow slope ascends more steeply for 200m (656ft) to reach the crater rim where you traverse left to the summit (5–8 hours ascent; 3–5 hours descent). It is best to get an

Cotopaxi as seen from near Sincholagua.

alpine start, as the snow becomes very wet in the early afternoon.

CLIMB ESSENTIALS

SUMMIT Cotopaxi 5897m (19348ft)
PRINCIPAL CAMP Refugio José Ribas 4800m (15748ft)
GRADE Alpine grade PD

frequently misty valley, these formations resemble wild animals of phenomenal size. After passing through the boulders, the trail climbs through a boggy valley to a camp at the base of Sincholagua (4150m/13615ft).

You'll have a short climb to a saddle between Cerro Chico and Sincholagua. The pass, at 4350m (14272ft), is marked by cairns and boasts great views of Cotopaxi, Antisana, Rumiñahui and the north and south Illiniza peaks. The trail now traverses Cerro Chico, descends to the Río Píta and crosses south, heading directly towards Cotopaxi and Lago Limpiopungo (3800m/12467ft) (4 hours to Lago Limpiopungo or 5 hours to the refuge at 4800m/15748ft on Cotopaxi). If camping by the lake, take good care of your equipment, as there have been a number of thefts in the area. If continuing to Cotopaxi from here, take the road to the turn-off for the refuge and follow this for approximately 9km (5½ miles).

Lago Limpiopungo is a superb area for bird-watching. It is also possible to see black ateolopus toads with their bright orange stomachs. There are a number of 'Andean wolves' in this area – actually foxes about the size of small German shepherd dogs.

Lago Limpiopungo is one of the main access points for ascents of Rumiñahui. Alternatively, you can extend the hike by continuing the trek around Cotopaxi via Mudadero, Río Tambo, Yacu, Hacienda El Tambo, and back to the park entrance at Río Daule, adding an additional 3–4 days to the trip.

SCRAMBLE OF RUMINAHUI

This is an easy ascent with a rocky scramble at the end. Go to Lago Limpiopungo and follow a path on the east shore until you reach some boggy ground to the north of the lake. From here, follow a path for about 1km (½ mile) to find some possible camping places. The trail heads west up a steep-sided valley and ascends the grassy ridge that runs down from the central peak. Follow this to the central peak summit. If you wish to continue to the main summit (4712m/15460ft), descend for a short section to some narrow arêtes. Traverse below these arêtes until you reach a big gully of very red sand and follow this to the summit ridge. Cross the ridge and descend a short way to the western side where you can scramble to the top fairly easily. Be careful of the rotten rock near the top. Descend via the same route (6-9 hours round trip).

COTOPAXI AND CHIMBORAZO DIRECTORY

REGIONAL TRANSPORT
To climb Cotopaxi: Private transport from Quito directly to below Refugio José Ribas (and then a 40-min walk to the refuge), or you can take a bus from Quito to Latacungo or Lasso and then take a pickup truck from there to the refuge.
To climb Chimborazo: Bus to Riobamba and then taxi from there to below Refugio Edward Whymper (45-min walk to refuge).

ACCOMMODATION
Hostería la Cienega, near Lasso, tel: (5933) 719052, fax: (5933) 719182.
Hostería La Andaluza, near Riobamba, tel/fax: (5933) 904223.

LOCAL ACTIVITIES
A visit to Zumbaghua, a market held every Saturday, where locals from the highlands meet with locals from the jungle to exchange news, animals, fruit and vegetables.
Guides:
It is advisable to take a recommended guide from Quito. Climbing

Hosteria la Cienega.

Cotopaxi and Chimborazo can be deceptive. The effects of high altitude combined with the frequent changes in weather on these mountains can be tough on climbers, especially novices. The agencies and guides in the Quito Directory are your best option.

TREK 24: THE PINAN LAKES

This area has much to offer with feral horses, paramo vegetation and tremendous views of the lakes. On a clear day, from the summit of Yanaurco, you can see the whole of the San Pablo Valley.

TREK ESSENTIALS

LENGTH 4–5-day trek. Approx 45km (27miles). Trek from San Francisco de Sachapampa to Lagunas Yanacocha and Burracocha, to finish at Hacienda El Hospital.
ACCESS *To start:* Either drive to the entrance of the Cotocachi Cayapas Nature Reserve, or take a bus to Ibarra and from here arrange transport to the small village of San Francisco de Sachapampa. *On finish:* There may be transport from Hacienda El Hospital, or you can hike uphill to Irunguchi for approx 1–2 hours and catch transport back to Ibarra from there.
HIGHEST POINT Side trip: Yanaurco de Pinan, 4535m (14879ft).
TREK STYLE Backpack/hire *arriero* and burros.
RESTRICTIONS None.
FURTHER OPTIONS Climb Yanaurco; visit Otavalo; ascend Fuya Fuya; ascend Cerro Imbaburra.
MAP Ecuadorean IGM 1: 50 000 Imantag

The trek starts from San Francisco de Sachapampa (2900m/9514ft) where it is possible to camp or, if you are lucky, you may be invited to stay with locals.

San Francisco de Sachapampa to Laguna Yanacocha

It is a 6-hour walk from San Francisco de Sachapampa to Laguna Yanacocha (Black Lake), set below Yanaurco. As you ascend into the layers of mist that cover the cloud forest, you may see local women carrying loads of firewood or taking small flocks of sheep out to pasture. The trail climbs steadily, following a series of ridges, passing through farmland into forest and cloud forest with a great number of epiphytes. Look out for white-tailed deer in this area.

A patchwork landscape in the high areas of Ecuador.

Finally, the trail reaches the paramo near Cerro Tumbatu before heading northwest to Laguna Yanacocha, where you can set up camp at the lake (3800m/12467ft). The area around here is home to many puna hawks, Andean lapwings and the cinerous harrier.

A possible option from this camp is to ascend

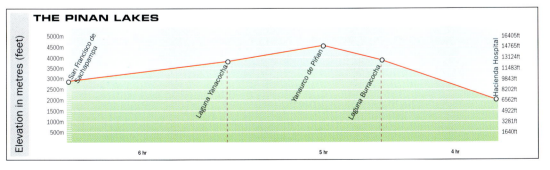

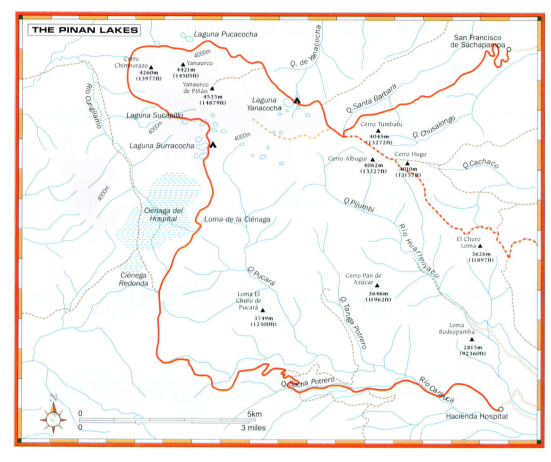

Volcán Yanaurco de Pinan (4535m/14879ft), following the distinct trail from the lake. Go up the scree slopes on the southeast ridge, which eventually leads to the summit ridge. Rocks near the summit are unstable, so watch your footing. From the summit, there are superb views of 40 lakes on the paramo of the Pinan lakeland. The climb takes 5–6 hours and is well worth the effort.

Laguna Yanacocha to Hacienda El Hospital

Trek south from Laguna Yanacocha towards Laguna Burracocha. Follow a trail that goes to the west of Cerro Chimborazo, and then head in a southerly direction across the paramo, following the Río Cungilamo for a short while before heading east.

On the trail from San Francisco.

You will pass Laguna Sucapillo and a number of smaller lakes before you arrive at Laguna Burracocha, where it is possible to camp.

The last day's walk will see you head south, skirting the vast boggy plains of Ciénaga del Hospital, which you keep to your west, and Loma de la Ciénaga to your east. Eventually, after several hours of bog trotting, you'll arrive at a distinctive track that takes you directly east to Hacienda El Hospital, a large working farm with cowboys, whom you will probably have seen out on the paramo, checking on sheep and cattle. There may be transport from Hacienda El Hospital, or you can hike uphill to Irunguchi for approx 1–2 hours and catch transport back to Ibarra from there.

Alternative exit route

An alternative exit is to take the trail from the lake that heads southeast, passing between Cerro Hugo and Cerro Albugui. After climbing steadily to 4000m (13123ft), the trail heads towards El Churo Loma (3626m/11897ft). There are numerous places to camp on the paramo. Don't panic if you wake to the sound of UFOs – it's more likely to be the *zumbador* or Andean snipe, which fly at night-time. Several *cerros* (hills) can be ascended here for views of the area; it is thought that there was once an Incan astro-observatory on Cerro Loma.

The trail heads east to the village of Irunbinc, where you can pick up transport to San Blass and Urcuqui, and back to Ibarra.

OTAVALO DIRECTORY

Local weaving.

Otavalo (2800m/9186ft) is a small town in the north, only 2–3 hours from Ecuador's capital, Quito. It offers a gentle start for trekking and climbing, with easy ascents of Fuya Fuya and Imbaburra volcanoes, and has the added attraction of some wonderfully attractive traditional villages, all within easy distance of the town. Otavalo holds the most famous Indian craft market in the country. The market is held on Saturdays, with the local Otaveleños wearing their traditional costumes of white shirts and trousers or skirts, and long pigtails with beautifully woven braids. The handicrafts are mostly made locally, frequently on back-strap looms in the surrounding villages of the San Pablo Valley (and particularly in the village of Peguche).

The market has a labyrinth of booths offering everything from blankets, jumpers, shirts and jewellery to all manner of items for tourists. There is also an excellent livestock market where you'll find pigs on leads, sheep, cows, lambs and a wide variety of meals that are typical of the area. The occasional llama is also sold here.

In the Andes, markets are an integral part of life and, for the people who spend their time working isolated patches of land or weaving colourful shawls for tourists, they are also a social occasion – a chance to buy and sell goods, but also an opportunity to visit friends and exchange stories and news.

REGIONAL TRANSPORT

Transport by bus from Quito is very easy, and there are frequent buses to Otavalo (2-3 hours) with Transport Otavalo or Transport Los Lagos. It is also very easy to take local transport to the surrounding villages (such as Peguche) or to travel up to Laguna Mojanda, or out to the Cotocachi and Imbaburra areas.

ACCOMMODATION

Hacienda Cusin, San Pablo del Lago, tel: (593) 691 8013, fax: (593) 918003.
Residencia El Rocio, Morales 1170, tel: (593) 920584.
Residencia Isabelita, Roca 11-07.
Hostal los Pendoneres, Calderon 5-10, tel: (593) 921258.
Hotel El Indio, Sucre 12-14, tel: (593) 920601.
Hostal Aya Huma, Peguche village (40 mins from Otavalo).
Hostal Ali Shungi, Calle Quito, tel: (593) 920750.

LOCAL ACTIVITIES

Many of the villages around Otavalo (such as Peguche, Illuman, and Agato) are worth visiting on foot. Care must be taken, however, around the Cascades Peguche, where there have been several robberies over the past couple of years. It is also well worth doing a trip to the Laguna Mojanda and trekking in this area. From Otavalo, it is possible to head south to Laguna Mojanda and Fuya Fuya by taxi. You can camp near the lake or ascend Cerro Fuya Fuya and return to Otavalo the same day. The ascent of Fuya Fuya is an easy scramble, but beware of loose rocks near the top (2-4 hours ascent). The view is excellent and well worth the effort of climbing.

7 VENEZUELA

Venezuela has over forty national parks, providing a mix of well-worn trails and jungle paths where some machete-wielding may be necessary. Whether you're into creeping stealthily around looking for unusual wildlife, or hauling yourself up some technical rock climbs, you will find something to suit in Venezuela.

Sierra Nevada de Mérida is Venezuela's best region for high-mountain trekking, where the possibilities are almost unlimited. And beyond the mountains themselves, many of the villages have preserved their historic architecture to such a degree that visiting them can feel like stepping back in time.

Pico Bolívar dominates the mountains of the Sierra Nevada above Mérida.

Caracas, Venezuela's capital city, was founded in 1560 only to be razed to the ground by the native Indians a year later. It was finally firmly settled by the Spanish conquistadors in 1567 when it gained its full name of Santiago de León de Caracas.

Despite numerous earthquakes, Caracas survived and grew as a stable political and economic centre, gaining its greatest wealth in the 20th-century oil boom. Caracas is now a buzzing metropolis that undoubtedly has its feet set firmly in the modern world, with some of the best contemporary architecture in the whole of South America. However, this wealth lies side by side with growing shanty towns.

The Land

Venezuela has a unique geography and one of the world's most diverse ecosystems. The Sierra Nevada occupies the heart of the Venezuelan Andes and, situated at the extreme northern end of the Andes Range, this section of the magnificent mountain range is severely affected by the weather from the Caribbean.

The Andean paramo is the natural habitat of many large, strangely shaped plants known as frailejones or espeletia.

The often humid winds off the coast cool the foothills at 1800–3000m (5906–9843ft) and greatly affect the vegetation found in the mountains. The hills support a variety of mixed forests – from subtropical rainforest to open pine and cloud forest. Above 3000m (9843ft) forest gives way to alpine meadows, and above 3700m (12139ft) the frailejones or espeletia, a tall, grey-leaved plant typical of the paramo, is found.

The best time for trekking and climbing in Venezuela is November through April. The glaciers here present few difficulties, though any climbing should be done early in the day, as the snow warms rapidly and becomes soggy by midday. In addition, the summits tend to become obscured early in the day, which can make route-finding difficult.

Politics

Despite a strong struggle by Venezuela's indigenous tribes, Spain's first permanent settlement, Nuevo Toledo, was established in Venezuela in 1522. Further resistance was soon subdued by the spread of European ailments, which wiped out two-thirds of the population in the Caracas Valley alone.

Venezuela soon became a neglected colony, as the Spanish crown focused on extracting gold from other areas of its South American empire. This prompted a series of uprisings by restive Venezuelan colonists, until independence was finally achieved in 1821 under the leadership of native son Simón Bolívar.

Having already brought independence to Colombia, Bolívar went on to liberate Ecuador, Peru and Bolivia, uniting them into the state of Gran Colombia. Bolívar's efforts did not survive his death, however, and Venezuela declared full independence in 1830.

Military dictators, political coups and economic instability characterized the country's post-independence period. The discovery of vast oil reserves just before World War I brought a degree of prosperity, but poverty was rife among the majority, and the state of education and health programmes was deplorable.

Military juntas continued to dominate Venezuelan politics until 1959, when civilian Rómulo Betancourt was elected president. Since then, the country has enjoyed an unbroken tradition of civilian democratic rule, with two parties – Accion Democratica and Christian Democrat – alternating in power.

Despite this recent political stability, corruption scandals and threats of military coup have plagued Venezuela's government. The economy, hit hard by the worldwide drop in oil prices, has also remained shaky. In 1998, Venezuelans signalled their frustration with the government by electing a fierce populist president, Hugo Chavez. Chavez argued that the existing political system had become isolated from the people and called for the creation of a National Constituent Assembly to write a new constitution. Chavez was re-elected with a comfortable margin in 2000.

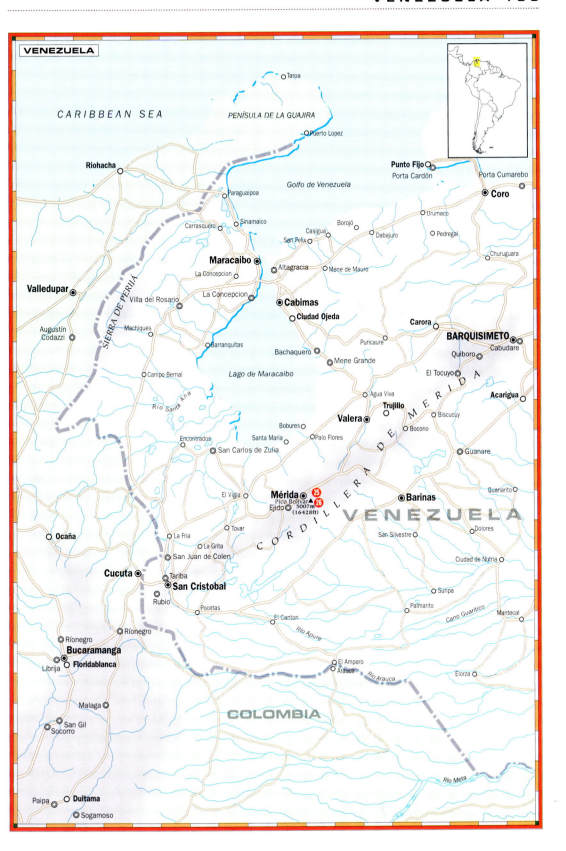

ARRIVING IN VENEZUELA

By Air
Iberia, American Airlines, TAP, Avianca, Air France, Alitalia, British Airways, Avensa and Continental all fly to Caracas from both Europe and North America.

Visas
All travellers should have a passport with at least six months' validity. The airline will issue you a free tourist card (*tarjeta de tourismo*), which is valid for 90 days. Extensions of up to 60 days can be obtained at the Dirección de Extranjeros, Departamento de Tourismo, 2nd floor Av Baralt and Este 8 for a fee.

Travellers who arrive overland must obtain a visa from the Venezuelan consulate. If you plan to enter the country in this way, it is best to sort out your visa before leaving for South America. Your passport must be stamped on entering and leaving the country. Always keep your tourist card and passport handy as ID is frequently asked for.

Time Difference
Venezuela is 4 hours behind Greenwich Mean Time – except during the summer, when the country is 5 hours behind Greenwich Mean Time.

Money
The Bolívar (Bs) is Venezuela's official unit of currency, but the US dollar ($) is widely accepted throughout the country.

Italcambio is one of the many exchange services; it is open 24 hours per day at the airport. Electronic funds can be sent to Italcambio, which offers a money transfer. Money exchanges (*casas de cambio*) are generally closed at weekends, with the exception of Italcambio, which opens until midday. Banks are becoming increasingly reluctant to exchange foreign currency and often restrict their services to clients only.

Treks in Venezuela will often take you through areas of dense vegetation.

EMBASSIES

Australia, Quinta Yolanda, Av Luis Roche (at Trans 6-7 Atamira), tel: (58 2) 261 4632
Canada, Edif Omni Av 6 (between Trans 6 Altamira), tel: (58 2) 264 0833/261 5680
France, Edif Embajada de Francia, Calle Madrid con Av La Trinidad, Las Mercedes, tel: (58 2) 993 6666/993 8592
Germany, Edif Panaven, Piso 12, Av San Juan Bosco con 3a Transversal, Altamira, tel: (58 2) 261 0181/261 1205
Italy, Edif Atrium, Pent House, Calle Sorocaima entre Av Tamanaco y Venezuela, El Rosal, tel: (58 2) 952 7311/952 893.
Netherlands, Edif San Juan, Piso 9, 2a Transversal con Av San Juan Bosco, Altamira, tel: (58 2) 263 3076/263 3622
Spain, Quinta Marmalejo, Av Mohedano entre 1a y 2a Transversal, La Castellana, tel: (58 2) 263 2855/263 3876
UK, Torres Las Mercedes, Piso 3, Av La Estancia Chuaotel, tel: (58 2) 993 4111
USA, Calle F at Calle Suapure Colinas de Valle Arriba, tel: (58 2) 977 2011

TRANSPORT

By Taxi
A system of taxi tickets regulated by the airport allows you to pay at your destination, depending on which zone you are going to. Fares are authorized. Travellers should use only registered taxis and must never accept offers of transportation or guide services from individuals seeking clients on the street.

By *Por Puesto*
Por puestos are vans where you pay by the seat. They ply long-distance routes between towns and

cities throughout the country. Routes have set fares but you can also buy all the seats for a particular journey.

By Bus
Buses go from the Terminal de Pasajeros in Caracas to all areas of the country. Rates are set per area. It is best to travel midweek, as weekends are fairly crazy.

Terminal de Oriente is the terminus for the long-distance buses for eastern Venezuela, whilst westward buses go from La Bandera Terminal on Av Nueva Grande. An airport bus runs to the Terminal de Pasajeros between 4am and 7pm.

By Air
There is an excellent national airline service – Avensa, Aeropostal, Aserca, Oriental and Santa Barbara all fly to Mérida.

ACCOMMODATION
Avila Centre, Av Washington San Bernardino, tel: (58 2) 555 3000, fax: (58 2) 552 8367. Very nice and quiet.
Hotel Residencia Montserrat, Av Avila, Sur Plaza Altamira, tel: (58 2) 263 3533, fax: (58 2) 261 1394. Central and reasonable.
Hotel Tampa, Av Francisco Solano, tel: (58 2) 762 3771, fax: (58 2) 762 0112.
El Cid, Av 2 las Delicias, tel: (58 2) 769 9961, fax: (58 2) 762 6606.
Campo Alegre, Calle 2 Campo Alegre, tel: (58 2) 265 558, fax: (58 2) 262 1243. Friendly and helpful.

FOOD
Food is generally a mix of beef, local fish, beans, steak, sausage, roast chicken and bananas. *Hervido* is a popular stew of beef or fish with chunks of onion, maize, yucca and yam, served with rice.

COMMUNICATIONS
Venezuela's country code is 58, and the city code for Caracas is 2.

Once you find an operable public telephone, it is very easy to place local and international calls. All telephones are operated by CANTV and require phone cards, *tarjetas magneticas*, which can be purchased at corner shops, pharmacies and at all CANTV offices. Most of the public phones are incorporated into the long-distance system, so it is possible to call anywhere in the world without placing your call through an operator. The best place to find a phone that works is in a hotel or metro station.

ELECTRICITY
110 volt/60 cycles AC is the standard electric current throughout Venezuela.

SECURITY
Visitors to Venezuela should be vigilant when spending time in the cities. Theft is the biggest problem, with pickpockets targeting crowded areas such as street markets, bus stations, train stations and airports.

If you are assaulted, you should report the crime to the police as soon as possible. Unfortunately, Venezuelan police have been known to demand bribes. Should you find yourself on the receiving end of such a demand, you should report the official's name and badge number to your embassy immediately.

A bust of Venezuelan hero, Símon Bolívar greets you at the summit of Pico Bolivar (5007m/16428ft), the country's highest point.

TREK 25: SIERRA NEVADA DE MERIDA

A stunning trek and the classic of the Venezuelan Andes, the Sierra Nevada de Mérida offers a great variety of vegetation systems – starting in cloud forest, passing through the paramo up into the high alpine – with spectacular views all the way. With everything from eucalyptus trees, scrub bushes, an amazing array of flowers and prickly pear plants, along with checkered fields of wheat, photographic opportunities are infinite. The local people are mostly farmers and are particularly helpful and keen on meeting foreigners, thus providing a great cultural opportunity which is not to be missed.

Mérida to Loma Redonda

Mérida is home to the highest cable car (teleférico) in the world on Pico Espejo. The trek starts by taking the cable car to La Montaña station at 2435m (7989ft). Once out of the confines of the cable car, look for the trail by the water pipe that lies below the cable way. The path heads up through the cloud forest. Keep an eye out for guans, large tropical birds. The trail emerges at Quebrada La Fría, where it is possible to camp in the forest.

The next day continues through a short section of cloud forest, which gradually changes to eucalyptus trees – a pleasant change from the humidity of the cloud forest – and brings you into the La Redonda area (by the Aguada teleférico station at

TREK ESSENTIALS

LENGTH 4-5-day trek. 50km (31 miles). From Mérida, trek to Quebrada La Fría, Loma Redonda, Los Nevados, El Morro and the Valle Los Calderones to finish at Mucunutan.
ACCESS To start Mérida teleférico to La Montaña; To finish Private transport or por puesto from Mucunutan to Mérida.
HIGHEST POINT Alto de la Cruz, 4540m (14895ft).
TREK STYLE Backpacking.
RESTRICTIONS It is possible to hire burros in El Morro and Los Nevados. Permits are necessary and cost approx US$1 per night. These should be returned at the end of the trip. The trip is best done between December and February.
FURTHER OPTIONS Climb Pico Bolívar.
MAP La Casa del Turista 1: 100 000 La Ciudad de Mérida

3450m/11319ft), where it is possible to camp. Alternatively, you can continue on the trail, which ascends through a series of rocks, to reach Loma Redonda at 4045m (13270ft).

Loma Redonda to Mucunutan

Next, head towards a pass, where the trail you want goes south to Los Nevados, passing through some rocky terrain and eventually into the paramo. It is worth visiting the beautiful Lagunas de Anteojos, set below the cable car. Work your way downhill to a beautiful village, Los Nevados, at 2700m (8858ft), where there are several options for camping or staying at local posadas such as the Gumanchi. If you

Frailejones or espeletias are a typical feature of the paramo.

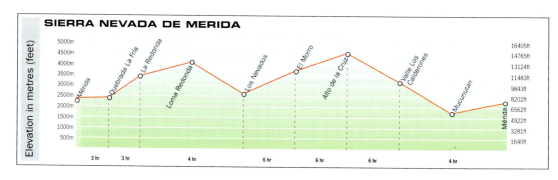

TREK 25: SIERRA NEVADA DE MERIDA 173

While you can take the easy way up into the Sierra Nevada via the *teleférico*, burros have to slog up the mountains.

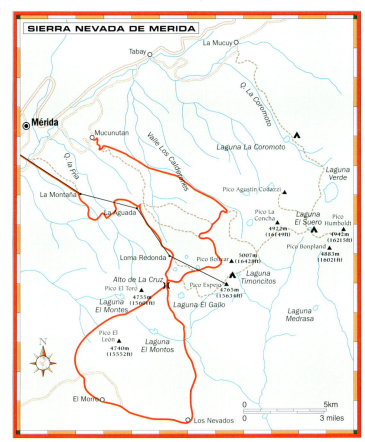

like, you can return to Mérida from here.

The trail, however, continues west to El Morro (from where you can return to Mérida by *por puesto*), passing through semi-desert landscape and staying above the Río Nuestra Señora. From here, it is a steep ascent to return to the paramo, with its numerous frailejones – giant plants that looks like monks in robes – to reach the Alto de la Cruz at 4540m (14895ft). From the pass, it is possible to see El Torro, El León, Pico Espejo and Pico Bolívar. The trail descends to Valle Los Calderones and then enters cloud forest. Camp can be made in a clearing at 3350m (10991ft) with tremendous views to the north.

The next morning, descend through more cloud forest with huge ferns, parrots, butterflies and giant snails. The trail eventually arrives at Mucunutan at 1700m (5577ft). From here, you can pick up transport to Mérida.

PEAK: PICO BOLIVAR

This, the highest peak in Venezuela at 5007m (16428ft), was named after Simón Bolívar, the liberator of many countries in South America. Access is best via the cable car (*teleférico*) from Mérida that runs to Loma Redonda at 4045m (13270ft). Follow a trail to Pico Espejo and camp at Laguna Timoncitos (4750m/15584ft).

You can climb the Normal Route or the Weiss Route. The Normal Route is mostly a rock scramble (Grade II–IV) with a very exposed summit ridge. The Weiss Route follows a gully (which can contain snow) from directly above the lake. At around the halfway mark, enter a chimney to gain the ridge. From here, move northwest and follow ledges to the summit. It takes around 4 hours to reach the summit. Descend via same route.

Pico Bolivar offers visitors a scramble or the choice of a more technical climb via the Weiss Route.

CLIMB ESSENTIALS

SUMMIT Pico Bolivar 5007m (16428ft)
ROUTE Normal/Weiss
PRINCIPAL CAMP Laguna Timoncitos 4700m (15420ft)
GRADE Alpine Grade PD (Weiss Route)

You will pass numerous beautiful, azure lakes on this trek.

Trek Extension

If you would like to extend your trip, you can head west from El Morro and enter Quebrada Mosnanda, and then Quebrada El Banco. There are places for camping in both valleys.

The trail then climbs and crosses several ridges to meet an old jeep road that goes to Mérida via Quebrada Mucusabacha. It is possible to follow an old track that eventually meets the main Mérida road. There are numerous possibilities for camping along this section.

TREK 26: PICO HUMBOLDT

Pico Humboldt (4942m/16215ft) is Venezuela's second highest peak. The summit of the country's highest peak, Pico Bolívar (5007m/16428ft), is 6km (4 miles) away and is long and technical compared to Humboldt, which is rounded and relatively straightforward. Bolívar is only covered in snow in the summer, whereas Humboldt has a permanent glacier. The area around Humboldt offers superb trekking, with a variety of terrain and scenery, and the ascent of the peak makes this a superb destination in the Venezuelan Andes.

La Mucuy to Laguna Verde

Drive to La Mucuy at 2300m (7546ft), a village famous for its wood carving and naïve sculptures, 30 mins from Mérida. Here is the entrance to the Sierra Nevada Park. The trail ascends through cloud forest with dense vegetation, parrots and giant snails. Crossing several streams and small waterfalls, you eventually break out of the forest at 3300m (10827ft) with a view of Laguna La Coromoto on the

Entering a cloud forest in the Sierra Nevada de Mérida.

TREK ESSENTIALS

LENGTH 4-5 days. 45km (29 miles). From La Mucuy, trek to Laguna Verde, Laguna Timoncitos, Pico Espejo Base Camp and Loma Redonda to Los Nevados, where you can pick up trek 25.
ACCESS *To start* Drive to La Mucuy by *por puesto*, taxi or 4-wheel drive. *On finish* Return from Los Nevados by *por puesto* or taxi to Mérida.
HIGHEST POINT Laguna Timoncitos, 4700m (15420ft).
TREK STYLE Backpack/burros; *arriero* recommended.
RESTRICTIONS Park fee payable and minimum of 2 people required to do the trip.
FURTHER OPTIONS Climb Pico Bolívar, Pico Humboldt and Pico Espejo.
MAPS La Casa del Turista 1: 100 000 La Ciudad de Mérida

PARQUE NACIONAL SIERRA LA CULATA

North of Mérida, there is a smaller range of mountains locally known as La Culata or 'the butt'. This is an area of paramo, with the peaks of Piedras Blancas (4762m/15623ft), Tucani (4400m/14436ft), and Los Conejos (4200m/13780ft). It was made a national park in 1989 and stretches from Timotes to La Azulita, boasting many varied, fascinating ecosystems. The rare spectacled bear and numerous different plants can be found in the area, especially frailejones. It is well worth a visit, and offers a variety of short treks.

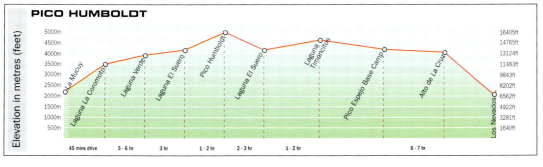

176 VENEZUELA

The red hot poker plant, Mérida.

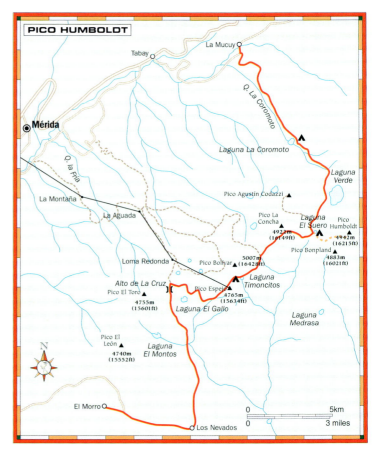

paramo. From here, the trail heads across open ground and initially climbs gradually to reach a rocky area that may require some scrambling on narrow exposed paths. It finally descends to Laguna Verde at 3900m (12795ft), where it is possible to camp.

Laguna Verde to Los Nevados

The trail then heads to Laguna El Suero at 4200m (13780ft) where it enters a hanging valley to the base of Pico Humboldt. From this valley, it is possible to ascend the peak. Follow a trail up to the glacier edge, where you should rope up. Follow the glacier up towards the summit with a final short section of 45° snow and ice just below the summit (4–5 hours ascent, descent via the same route).

If you don't wish to climb Pico Humboldt, follow the vague trail out of the valley and scramble over loose rocks. Then you will finally descend to the paramo and hike towards Pico Bolívar. Camp can be made at Laguna Timoncitos at 4750m (15584ft), with an easy side-trip scramble to the top of Pico Espejo (4765m/15634ft). It is also possible to descend to Los Nevados via Alto de La Cruz. From Los Nevados, you can follow the Sierra Nevada de Mérida trek (trek 25) or return to Mérida.

Alternatively, you can descend to Mucunutan, from where it is possible to go to Curbati where you can take transport back to Mérida.

VENEZUELA'S SNOW-CAPPED PEAKS

The Indians of the Venezuelan Andes believe that the country's snow-capped peaks were formed by giant white eagles. According to legend, Caraby, the daughter of the Sun and the Moon, saw white eagles perched high on some rock cliffs on the summit of the peaks. She decided to investigate and see for herself their brilliant plumage. Up she climbed until she finally arrived at their perch. Extending her hand to grab some feathers, she frightened the eagles, who screeched and flapped their wings. Many feathers rained down over five peaks. Caraby fled, not stopping until she returned to the valley floor. Looking back, the eagles had disappeared, and the only trace was the sprinkling of white feathers, which now form the snow-capped peaks of Venezuela.

MERIDA DIRECTORY

The treks and climbs described in this chapter are based out of the small university city of Mérida. Originally founded in 1558, Mérida is very proud of its Spanish roots and its distinct Andean heritage.

ARRIVING IN MERIDA
By Air
There are daily flights from Caracas, Maracaibo, Cumana and Puerto Ayacucho with Avensa, Lai and Air Venezuela.

By Bus
The bus terminal is on Av Las Americas, about 3km (2 miles) from the city centre. A bus to Caracas takes 12 hours on the Trans-Andean route via Valera and Pico.

ACCOMMODATION
This consists mainly of *posadas* (bed and breakfasts). In some villages families offer bed and either breakfast and/or an evening meal at reasonable prices, such as Gumanchi in Los Nevados.

Hotels and Posadas:
Hotel Prado, Rio Av 1, la Hoyada de Milla, tel: (58 74) 520704, fax: (58 74) 525192. Luxury hotel, run by the University's hotel school.
Hotel Gran Balcon, Av Domingo Pena, tel: (58 74) 520366, fax: (58 74) 529055. Quiet and friendly. Ask for a room with a view. Good storage for luggage.
Hotel Teleférico, Plaza Las Heronias, tel: (58 74) 527370. Popular with young travellers.
Hotel Italia, Calle 19, Av –3, tel: (58 74) 525737. Also popular with young travellers.
Posada La Casona de Margot, Av 4, Calles 15-1, tel: (58 74) 513312. Nice and quiet.
Luz Carabello, Av 2, Plaza Sucre, tel: (58 74) 525411. Very popular and well run.
Posada Calle 18, tel: (58 74) 522986. Pleasant, family-run place. English spoken.
Posada Las Heronias, Calle 24, tel: (58 74) 522665. Very well run; excellent information on trekking in the area; great views.
Finca la Trintera, tel: (58 74) 440760, email: bratt@ing.ula.ve. Magical farmhouse setting. Contact Mary Woodward.

LOCAL ACTIVITIES
Astrophysical Observatory (3600m/11811ft), Sierra del Norte, near Apartaderos and Pico Aguiles, tel: (58 74) 712459, www.cida.ve. Open 9 July–20 Sept. Entrance fee US$3.
Xamu Pueblo, Indigena, near Lagunillas, 25km (15½ miles) west of Mérida. This explores Andean customs since the Spanish conquest, and shows how the Mucujin people lived, farmed and wove.
Laguna de Urao, near Lagunillas. This lake is a source of soda crystals, which are used in the making of *chimo,* a paste of tobacco and soda that some locals use as a stimulant and to avoid hunger.
Jaji, A reconstructed colonial village, about 45 mins drive from Mérida. It is possible to stay at one of several *posadas* (bed and breakfasts) near here.

A typical paramo cloud hangs low over the town of Mérida.

Piedras Blancas, tel/fax: (58 74) 635633, contact: Yves Lesenfants. Ecological Reserve northwest of Mucuchies. There is a refuge here and it is also possible to camp.

Trekking:
Gumanchi Expeditions, Calle 24, tel/fax: (58 74) 522080, email: geca@bolivar.funrmd.gov.ve, www.ftech.net/~geca. Excellent organization, guides and reasonable rates (ask Patricia, the manager, for information). They also run a *posada* in Los Nevados.
Montana Adventure, Apartado Postal 645, Mérida, tel: (58 74) 662867, email: andes@telcel.net.ve.
Natoura, Calle 24, No 8-237, email: emailnatoura@telcel.net.ve.

USEFUL ADDRESSES
El Canvite Centro Campesino, Calle Bolivar 1, tel/fax: (58 74) 81163. This is a training centre for local *campesinos* that produces a list and map of local farmers and homeowners offering guest rooms in return for planning and administration advice from the centre. This is part of a self-help programme to improve standards of living and earning capabilities, along with improving farming practices. Also offers guiding for trekkers and craft-making.
Inparque, Calle 19, Av 5-6. Open: Mon-Fri, 8.30am-noon, 1.30pm-5pm. You must get permits (you will need your passport) from Inparque for all camping trips and day trips. They also sell maps of the national parks.
Federacion Venezolana de Montanismo and Escalada, tel: (58 74) 521665.
Andino de Rescate GAR, tel: (58 74) 444666.
Association Meridena de Andinismo, tel: (58 74) 526886.
Teleférico, The *teleférico* is the highest cable car in the world (4765m/15633ft) and covers 12km (7½ miles). You must make reservations to use the *teleférico* to access any treks or climbs. It is possible to get off at any of the intermediate stages.

MAPS
La Casa Turista, Av 3, near Plaza Bolivar. Has a selection of maps.

THE ANDEAN ENVIRONMENT

GEOLOGY
By Stuart Holmes

South America may once have been part of the ancient landmass known as Gondwanaland. About 150 million years ago, it broke away from what is now Africa and began to drift westwards to its present position. During the Cretaceous geological period, between 136 million and 65 million years ago, the Pacific tectonic plate collided with the South American plate. The denser rocks of the oceanic plate started to, and still continue to, slide beneath the more buoyant continental plate in a process called subduction. The descending plate acts like a bulldozer on a conveyor belt, folding and uplifting the existing sedimentary rocks on the land. This geological action created the longest mountain chain above sea level in the world – the Andes.

The Andes run like a 7000-km (4350-mile) back bone down the length of South America, from northern Colombia and Venezuela to the far south of Chile, where they disappear into the sea. The mountains exceed a height of 3600m (11811ft) for more than half their length, reaching a maximum height of 6960m (22836ft) on Aconcagua in Argentina. Perhaps the most surprising aspect of this range is how narrow it is over much of its length – the high part of the range is typically less than 150km (93 miles) across.

The oldest and most stable structural element of the continent is the shield area of the Brazilian and Guiana highlands of the east and northeast. It comprises a pre-Cambrian (before 570 million years ago) complex of igneous and metamorphic rocks. In most places, the shield is overlaid by sedimentary rocks, mostly of Paleozoic age (570 million to 225 million years ago), although some areas of younger basalts occur, notably in south Brazil. Fossils found in the Brazilian highlands offer evidence of continental drift, lending support to the theory that, in the past, the continent was linked to Gondwanaland, the great landmass incorporating Africa and Asia.

The complex that underlies the Patagonian plateau is largely mantled by sediments deposited in the Mesozoic era (225 million to 65 million years ago) and Tertiary period (65 million to 2.5 million years ago) and by basalts of recent formation.

Material eroded from the old shield areas contributed to the thick deposits of sediments in the surrounding seas. These sedimentary formations were uplifted repeatedly in the Mesozoic era to form the coastal ranges of Chile and south Peru, and the higher and more extensive Andes. This mountain-building process, which continued through the Tertiary period, was accompanied by intrusions of magma (molten rock) and the formation of volcanoes. The glaciers of the southernmost Andes are remnants of the great ages of glaciation of the Quaternary period (beginning 2.5 million years ago). The erosion of the highlands continues to contribute sediments to surrounding lowlands.

The Ring of Fire

As the Pacific slab slides down the subduction zone, it warms slowly. Partial melting takes place in the mantle (the part of the earth between the crust and the core), with the most volatile compounds rising and erupting from volcanoes on the surface. The active Andean volcanoes form a line parallel to the plate boundary and represent part of the 'Ring of Fire', the string of volcanoes that mark the tectonic plate margins around the Pacific Ocean. The composition of the lava depends on the depth from which it comes. The older and deeper the descending slab, the longer the mantle has been subjected to partial melting, and the more silica-rich the magmas, or hot molten rock, produced.

The Andean volcanoes represent some of the highest peaks in the range. Ojos del Salado, at 6908m (22664ft), on the border between Chile and Argentina, is the world's highest volcano (now dormant).

Movement between the Pacific tectonic plate and the South American plate is not smooth and is characterized by long periods of relative equilibrium followed by the sudden release of stress or strain energy. The resultant shock waves, originating as deep as 700km (435 miles) below the surface, cause the earth tremors and earthquakes that are regularly felt on the surface. This is one of the most geologically active areas in the world.

The most catastrophic seismic disaster (earthquake) yet experienced in the western hemisphere occurred in Peru on 31 May 1970, killing more than 80,000 people. The resulting Huascarán landslide destroyed the cities of Yungay and Ranrahirca, killing 18,000 people. As much as 50–100 million cubic metres fell 600m (1969ft) off the mountain and then travelled 4.5km (2¾ miles) down a valley in 3 minutes at velocities of 280km per hour (174 miles per hour). It left virtually no debris but it must have moved as a 100-m (328-ft) thick flow. As the flow continued, it slowed, depositing boulders of 700–14000 tonnes. An examination of the local geology revealed that this was not the biggest fall to have come off Huascarán.

Geologically speaking, the Andes are new mountains. The landscape we see today is the result of on-going geological and weathering processes. Continental plates are still colliding and the vertical upheaval of the mountains continues. As the rivers cut into the relatively soft sediments they create some of the biggest canyons in the world. Glaciers continue to carve their characteristic valleys, as well as some of the most spectacular sheer-walled granite pinnacles anywhere.

The picture-postcard snow-covered cone of Volcan Villarrica.

The Lie of the Land

The Andes are not a single line of high peaks but rather are subdivided into many smaller units: cordilleras (mountain ranges); *nudos* (knots or clusters of peaks); and the Altiplano (high plateaux).

Just north of the Colombia–Ecuador border is the Nudo de Pasto, a complex knot of volcanic peaks, out of which run the three main ranges of the Colombian Andes. The Cordillera Occidental (the western range) runs parallel to the Pacific Ocean and is moderately high, with most peaks below 3700m (12139ft). The Cordillera Central, which extends northwards to about 9°N latitude, is a high, rough range – and a barrier to modern transportation in Colombia; many of the mountains here are volcanic. The Cordillera Oriental (the eastern range) is wider and longer than the other two ranges. It extends to about 12°N latitude at the Guajira Peninsula, which juts into the Caribbean Sea at the Colombia–Venezuela border. Within the Cordillera Oriental, there are a number of wide, flat plateaux, which are the home of about one third of Colombia's population. The national capital, Bogotá, is located here.

A branch of the Cordillera Oriental runs eastwards into Venezuela, where it is known as the Cordillera de Mérida. There are several snow-capped peaks (the highest, Pico Bolívar, reaches 5007m/16428ft) and the range is generally rough. Outlying parts of the Cordillera do Mérida extend eastwards in Venezuela, but they are lower and have gentler slopes than the mountains in the western part of the country.

In Ecuador, the Andes are composed of two parallel ranges – both volcanic – and a series of basins. The western range, the Cordillera Occidental, is generally lower than the eastern range, the Cordillera Oriental, though the highest peak in Ecuador (Chimborazo, at 6310m/20702ft) is located in the Cordillera Occidental. Repeated volcanic eruptions have filled the rift valley that separates the two cordilleras. Transverse ridges also tend to divide the valley into a series of discrete basins. The floors of these basins are more than 2700m (8858ft) high in the north, whereas the basins in southern Ecuador are at elevations of less than 1800m (5906ft). In the past, most of Ecuador's population lived in the highland basins, but today, fewer than half of its people live there.

A large number of separate ranges, surrounding several areas of high plateau country, make up the Andes in Peru. In contrast to the northern Andes of Ecuador and Colombia, most of Peru's mountains are not volcanic in origin. Volcanoes are found only in the southwestern part of Peru. There are many areas of extremely rough terrain in the country, however, and some of the mountains are very high and snow-covered throughout the year. The Peruvian Andes are much wider than the ranges to the north.

Several of the cordilleras in Peru are made up of sharp peaks that are famous among the world's mountaineers. Such chains as the Cordillera Blanca and the Cordillera de Vilcabamba are made up of magnificent peaks. The highest mountain in Peru, Huascarán (6786m/22264ft), is part of the Cordillera Blanca.

In southern Peru, western Bolivia and northernmost Chile and Argentina, high plateaux are the major feature of the Andes. These high plains are called the Altiplano. The Altiplano ranges in elevation from about 4570m (14993ft) in the north to about 3800m (12467ft) in the south; east and west of it, there are high mountain ranges. The Andes are at their widest here – stretching almost 640km (398 miles) from east to west. The most interesting feature of the Altiplano is Lake Titikaka, which lies along the border of Peru and Bolivia. Titikaka is the highest navigable lake in the world and the largest lake in South America.

From the Altiplano, the Andes extend southwards through Argentina and Chile to the tip of the continent. In general, the chain becomes lower as it runs southward, though the Andes' highest peak, Aconcagua, is in Argentina, near the Chile–Argentina border, at latitude 33°S. In northern and south-central Chile, many of the peaks are volcanoes, some of which are fairly active. Passes through these mountains are usually high and difficult; the southern Andes are a barrier to trade and transportation. Climatic conditions also make the Andes in Chile and Argentina relatively inhospitable.

Mines and Minerals

The melting of the subducted ocean crust is responsible for the formation of rich metallic ore deposits of gold, silver, tin, tungsten, bismuth, vanadium, copper and lead. Hence, the Andes contain many rich mines. Copper is found in several parts of Peru and Chile. Chuquicamata in northern Chile is the largest single lode of copper-bearing ore. Peru and Chile control about one quarter of the world's reserves of copper. Bolivia is the main producer of tin, while Peru produces lead and zinc.

FLORA AND FAUNA
By Val Pitkethly

The region from the eastern Andes down to the Amazon basin is one of the most species-rich and diverse areas on earth. In comparison, the western Andes is dry and barren, with paramos and punas – high plateaux with shrubland and grassland.

The paramo, which lies at 3700–4500m (12139–14764ft), runs north into Ecuador, Colombia and Venezuela. The Andes are divided in the middle by the 1000-km long (621-mile long) Altiplano, a high plain at 3200–4000m (10499–13123ft) which stretches from southern Peru to northern Bolivia as well as south into parts of Chile and Argentina.

The Altiplano has a high level of UV radiation and incredible evaporation rates. For example, Lake Titikaka can drop by 1–3m (3–9ft) over a 240-km (149-mile) surface area in a season. The Altiplano is home to many of the indigenous peoples, as well as llamas, alpacas and pre-Hispanic ruins.

Higher still is the puna, at 4400m (13123ft), where the snowline varies with the latitude. In Peru, Ecuador and Bolivia it is often around the 4900m (16076ft) mark, whilst in Chile and Argentina it is much lower. Here, hardy vegetation such as ichu grass, cushion plants, dwarf trees and herbaceous plants have made adaptations to the climate, such as small thick leaves that make them less susceptible to the frost. The leaves often have waxy skins to reflect solar radiation, and fine hairy down for insulation. Leaves are often rosette-shaped, to prevent them from shadowing each other during the day, and to protect their delicate centres. Plants are usually compact and close to the ground, where the temperature tends to be more constant. The chemical composition of some leaves changes, and acts like an antifreeze.

You will find espeletias, bromeliads, gentians, orchids, Rima Rima and many other plants such as those in the pea and snapdragon families. Quenal, or polylepsis trees, hold the record for altitude amongst trees and are found growing at up to 5000m (16404ft).

Plants and the People

Many of the plants found growing in the Andes are used as natural medicines, for dyes or as tools. For example, Wancu wancu, or Angel's Hair, is used as a treatment for liver ailments, whilst the leaves are dried and used to cauterize wounds. Garbanzillo, of the sweet pea family, is used as a soap for washing fine woollens; it is also used for treating fractures in animals. Puya Raimondii is rare and flowers only once every 28–30 years. The stems are dried and often used as lightweight benches for children at school. The plant has other uses too: to insulate ceilings in buildings in the puna area and as a buffer at boat landing sites on Lake Titikaka. Barberry fruit is used as blue dye, whilst the roots create a yellow dye. In remote Peruvian villages, Rima Rima flowers are placed on the tongues and under the chins of mute children to encourage speech. Various sedges are used for roofing material.

Related to llamas, alpacas are famous for their soft wool.

Fauna

The fauna of the Andes includes vicuñas, guanacos, llamas and alpacas, all members of the cameloid family. Vicuña are a protected species, having been hunted almost to extinction, particularly in Peru. Puma are very rarely seen today, although they do still exist. There are the Fuegian Fox (actually a wolf) and the Patagonian Fox. The tapir, a wild animal which inhabits the dense forests of Ecuador (especially the eastern highland cloud forest), is particularly difficult to catch a glimpse of. Viscachas, which look like a small rabbit crossed with a squirrel, and make high piercing whistles, are found in the rocky areas around Base Camps and high passes in Peru and Bolivia. White-tailed deer or huemul inhabit highland puna slopes with dense quenal forest nearby. Giant toads can be found in the Lake Titikaka area, where dwarf Andean pudu deer are also to be found. The spectacled bear is another rarity that has been ruthlessly hunted. There are also armadillos, whose skins are often used in the construction of churangos, the guitars famous throughout Peru and Bolivia. The Andes also have a full complement of snakes and lizards.

The birdlife of the Andes is phenomenal – Andean lapwings, condors, teal, hummingbirds, caracaras, torrent ducks, flycatchers, Zumbador (Andean snipe), gulls, coots, geese, ibises, black necked swans. Aplomado falcons, royal eagles and Magellenic woodpeckers are just a few of the species you are likely to encounter.

MINIMAL IMPACT TREKKING

Trekking and climbing have a big impact on the lives of South America's indigenous peoples. Both your attitude and your behaviour are important culturally and enviromentally. Start by remembering that you are a guest in someone else's country and being respectful of local customs and lifestyles. Be prepared to be patient and friendly – a smile and a genuine interest in the people goes a long way. Remember that each country has its own customs. They may seem strange to you, but the South American people would probably feel the same way if they had the opportunity to visit your home country.

Locals have a right to privacy and respect; shoving a camera in someone's face may mean a great photo that you can boast about at home, but imagine what it's like on the receiving end. Please avoid being obtrusive with your camera, particularly with older women in the mountain areas of Peru, Bolivia and Ecuador.

You can also make an effort to minimize your impact on the environment. Leave no trace of your trip, by following some simple dos and don'ts.

No matter what type of trip you are doing, be it backpacking or a full-service trek and climb with guides and cooks, remember that just because you have paid does not mean that you are no longer responsible for how you travel and the effect you have on the local people and environment: the buck stops with you.

Do remove any excess packaging (such as film boxes and battery cardboard) before you travel. Do make sure you take used batteries to a main centre or your home country. Dispose of any waste at a suitable place. Leave places as you found them – or, better still, clean up your camping areas (including rubbish left by others less responsible than yourself). Encourage others to behave responsibly.

When taking internal road or air transport, remove all the labels as soon as you arrive at your destination so that they are not ripped off as your bags are carried along a trail by burros or porters.

Make sure you take your litter away with you, leaving the environment clean for those who follow.

Try to use local produce whenever possible, as it saves on rubbish. Some of the Base Camps in the Cordillera Blanca's most popular climbs are filled with foil packets from dehydrated food brought from all over the world. If you must use freeze-dried food, make sure you remove all signs of its use. Take it back to the centre where you are based or take it home.

Take care to avoid contaminating water supplies (for example, make sure your toilet is at least 30m/98ft away from any water source). Burn toilet paper or carry it with you. Tampons, napkins and cotton buds are not biodegradable and make awful litter. Wrap them up carefully and return them to the city or main centre where you are based.

Using firewood on a trek is a big problem in many areas. There is such a huge pressure on the forested areas from their use by locals that deforestation is a major concern in many countries. Please ensure that you use an alternative fuel source such as white gas (*benzina blanca*), petrol or kerosene and make sure you have enough to provide your staff with fuel to cook for themselves (along with a tent and warm clothing) so that the temptation to collect wood to burn for warmth is removed.

Think about the impact of your actions. Dress accordingly: as a general rule, tight, revealing clothing is offensive, particularly in the highland areas of Ecuador, Peru and Bolivia. Learn some of the local language, such as 'hello', 'goodbye' and 'thank you'. Don't cause unnecessary noise.

As far as medical aid for local people is concerned, consider where you are and whether it is appropriate. Is there a local doctor or health post nearby? In many areas, there are no facilities and to get to one for a local is very expensive. Medicines are also costly, so you must assess the situation in each case and decide what is helpful. Don't give out antibiotics unless you have sufficient medicine to cover a full course – there is little point in giving one or two tablets. Consider whether you can explain well enough to the patient what you are giving them and how to use it correctly. Is there a local with you who could help explain? In the Cordilleras Huayhuash and Blanca of Peru, many of the women only speak Quechua and understand little Spanish, and in Bolivia the locals speak Aymara. If you have a local *arriero* with you, ask him to explain what the medicine is for and how to take it.

CULTURAL CONSIDERATIONS

The mountain areas you will be travelling through (with the exception of some of the treks in Chile and Argentina) are not wilderness areas. They have been

The warm welcome given by the mountain people is one of the best reasons to visit the Andes.

populated for centuries and used for growing crops and grazing animals. The mountain trails often pass fair-sized villages, though many families live in one- or two-house settlements scattered throughout the mountain valleys. People usually speak Quechua or Aymara (their first language) along with Spanish. The older women often speak only the indigenous language and are often very shy or even rather frightened of foreigners, especially when their men are not around. Smile and say hello. These people live in a small, traditional world lacking technology and modern conveniences but this does not mean they are not intelligent. Bear in mind when you talk to them that they are probably conversing in their second language – usually fairly fluently.

Communication is always possible and does not require fluency in another language. People will know if you are taking a genuine interest in them. The common word 'gringo' is neither positive or negative but just a way of describing you. You will often find yourself the centre of attention; accept this – you are often a welcome change, just like having television for the day.

If invited into people's homes, be respectful. You may be invited to share a meal, and the best idea in terms of 'payment' is to try and offer something in return such as a souvenir from your country or some treat that they cannot find locally. When offering money, use your common sense. Do they need it? Is it helpful? Would it cause offence? When eating with locals, you will generally be fed first, often in a separate room. This is the custom with all guests but, with some extra effort, you can usually persuade them to sit and eat with you – or at least in the same room.

People often want to buy equipment that you have but they usually have little idea of its actual cost (camp stoves are especially popular). Explain carefully why you need it and try and equate it to something that they use in their daily life that would be difficult to do without or replace. Mountain folks have little sense of time so be careful when asking how long it will take to get from A to B or when asking for directions. Having often lived all their lives in the area they will overlook simple things, as they seem of no significance to them. Also, keep your questions specific.

Photography is a major interest with most trekkers and climbers and this is often a major cause of problems with locals, as they get tired of having cameras stuck in their faces. Think before you take a picture and always show respect.

Handing out sweets and balloons on the trail is not a good idea. Sure, you'll get great smiles for the photos, but you are making beggars out of the children and causing cultural degradation. Think before you give out anything for nothing; are you actually helping the children or just making yourself feel good? It's better to carry some pens and books and then, if a child helps you with something, you can give him or her something or drop the pens at the local school.

Trekking offers you a unique chance to see the world through the eyes of the locals. Take this chance and it will open up a whole new world.

ASKING LOCALS QUESTIONS

People like to please and rather than say 'no' will often agree in order not to offend. In the northern part of the Cordillera Blanca, I once asked directions to the next village, pointing to an obvious looking pass and saying 'is that the way to...?'. The answer was 'yes', so off I went, only to meet the same person much later in the next village. As we talked, I asked him which way he had come and why I hadn't seen him on the trail. 'Oh, senorita, I came the quick way over a different pass. It's much faster.' 'Well why didn't you mention it?' I replied. 'Oh, well you asked if the other pass came here, and it does, and I would make you angry if I told you you were wrong!'

MOUNTAIN PHOTOGRAPHY

[By STEVE RAZZETTI]

In conjunction with a meticulously kept journal, a collection of photographs is the best way of recording your impressions of the Andes – for capturing those precious moments of scenic splendour and remembering the people encountered along the way. Few travel these days without a camera, but attitudes to photography vary from the casual to the complete obsessive. As you will be carrying your camera equipment for many weeks or months during a season trekking, careful consideration should be given to both the type of camera chosen and the film stock used.

PRINT PHOTOGRAPHY

If all you require at the end of your trip is a set of prints to pass round amongst your family and friends, then using one of the middle speed (100–200ASA) print films and having it processed by a normal commercial service should be adequate. In this case, a compact auto-focus camera with a zoom lens and built-in flash is ideal. There are hundreds to choose from, but for mountain and general outdoor use go for a waterproof or 'splash-proof' model, as these tend to have rubber seals that also serve to keep dust at bay.

If you go for the print option it is not really worth carrying a heavy professional SLR system unless you are prepared to pay for expensive specialist processing and printing. However beautifully you may monitor your exposures – to capture particular features of a landscape, for example, or detail in a wonderful shadowy forest – using the sophisticated exposure meter on a modern SLR, all this will be lost when you come to have the film processed and printed by a standard service, which simply take an average exposure value for the print, thus losing any high degree of contrast.

SLIDE PHOTOGRAPHY

If you think you may want to give the odd slide show, reproduce some of your images for framing or even consider publishing the odd shot you should opt for colour slides. The total contrast capable of being accurately rendered by a slide film is over 10 times that which a print can reproduce. In a mountain environment, where scenes often include snow slopes in bright sunshine and valleys in deep shadow, the benefits of reversal or slide films are enormous. As this type of film is developed by a set process, any subtle exposure variations made with the camera are faithfully reproduced in the final transparency.

By 'bracketing', ie. making one exposure at the value indicated by your camera's meter, and then another either side of it by up to one f-stop, you can be sure of capturing the effect you want. For example, if the meter indicates an exposure of $1/250$ sec @ f8, also shoot $1/250$ @ f5.6 and $1/250$ @ f11. Many new cameras have the facility to do this automatically.

A couple of other factors should be considered for slide photography. The exposure meters of most SLR cameras are calibrated for print film, and slide emulsions tend to be more sensitive. As a rule of thumb, I always underexpose slide film by a third or two-thirds of a stop – that is, I shoot 50ASA film at 64ASA or 80ASA. This is only a very minor adjustment, but it does allow the film to produce maximum colour saturation. Every camera's meter is slightly different, so if you are taking your photography seriously, shoot a roll of your chosen film at home and bracket each exposure by up to two whole stops and observe the results. This will also give you a good idea of how the film handles over- and under-exposure.

CHOICE OF FILM AND LENSES

The choice of film is always a matter that provokes debate. The faster the film (the more sensitive to light), the less capable it is of reproducing colour saturation or contrast. Slower films are richer, sharper and have greater latitude. They also require more light to create an image, and in low-light conditions this can be problematic as your shutter-speeds decrease, introducing the possibility of camera-shake blurring the picture. The longer the focal length of the lens, the more pronounced this effect becomes, and for sharp hand-held exposures your shutter speed should be a value higher than the focal length of your lens in mm. Don't shoot slower than $1/125$ sec with a 135mm lens. High in the Andes the light is often intense. This problem only really occurs at dawn and dusk, but enthusiasts will want to capture precisely these times of day and thus the choice of lens is crucial.

The speed of film you choose will affect the type of lens you need. Let us assume that you want perfectly exposed, pin-sharp slides with rich colour saturation. Fuji's Velvia is an obvious choice, but it's only rated at 50ASA, and by the time you've put a polarizing filter on your camera you've effectively reduced this to 18ASA. Most zoom lenses have maximum apertures in the f3.5–f5.6 range, and in low light, shooting slow film, you would be struggling with shutter-speeds of $1/4$ sec or slower, which is much too slow for hand-held exposures. To allow yourself flexibility in these light levels, you should use a faster lens (ie one capable of transmitting more light). Professional photographers always choose this option and use lenses with maximum apertures of f2, f1.8 or even f1.4 (and even then often in conjunction with a tripod). It is possible to buy faster-than-average zoom lenses, but they are prohibitively expensive. Almost 99 per cent of pictures taken with a zoom tend to be at one or other

Storm clouds gather over the Cordillera Blanca Tranquilo (trek 18).

end of its range, where a zoom lens is at its least efficient. I would always argue for carrying two or three fast lenses with fixed focal lengths akin to the extent of a zoom. Use a 28mm f2.8, a 50mm f1.4 and a 90mm f2 rather than a 28–80mm f5.6 zoom. You may have to think about your photography a little more, but your results will be vastly improved.

BATTERIES AND CAMERA CARE

Another key point to consider when choosing a camera for the mountains is the type of battery required. Modern auto-focus, power-wind cameras of all types rely totally on battery power to function. There is actually a strong argument for using vintage mechanical cameras. Alkaline cells perform very poorly in low temperatures, though a camera that runs on lithium cells performs better and will be happily snapping away before dawn at 5000m (16405ft) when the thermometer is showing -25°C. All batteries drain more quickly at low temperatures, so keep them warm in your tent overnight.

Dust, water and physical violence are the enemies of both photographic film and the delicate mechanisms inside every camera. Use a modern padded camera case, preferably one with a dust-gusset. Carry a blower-brush and lens tissues and use them meticulously. Clean the back of the camera every time you open it to change a film – the slightest specks of dust on the pressure-plate inside will give you skies bisected by perfect tram-lines. Heat and humidity both ruin any kind of film, so carry yours in a proper waterproof bag – especially the exposed rolls.

TECHNIQUE

However many books you read, seminars you attend or friends you discuss it with, you'll only ever define your own photographic style and find out what pleases you by pointing your camera at the world and contemplating the results. Mountain photography requires a certain element of technical accomplishment, but most of it is the result of the vision of the photographer.

One essential point to remember is that the definitive mountain photograph does not depend on form and composition, but on light. Mountain light. In the rarefied air of the high mountains, nature puts on a daily light show that often defies language to describe it. Most of the time it defies the photographer to capture it as well, but there are two 'magic hours', around sunrise and sunset, when colour and contrast and shadow combine to bring the contours of any vista alive. Those seeking further inspiration should start by looking at Galen Rowell's superlative essay on the subject of mountain photography, *Mountain Light*.

PHOTOGRAPHING PEOPLE

Perhaps the most contentious and potentially negative aspect of travelling with a camera, is the insatiable appetite of the average traveller for pictures of 'exotic' people. If you cannot spare the time and effort to befriend and talk to people on the trail don't be surprised if they don't consent to being photographed. Successful portraiture is a dynamic, intense process, demanding input from both sides of the camera and a sympathetic eye on the part of the photographer. The essential ingredient is time.

HEALTH AND SAFETY
[By DR RACHEL BISHOP and DR JIM LITCH]

Prevention is better than cure. There are a lot of nasties lying in wait for you on your trip to South America, but with some simple precautions and sensible behaviour there is no reason why the sights and scenes of South America should not be your abiding memory, rather than the inside of a bathroom, clinic or hospital.

FOOD AND WATER
Suspect the worst. Human waste is used as a fertilizer for growing food, and there is no doubt that this finds its way into public water supplies.

In major cities drinking bottled water is probably fine. Make sure that the seal is intact on the bottle. Do not drink tap water. Avoid ice cubes and ice cream. Whilst trekking, boiling or filtering water, or treating local water with iodine, are the best options. Boiling water will kill bacteria, even at altitude. The duration of the boil is only important in areas where there are dogs and sheep. In these areas, there may be hydatid cysts in the water and the water must be boiled for 20 mins. Filtering also reliably removes the cysts. Iodine will kill bacteria, but it does not kill hydatid cysts.

For food in general, boil it, cook it, peel it or forget it. When peeling fruit, make sure you peel it yourself, with a clean knife. And before you eat anything, wash your hands with soap and water.

Do not buy food from street vendors, and choose restaurants carefully. As a rough guide, ask to use the toilets. If they are filthy, the kitchens are unlikely to be much better.

PERSONAL HYGIENE
Trekking provides challenges to personal hygiene, but there is no excuse for getting sick. Wash your hands after going to the toilet and wash the rest of your body when possible, concentrating on personal sweaty areas, such as groin, armpits and feet, which are at risk of bacterial, fungal and parasitic infections.

INSECTS
Mosquitoes that bite at night spread malaria, and mosquitoes that bite in the day spread dengue fever, yellow fever and Japanese encephalitis. Protect yourself by wearing a long-sleeved shirt and trousers whenever outside. Insect repellents can help, particularly those containing DEET, but be careful not to get them in your eyes or mouth. At night, sleep under a net, if possible a net that has been impregnated with permethrin. If your room has a fan, turn it on, as the mosquitoes cannot land with the turbulence. As you trek higher, the presence of mosquitoes and the risk of disease become lower.

SEX
Bring condoms from home and use them to prevent Hepatitis B, HIV and other sexually transmitted diseases prevalent in South America. The condom must be put on before penetration to prevent infection.

SPECIFIC ADVICE
Altitude Illness
The higher you trek, the less oxygen is available to the body. Gradual ascent is necessary to allow the body to adjust or acclimatize to this lack of oxygen. The recommended rate of ascent is 300m (984ft) each day with a rest day for every 1000m (3280ft) of ascent. If you gain altitude too quickly, the body has no time to adjust. There are several potential consequences.

Acute Mountain Sickness. AMS is a mild reaction to being at altitude. The symptoms resemble many other holiday afflictions and include headache plus poor appetite, lassitude (physical or mental weariness), fatigue and nausea. Mild AMS is not dangerous as long as you do not go higher until you have recovered. Rest for at least 24 hours and drink plenty of fluids. If you wake the next morning without a headache, then continue to ascend. If you still have a headache that is not relieved by paracetamol, do not go higher until you are better. Acetazolamide (Diamox) – 250mg twice daily for two to three days – may relieve symptoms and aid acclimatization.

Severe Mountain Sickness. There are two forms of severe mountain sickness, High Altitude Pulmonary Edema (HAPE) and High Altitude Cerebral Edema (HACE). Both are life-threatening.

The term HAPE means that fluid collects in the lungs at high altitude. Everyone gets breathless when trekking at altitude, but after a few minutes of rest this settles to a level where one can hold a normal conversation. If a member of your party is persistently breathless at rest he or she may have HAPE. The treatment is descent. This should be immediate; don't wait for daylight.

The term HACE means excessive fluid collects in the brain at high altitude. The symptoms range from confusion to coma. If the patient is conscious, ask him or her to walk in a straight line, putting the heel of one foot in front of the toe of the other. If the patient is unsteady or falls, he or she may have HACE. The treatment is immediate descent. If you have acetazolamide (Diamox), give 250mg every 12 hours. If you have dexamethasone give 8mg, and then a further 4mg every 6 hours. These medicines are no substitute for descent, but can be given while you descend.

You must descend to the point where the patient last slept well without a headache or other symptoms of AMS. Descent is the best treatment because, as you go lower, more oxygen is available. Oxygen can also be given from a cylinder or by using a portable hyperbaric chamber such as a GAMOW bag or a PAC bag.

Follow these simple rules:
1. Learn the symptoms of AMS and recognize when you have them.
2. If you have any symptoms of mild altitude sickness do not ascend until they have disappeared.
3. If the AMS symptoms continue, descend.
4. If you have symptoms of severe altitude sickness, descend immediately.
5. Do not leave a person with altitude sickness alone.

If you are having difficulty acclimatizing, then taking Diamox may help. However, for the majority of people who follow the recognized guidelines for ascent, it is not necessary to take Diamox, so why take a drug you do not need?

Diarrhoea
Diarrhoea is the most common medical problem for travellers. Remember that prevention is better than cure and take heed of the advice on food and water given above. Some 85 per cent of diarrhoea is caused by bacteria. Antibiotics can dramatically reduce the course of the illness. The most useful is ciprofloxacin. Take 500mg when you have your second loose stool, and continue to take 500mg twice daily for three days (or a total of six doses). Keeping well hydrated is very important. You need to drink at least 3 litres per day, or more if you are having frequent diarrhoea. Add oral rehydration salts (dioralyte, gastrolyte) to 1 litre of water per day, and drink an extra 2–3 litres of water a day. If you are going on a long road journey, where toilet facilities will be limited, then Immodium will control your diarrhoea. Take 1 tablet after each bowel movement. It will not, however, cure your diarrhoea, so limit its use to extenuating circumstances.

Giardia is the other main cause of diarrhoea. This is a protozoa found in water, which causes diarrhoea, with abdominal rumbling and cramps, eggy tasting burps and flatus. It takes a week to develop the symptoms so is likely to occur once you have started your trek. Treatment is with tinidazole, 2 grams taken on two consecutive days. This tablet can make you feel a little nauseous so take it in the evening after your meal. You may wake up with a metallic taste in your mouth which will last for 24 hours.

Malaria
Malaria is a disease spread by the female anopheles mosquito, which bites in the evening and at night. There are four forms, and falciparum, or cerebral malaria, is by far the most serious and life threatening. The best protection is not to get bitten, by following the advice given in the insect section above.

In the highland areas of South America above 2500m (8202ft) there is no malaria risk. However, if travel to these areas takes you through the rural lowlands then antimalarials are recommended. For Bolivia, Ecuador and the provinces of Peru bordering Ecuador and Brazil, mefloquine is recommended. The dose is 250mg and should be taken once a week from a week before travel, throughout the trip and for four weeks afterwards. It should be taken after food. For the rest of Peru, chloroquine is recommended. The dose is 500mg and should be taken once a week from one week before travel, during your trip and for four weeks afterwards. Both these drugs have some minor side effects and are not tolerated by everyone. Always check with your doctor before starting a course of antimalarials.

These recommendations are updated regularly and can be found on the Center for Disease Control (CDC) website: www.cdc.gov/travel/regionalmalaria/tropsam.htm.

Yellow Fever
This is a virus spread by the bite of a daytime biting mosquito, causing a flu-like illness leading to jaundice and then haemorrhage. It occurs in certain jungle areas of South America. Yellow fever is a rare cause of illness in travellers. However, many countries require you to have evidence of immunization if you arrive from countries with known yellow fever cases. These regulations change regularly and an up-to-date country specific can be found at the CDC website: www.cdc.gov/travel/yelfever.htm If you have no yellow fever certificate you may find yourself refused entry, quarantined for six days or being offered a yellow fever vaccine.

Immunization is currently recommended for travel to Bolivia, Colombia, Ecuador, Venezuela and Peru. It is a single injection, which gives protection and a valid certificate for 10 years. The vaccine is only available at registered yellow fever centres. Contact your local health services for details.

INOCULATIONS

At least six weeks before your trip, you should have a check up with both your doctor and your dentist. You should get inoculations for tetanus, polio, typhoid, hepatitis A+B and meningitis. Rabies and yellow fever are also worth considering if you are thinking of visiting the jungle areas, along with anti-malarial medication if you plan to climb or trek in areas below 2500m (8202ft) on the eastern side of the Andes. Check with your local travel clinic or doctor's surgery.

A rough guide for an immunization programme is as follows:
Polio (normally just a booster)
Tetanus (a booster every 10 years)
Typhoid (two injections separated by an interval of 4-6 weeks)
Hepatitis A (Gama globulin injection taken just prior to commencement of trip; an alternative serum [Havrix] is available which gives 10 years' cover, but requires two injections over six months)
Anti-malarial prophylaxis
Meningitis A+C

SECURITY IN SOUTH AMERICA

On the whole, safety and security are both a matter of using your common sense and not attracting unnecessary attention to yourself. Due to the disparity in monetary wealth between most foreign tourists and the locals in the countries visited, petty theft is not uncommon. There has also been an increase in the incidence of assault, armed robbery and rape over the past few years in various countries, despite the fact that this is still less than in many cities in Europe and the USA. Travellers should be aware of problem areas and avoid dangerous situations. If you show consideration and are sensible you will generally find you are treated likewise.

The various strategies for separating tourists from their money and possessions are well developed, particularly in Cuzco, Peru and Quito, Ecuador. You are most likely to be at risk when you are loaded down with gear in crowds, or when leaving buses and trains. Take care, also, just after changing money and especially when walking alone at night. Some neighbourhoods are more dangerous than others and some should be avoided altogether, such as the Panacillo in the old part of Quito, unless you are in a large, well-organized group. However, it must be remembered that in all the countries described in this book, pickpockets operate in the major cities and razor blades are often used to slash bags and pockets.

A splash of local colour on Campesino day, Peru. Sadly, busy streets on fiesta days are ripe situations for petty thieves - be aware.

Don't let yourself be distracted too easily by someone or something. Think before you go to check out some unusual situation, or start a conversation with a total stranger who appears particularly friendly. Be careful of clean-up tricks, where you may have shampoo, or something similar, 'accidently' dropped on your shoulder and a kind local offers to help clean you up.

Lost money is another trick to avoid. Be careful of the kind soul who asks if you've lost your wallet, as their friend is probably helping himself to the rest of your gear. When changing money on the street, check for counterfeits and also that the calculator isn't rigged. Count your money before you hand over your cash. Any honest money changer will expect you to do this.

If you lose equipment or documents and have to go to the police, you will often be asked for a bribe. You can try and avoid this by playing dumb, but be prepared. Although illegal in all of the countries in this book, it is accepted practice so don't be surprised. Always carry identification and try to avoid encounters of any kind with the police or military. If you are approached by anyone trying to sell drugs in the street, keep walking and do not respond in any way.

Women travellers, especially those travelling alone, may encounter some harassment as machismo is very much alive in South America. Again, common sense is more helpful than anything else. Be prepared to deal with any situations that occur: verbal abuse is generally best ignored; embarrassing the offending party often works, too. Carrying a whistle to attract attention if threatened could also be useful.

EMERGENCIES

1. Inform your embassy as soon as possible. You are much better off letting them deal with the police.
2. Always keep a copy of your passport with you and preferably also leave a copy with your embassy before travelling from a main centre.
3. If you have an accident, especially if someone is killed, you must inform the police and local magistrates' office. You should try to organize the retrieval of the body and its removal to a morgue (if available) as soon as possible, preferably with a member of the police. You will need a coroner's report, and you must have a copy of this to return to the deceased's country of residence.
In all of the countries covered in this book, there will be a lot of bureaucracy and form filling for any accident or death. Stay calm and try to remain patient. It can be very frustrating but losing your temper will not help.
4. If you are asked for bribes to do with any of the form filling, playing dumb is the best option.

Bibliography

Bernhardson, Wayne: *Argentina, Uruguay & Paraguay* (1999 3rd Edition) Lonely Planet Publications.
Bernhardson, Wayne: *Chile & Easter Island* (2000 5th Edition) Lonely Planet Publications.
Biggar, John: *The High Andes: A Guide for Climbers* (1996) Andes.
Box, Ben: *South American Handbook* (1997) Footprint Handbooks (UK), Passport Books (USA).
Brain, Yossi; North, Andrew; Stoddart, Isobel: *Trekking in Bolivia* (1997) Cordee.
Brain, Yossi: *Bolivia: A Climbing Guide* (1999) Cordee.
Burford, Jim: *Chile and Argentina: Backpacking and Hiking* (1998) Bradt Publications.
Chatwin, Bruce: *In Patagonia* (1998 New Edition) Vintage.
Clark, Simon: *The Puma's Claw* (1959) Hutchinson.
Cumes, Carol: *Journey to Machu Picchu* (1988) Llewelyn Publications.
Dydynski, Krzysztof: *Venezuela* (1998 2nd Edition) Lonely Planet Publications.
Frost, Peter: *Exploring Cusco* (1989) Nuevas Imagenes.
Galeano, Eduardo: *Open Veins of Latin America* (1998, 25th Anniversary Edition) Latin American Bureau.
Hemming, John: *The Conquest of the Incas* (1993) Papermac.
Jarvis, Kathy: *Ecuador, Peru and Bolivia: The Backpackers Manual* (2000) Bradt Publications (UK), The Globe Pequot Press Inc. (USA).
Keenan, Brian & McCarthy, John: *Between Extremes* (2000 New Edition) Black Swan.
Lindenmayer, Clem: *Trekking in the Patagonian Andes* (1998 2nd Edition) Lonely Planet Publications.
Murphy, Dervla: *Eight Feet in the Andes* (1995 New Edition) Flamingo.
Neate, Jill: *Mountaineering in the Andes* (1994 2nd Edition) Expedition Advisory Centre.
Pollard, Andrew; Murdoch, David; Hillary Edmund; Milledge, James S.: *The High Altitude Medicine Handbook* (1996) Radcliffe Medical Press.
Rachowieki, Rob: *Ecuador & the Galapagos Islands* (2001 5th Edition) Lonely Planet Publications.
Rachowieki, Rob; Thurber, Mark; Wagenhauser, Betsy: *Climbing & Hiking in Ecuador* (1997 4th Edition) Bradt Publications (UK), The Globe Pequot Press, Inc. (USA)
Simpson, Joe: *Touching the Void* (1998 New Edition) Vintage.
Slesser, Malcolm: *The Andes are Prickly* (1966) Victor Gollancz.
Swaney, Deanna: *Bolivia* (1996) Lonely Planet Publications.
Wheeler, Sara: *Travels in a Thin Country* (1995 New Edition) Abacus.

Glossary

abra = pass
alasitas = miniature objects for blessings
alberge juventude = youth hostel
alcalde = mayor/village headman
alojamiento = lodgings (cheap)
alpaca = related to the llama, reared for wool
apacheta = cairn
apus/achachilas = Aymara mountain spirits
auracaria = monkey puzzle tree
arriero = muleteer
arroyo = stream
baños = bathroom/washroom/springs
bosque = forest
casa de cambio = bureau de change
campesino = peasant
canaleta = gully
cenega = swamp
cerro = hill that is not glaciated
cholo/chola = Quechua/Aymara person who has migrated to the city, but still wears traditional dress
cocinero = cook
coigüe = three types of evergreen southern beech
collectivo = taxi that picks up passengers along a fixed route
comedor popular = market-place restaurant (cheap)
confiteria = teashop/café
cordillera = mountain range
cresta (arista) = ridge/crest
criollos = native-born Hispanics
cumbre = summit
estancia = large cattle/sheep ranch
estero (arroyo) = stream
gaucho = cowboy
guanaco = Patagonian cameloid, related to the llama, found below 2000m
hacer el dedo = hitchhiking
hacienda = farm
hospedaje/hostería = small, family-run hotel
hostal = hostel
huemul = rare Andean deer
jukumari = Andean spectacled bear
lago = lake
laguna = small lake
lenga = deciduous southern beech

llamero = llama man
mallín = swamp/bog
mapoteca = map shop
mazorca = Argentinian secret police
mestizo = person of mixed race (Hispanic and Indian)
mirador = viewpoint
mochilero = backpacker
nevado = snow-covered mountain
oca = type of potato
pampas = grassland
penitentes = vertical spikes of snow/ice
pension = hostel
piedra = rock/stone
polylepsis/quenal = tree with multilayered reddish bark
portada = entrance to a valley (usually with a gate)
puente = bridge
puna = area above 4000m but below the glaciers
punta/paso/portachuello = pass
quebrada = valley/ravine/gorge
refresco = fizzy drink
residencial = guest house, bed & breakfast
salto = waterfall
sendero = path
soroche = altitude sickness
subida = ascent
termas (baños termales) = thermal springs
ventisquero = glacier
vicuña = the smallest of the cameloids, lives above 4000m
viscacha = Andean long-eared, bushy-tailed rabbit
zunbador = snipe

Index

Numbers in *italics* refer to photographs. Note: most locations begin with a descriptive term, for example Río Alerce, rather than Alerce River.

Abra Illampu 94
Abra Pacuani 86
Abra San Enrique 83
Abrada de Malaga 123
Abrada Runturakay 126
Abrada de Wuarimahuasaca 126
accommodation *see* individual countries
Achupallas 153
Achura (Chucura) 91
Acobamba 125
Aconcagua 68–9
acute mountain sickness (AMS) 185, 185–6
Aguas Calientes 127, 129
airlines 25, 30, 76, 116, 150, 170
Alausí 153
Alpamayo 140, 141, *142*
Altiplano 10, 89, 179, 180
altitude illness 185–6
Alto de la Cruz 173, 176
Alto de Puccara 139, 141
AMS (acute mountain sickness) 185, 185–6
Ancohuma 95, *104*, 105
Antaquilla 111
Antisana 160
Apacheta Pass 98
Apaneta Pass 119
Apolobamba 107–11
Arapa Pass 119
Araucanía 22, 63
Arenal Grande sand pit 158
Argentina 23, 28–9
 accommodation 32, 46, 62
 local information 32–3
 transport 31–2, 46, 62
 travel to 30–1
arrieros 16–17, 145

Arroyo Casa de Piedra 51
Arroyo Fresco 51
Arroyo Goye 52
Arroyo Huancasayani 109
Arroyo López 52
Arroyo Navidad 52
Arroyo Van Titter 50

Banos Huancarhuas 144
Bariloche 53, 56, 58, 62
Batea Paquisha 124
Bolívar, Símon 24, 168, *171*
Bolivia 10, 74–6, *75*
 accommodation 78, 101, 111
 fiestas 80–1, *81*
 local information 76–7, 78–9
 mining 85
 transport 77–8, 101, 111
 travel to 76–7
Botijlaca 98
Buenos Aires 28, 31
burros *10*, 16

Cañar 154
Cajatambo 132, 133
Camino Calzada 95, 103
Campa pass 121
Campamento Bridwell 43, 44
Campamento Británico 39
Campamento las Carretas 34
Campamento Chileno 38
Campamento Coirón 37
Campamento Los Guardas 36
Campamento Italiano 39
Campamento Japonés 38
Campamento Madsen 44
Campamento Maestri *41*, 43
Campamento Neozelandés 49
Campamento Paso 36–7
Campamento los Perros 37
Campamento Poincenot 44
Campamento Serón 38
Campamento Torres 38
Camping los Cuernos 39
Cancha de Futbol 50, 51

Caraby 176
Caracas 168
Caraz 144
Carihuairazo 156
Carretera Austral 49
Casa Pangue 56
Cashapampa 137, 139, 140, 142, 144, *144*
Cerro Bengala 82
Cerro Castillo 47–9, *48*
Cerro Cella 51
Cerro Chico 162
Cerro El Tambo 159
Cerro Electrico ridge 45
Cerro Lomo 121
Cerro Lomo Chosalago 160
Cerro Madsen 44
Cerro Mapahuiña 153
Cerro Navidad 52
Cerro Piedra Negra 156
Cerro Torre 43
Cerro Yaypuri 84, *84*
Chachabamba 125
Chairo 92
Chajolpaya 74, 95, 103
Challapampa 92
Charazani 107, 111
Chavin de Huantar 138
Chihuani 105
Chilca 126
Chile 23, 24
 accommodation 27, 40, 49, 67, 71
 local information 27–8, 33
 transport 25, 26–7, 40, 49, 67, 71
 travel to 25–6
Chillca 122
Chimborazo 156–8, *158*, 162, *179*
Chiqapa Jawira Valley 97
Chiquian 130, 133, 145
Cholin 144
Chopicaiqui 138, 139
Choquetacarpo Pass 124
Choro Trail 91, 92
Chorrillo del Salto 44

Chulloca 122
Chuquipogyo 157
Ciénaga del Hospital 165
climate 12, 148
climbing 17, 18
coca leaf 93
Cocoyo 95
Cohoni 86, 88
Colcabamba 137, 138
Collpampa 125
Colombia 12, 13
Colonia Suiza 52
communications 28, 33, 79, 118, 152, 171
Condoriri 98, *98*, 100, *100*
Cora 130
Cordillera Auzungate 119–22, *121*, 129
Cordillera Blanca 137–9, 140–1, 179
Cordillera Blanca Tranquilo 134–6, *184*
Cordillera Carabaya 121
Cordillera Huayhuash 130–3
Cordillera do Mérida 10, 179
Cordillera Occidental 10, 179
Cordillera Oriental 10, 179
Cordillera Real 10, 85, 94–101, 103–5
Cordillera Vilcabamba 126
Cordillera Vilcanota 121
Cordón de Caulle 58
Cotopaxi 161, *161*, 162
Coyhaique 47, 49
Cuchilla Tres Cruces 153
Cuenca 154, 155
Cuernos de Paine 34, *35*
Curbati 176
currency *see* money
Curva 107
customs/immigration 26, 30–1, 76, 117
cuy (guinea pigs) 131
Cuzco 122, 123, 129

Descanso de los Potros 54
Diablo Mundo 132, *132*, 133

Diamox 186
diarrhoea 186
drink *see* food and drink

Ecuador 10, 148–50, *149*
  accommodation 151, 155, 162, 165
  local information 151–2
  transport 151, 155, 162, 165
  travel to 150–1
El Alto 74
El Calafate 43, 46
El Camino del Inca 153–5
El Chaltén 43, 45, 46
El Churo Loma 165
El Morro 173, 174
El Rodeo 154
electricity 33, 79, 118, 152, 171
embassies 26, 31, 78, 117, 150, 170
Estancia Totoral Pampa 86, 87
Estancia Tuni 100
Estancia Una 88
Estanciá Urbanas 157
Estancia Utaña Pampa 95, 105
Estero Aihue 65
Estero Aislado 47
Estero Blanco Chico 47
Estero Challupen 63
Estero del Bosque 48, 49
Estero La Lima 47
Estero Ñilfe 63
Estero Paso de las Mulas 47
Estero Traico 63

Fabulosa Pass 97
fiestas, Bolivian 80–1, *81*
first-aid kit 19
flora and fauna 180
food and drink 18–19, 27–8, 32–3, 33, 78–9, 171, 185
Fortaleza 38, 39

Gara Gara pass 143
geology 10, 12, 178–80
giardia 186
Glaciar Francés 39
Glaciar Grey 36, *39*
Glaciar Olvidado 37
Glaciar Peñón 47
Glaciar Peulla 56
Guardería Anticura 58
Guardería Chinay 65
guides 17, 129, 155, 162
guinea pigs (cuy) 131

HACE (High Altitude Cerebral Edema) 185
Haciana Uchuy Finaya 121
Hacienda Callanges 138
Hacienda El Hato 160–1
Hacienda El Hospital 165
Hacienda El Tambo 162
Hanamura, Tamiji 92
Hankolokhaya 97
HAPE (High Altitude Pulmonary Edema) 185
health 33, 185–6
Hilo Hilo 108
Hostería las Torres 34, 38
Huallanca 144
Huamasaraju 136

Huancacalle 123, 124
Huaráz 137, 145
Huascarán 10, 144, *144*
Huayllabamba 126
Huayna Picchu 127
Huayna Potosí 98, 99, *99*
Huayracmachay 125
Huilca 143
Huinay Huayna 125, 127
hummingbirds 106
Huyallapa 133

Ibarra 165
Illampu 94–5, 103–5, *104*, *105*
Illimani 86–8
Inca Trail 125, 126–8
Incacancha 107
Incachiriasca Pass 125
Incaracay 124
Incas 85, 114, 122, 125, 128
Ingapirca *152*, 154, *154*, 155
inoculations 186
insects 185
insurance 18
Intipunku 127
Irunbinc 165
Irunguchi 165

Jampa 121, 122
Janca 131, 136
Janpaucacocha 119
Jatunpampa 107
Jurikhota 97, 98, *98*

Kallwayas medicine men 107
Khori Chuma Cirque 84
knots, language of 125
Kotia 97

La Mucuy 175
La Paz 74, 76, 77
La Piedra Grande 107
Lago Dickson 37
Lago Electrico 45
Lago Escondido 37
Lago Grey 34, 36, 39
Lago Limpiopungo 162
Lago Nordenskjold 38
Lago Paine 34, 37
Lago Pehoé 34, 36, 39
Lago Pingo 39
Lago Skottsberg 39
Laguna '69' 137
Laguna Abutardas 67
Laguna Alejandra 38
Laguna Alerce 55
Laguna Alka Khota 98
Laguna Amarga 38
Laguna Atochaico 132
Laguna Auzungatecocha 119
Laguna Azul 67
Laguna Azulacocha 143
Laguna Burrococha 165
Laguna Capri 44
Laguna Carhuacocha 131–2
Laguna Celeste 109
Laguna Cerro Castillo 48
Laguna Chatamarca 82, 83
Laguna Chiar Khota 98, 100
Laguna Choco Khota 84
Laguna Churup 134
Laguna Colorado 156
Laguna Cuerococha 141
Laguna Culebrillas 154

Laguna Culliacocha 134, 143
Laguna Frías 56
Laguna Hualatani 103
Laguna Jahuacocha 133
Laguna Jancarurish 143
Laguna Jurau 133
Laguna Kacha 103
Laguna Kaiko 143
Laguna Khota Khuchu 83
Laguna Margarita 56
Laguna Miguillas 83
Laguna Mitcocha 131, *131*
Laguna Negra 52
Laguna del Perro 44
Laguna los Perros 34, 37
Laguna Piedras Blancas 44, *44*
Laguna Pocura 60
Laguna Quitarasca 143
Laguna Roca 36
Laguna Safuna Baja 143
Laguna San Francisco 103
Laguna Santa Lucia 160
Laguna Schmoll 50, 51
Laguna Sibinacocha 121
Laguna Solteracocha 133
Laguna Soral 109
Laguna Sucapillo 165
Laguna Suches 111, *111*
Laguna El Suero 176
Laguna Susacocha 133
Laguna Tambillo 135
Laguna los Témpanos 51, 52
Laguna Ticllacocha 121
Laguna Timoncitos 174, 176
Laguna Tocllacocha 139
Laguna Tonchek 50, 51
Laguna Tres Cruces 153
Laguna de los Tres 44
Laguna Tullparaju 134
Laguna Verde 175
Laguna Viconga 132
Laguna Viscachani 90
Laguna Volcán 159
Laguna Yamaca 109
Laguna Yanacocha 163, 164
Laguna Zongo 99
Lagunas de Anteojos 172
Lagunas Jatunacocha 139, 140
Lagunas Madre e Hija 44
Lagunas Morococha 139, 141
Lakathiya 94, 105
Lake District 22
Lake Titikaka 10, 89, 179
Lambate 87
language 19, 28, 33, 79, 182
Las Horquetas Grandes 47
Liviñosa Valley 98
Llactapata 125, 126
Llamac 130, 133
Llamac Corral 139, 140
Llanganuco 136, 137, 138
Llulluchapampa 126
Llupa 134
Loma Redonda 172, 174
Lomo Piedra Negra 156
Loriacani 104
Los Andenes 124
Los Baños 59
Los Baños Neuvos 60
Los Cedros 143
Los Geisires 60
Los Nevados 172, 176
Lusani Pass 109

Machu Picchu *114*, 125, 127, 128, *128*, 129
Macusani 121
malaria 186
Mancos 144
maps 17
Mapuche Indians 22, 70
medicine men 107
Mendoza 68, 71
Mérida 172, 173, 174, 176, 177
Millipaya 104
mining 12, 85, 97, 108–9, 133, 179–80
Mirador Laguna Torre 43, 44
money 26, 31, 33, 76, 118, 151–2, 171
Monte Almirante Nieto 38
Monte Fitz Roy 41–6, *45*
Monte Tronador 57
mosquitoes 185, 186
Mucunutan 173, 176

Nahuel Haupi *20–1*, 22, 50–2
Nevados San Felipe 82
Nido de Cóndores 86, 88
Nusta Hispaña ruins 123

Osorno 58, 60
Otavalo 165

Paccha 124
Pacchanta 121
Pacchaspata 121
Pachamama (Mother Earth) 120
Paco 121
Pacuni 83
Palca 95
Palcoyo 122
Palguín-Coñarip road 65, 67
Palomani Pass 119
Pampa Cahuana 125
Pampa Linda 53, 53–4, 55
Pampacancha 121
Papallacta 159
paramo 170
Paredones ruins 154
park fees 17
Parque Nacional Cajas 155
Parque Nacional los Glaciares 41–6
Parque Nacional Nahuel Haupi 22, 50–2
Parque Nacional Sierra La Culata 175
Parque Nacional Villarrica 63–7
Pasada Peñón 47
Pasaje de Yaṇajacu 138
Paso Aguja Negra 98
Paso Brecha Negra 51
Paso Calzada 103
Paso Huila Khota 105
Paso John Garner 34, 37
Paso Korahuasi 95
Paso de las Nubes 55
Paso Negruni 95, 96
Paso de Pérez Rosales 56
Paso Pura Pura 109
Paso Quera (Sanches) 109
Paso Yanacocha 109
Paso Zongo 99
Paso Zongo Sistaño 98

Patagonia 21, 22, *23*
   see also Argentina; Chile
Paucaros 122
peak fees 17
peaks, grading 17
Pelechuco 108–9, 111
people of the Andes 12–13
Pequeño Alpamayo 101, *101*
Peru 10, 114–15, *115*
   accommodation 117, 129, 145
   local information 117, 118
   mining 133
   transport 116–17, 129, 145
   travel to 116, 117
Petrohué 56
Peulla 56
photography 182, 183–5
Phuyupatamarca ruins 127
Pico Bolivar *166-7*, 174, *174*, 176
Pico Espejo 172, 174, 176
Pico Humboldt 175–6
Piedra del Fraile 45
Piedra Peréz 54
Pinan Lakes 163–5, *164*
Pinaya 88
Pisco 136, 137
pisco sour 118
Pitec 134, 136
Pitumarca 121, 122
Pocpa 130
Pogyos 156, 158
politics and history 24, 28–9, 74, 114–16, 148, 168
Pomabamba 141, 144
Portacheullo Huayhuash 132
Portachuello de Llanganuco 137, 139, 141
Portero Pass 97
porters 17
potatoes 78
Pucacocha 143
Pucón 65, 67
Puente López 52
Puente Roto 86, 87, 88
Puerto Frías *29*, 55
Puerto Montt 56
Puerto Natales 40
Puesco 67
Pulpera 122
puna 180
Punta Carhuac 131
Punta Carnicero 132
Punta Cuyoc 132–3
Punta Llamac 133
Punta Tarpush 132, 133
Punta Union 137, 139, 141
Puyehue National Park 58–60, *61*

Qortelhuian 130
Quebrada Abraspungo 156
Quebrada Alpamayo 143
Quebrada Ancococha 133
Quebrada Arhayacocha 139, 140, 142
Quebrada Auaican 156
Quebrada Cayesh 134
Quebrada Chillcamayo 122
Quebrada Colpa 124
Quebrada Cunturacahuayjo 121
Quebrada Estero Parada 49

Quebrada La Fría 172
Quebrada Gadrui 153
Quebrada Guanacpatay 133
Quebrada Hacris 133
Quebrada Huampunimayo 121
Quebrada Huaripampa 138, 139, 141
Quebrada Illampu 94–5
Quebrada Jampamayo 121, 122
Quebrada de Kote 103
Quebrada Mayobamba 143
Quebrada Mayuyoc 124
Quebrada Mosnanda 174
Quebrada Mucusabacha 174
Quebrada Paria 138, 139
Quebrada Qelcamachay 124
Quebrada Rajucolta 135
Quebrada Rondoy 130
Quebrada Santa Cruz 140, 142, *143*
Quebrada Shallap *112-13*, 134–5
Quebrada Sunfohuayacu 159
Quebrada Tayapampa 139, 143
Quebrada Tigre Saltana 156
Quebrada Yanacolpa 143
Quebrada Yanamayo 121
Quebrada Yanapacha 137
Quilahuaya 88
Quilambaya 94
Quillo Loma 153
Quimsa Cruz 82–3, 84, 88
quinoa 102, *102*
Quirrasco 60
Quisipata 130
Quito 150

Rajucolta 136
Rancho Huarantara 109
Raqchi 122
Refugio Dickson 37
Refugio Edward Whymper 157, *157*, 158
Refugio Fabian Zurita 158
Refugio Frey 50, 51
Refugio Lago Pehoé 34, 36
Refugio López 52
Refugio Lynch 50
Refugio Otto Meiling 54, 57
Refugio Piedritas 50
Refugio Pingo 39
Refugio Pudeto 39
Refugio San Martín (Jakob) 50, 51, 52
Refugio Segré (Italia) 52
Refugio los Troncos 45
Refugio Villarrica 63, 66
Refugio Volcán Puyehue 58–9, *60*
Refugio Zapata 39
rescues 18, 145
Reserva Nacional Cerro Castillo 47–9
Riñinahue 60
Río Alerce 55
Río Aobamba 125, 127
Río Ascensio 38
Río Blanco *43*, 44, 45, 47
Río Cabeza del Indio 37
Río Cadrul 153
Río Caracoles 83
Río Carhuacocha 132

Río Castaño Overa 54
Río Chajolpaya 103
Río Challiri 87
Río Contrafuerte 60
Río Cuischaca 126
Río Cullcamayo 121
Río Cullirama 161
Río Cullupampa 141
Río Cungilamo 164
Río Daule 162
Río Electrico 45
Río Fitz Roy 43
Río del Francés 39
Río Huacanasca 86
Río Ibáñez 49
Río Llamac 130, 133
Río Llancahue 66, 67
Río Malpaso 87
Río Nakara 109
Río Nilahue 60
Río Pacamayo 126
Río Palguín 66
Río Pasto Grande 87
Río de los Perros 37
Río Peulla 56
Río Pichillaneahue 65
Río Pinaya Jahuira 86
Río Píta 162
Río Pitumarca 122
Río Quero 130
Río Salca 130
Río San Cristobál 105
Rio Shiulla 143
Río Tambo 159, 162
Río Turbio 47
Río los Venados 60
Riobamba valley 157
Rosaspata 124
Rumiñahui 162
Runturakay 126

safety 18, 28, 33, 79, 118, 171, 187
   health 185–6
Salca Valley 122
Salcantay Casa Pass 125
Salloca 122
Salto del Indio 58
Salto Garganta del Diablo 54
San Blass 165
San Francisco 92
San Francisco de Sachapampa 163
San José 154
Sandillani 92
Sanja Pampa 91
Santiago 26
Sarani Valley 95
Sarapacocha 133
Sayacmarka ruins 126
security see safety
sex 185
Sierra Nevada de Mérida 172–4, *175*
Sierra de Perijá 10
Sistaña Pass 98
Siulacocha 132
Sorata 94, 95, 101, 104, *104*
Spaniards 13, 85, 93, 114, 148
Sunchuli 108

Tansana 109
Termas de Palguín 65

time differences 33, 76, 118, 152, 171
Tinqui 119, 121, 122
Tiwanaku civilization 89
torrent ducks 56
Torres del Paine *8-9*, 34–40, *36*, *37*
Totoras 157
transport, local see individual countries
Trapiche 111
travel insurance 45
travel to Andean countries 25–6, 30–1, 76–7, 116, 117, 150–1
trekking 16–17, 181–2
   agencies 27, 32, 77, 151
   equipment 17–18
   permits 17
   trek grades 17
Tres Ríos 86

Uchulluclло 122
Uma Palca 90
Unchus 135
Upis 119
Urcuqui 165
Uyuni 122

Valle del Río de las Vueltas 45
Valle del Silencio 38
Valle Escondido 37
Valle del Francés 34, 39
Valle Los Calderones 173
Vaqueria 138
Venezuela 168, *169*
   accommodation 171, 177
   local information 171
   transport 170, 177
   travel to 170
Ventisquero Negro 54, *55*
vicuñas 84, *125*, 132, 180
Villa Catedral 50
Villa Cerro Castillo 49
Villarrica traverse 63–7
Viloco 82
Viracocha 122
visas 26, 30, 76, 117, 150–1, 170
Viscachani gold mine 108
viscachas 121
Vitcos 124
Volcán Choshuenco 67
Volcán Puyehue 58, 59, 61
Volcán Quetrupillán 66
Volcán Villarrica 63, 66, 66
Volcán Yanaurco de Pinan 164
Volcano Sincholagua 160, 161–2
volcanoes 61, 179

water see food and drink
Whymper, Edward 158
Wila Llojeta Pass 97

Yacu 162
Yaino ruins 141
Yanacolpa 143
Yanama 124, 138
yellow fever 186
Yolosa 92
Yurac Corral 137
Yurac Rumi ruins 123

Zanjón Pino Huacho 63

AUTHORS' ACKNOWLEDGEMENTS

Thanks to Marg Saul and Jim Baker for their much appreciated help with reading the text and correcting it, especially my dreadful punctuation; and to Stuart Holmes, Dr Rachel Bishop and Dr Jim Litch for their help with the geology and medical advice information.

Many thanks to all my friends with whom I've trekked and climbed in South America over the years, especially Lisa Richardson, Brian Mugridge, Mark Klassen, Richard Lindsay, Patty Rosendaal, Mark Williams, Betsy Wagenhauser, Natalie Poulin, Kate Charles, Jack Allen, Tony Farrel and Murray Wilson.

A very special thank you to the Bedon family of Chiquian and Huaráz for their fantastic hospitality and friendship over the years, particularly Natividad, Melky, Salsado Antonia and Flora.

Thanks to Manuel Serafin and his family Sylvena and Lucho for the always warm welcome and hospitality at the Hostal Colomba in Huaráz; the Figueroa family of Edwards Inn, Huaráz; Pablo Segovia for his help with details of the Cordillera Vilcabamba; and Camillo Andrade for his help and great service on treks and climbs in Ecuador.

Thanks also to the many friends and acquaintances I've met on all the trips I've worked on for both Sherpa and KE Adventure; and to Kate Michell for her help and advice with the general details of the book.

Val Pitkethly

Special thanks must go, firstly, to Jennie Roberts, who was not only an uncomplaining travelling companion one very snowy autumn in Patagonia, but who has also spent many hours at her computer gathering information for me. Secondly, special thanks to Pete Harrop for his support and patience throughout the writing of this book. And thirdly, thanks to Mario Nina Quispe, whose knowledge of all cultural, political and historical aspects of Bolivia is probably unsurpassed and who opened my eyes to Bolivia's rich heritage and diversity; he is largely responsible for the feature on Tiwanaku and for the story of the humming birds! Thanks, too, to Piter Barron Camacho, for all his help.

I would like to thank KE Adventure Travel, who gave me the opportunity to visit South America in the first place, and all those who have accompanied me on trips over the years.

From Chile, I have to thank Dagoberto Pena, not forgetting Luis and Juan, Park Rangers in Torres del Paine, who stored bags for me and made backpacking in the park much more pleasant.

From Argentina, my thanks to Caltur. From Bolivia, I would like to thank all those who have made me so welcome over the years, especially Juan Villaroel, who has shared his extensive knowledge of the mountains with me, Carlos Escóbar, with whom I first trekked, Oswaldo Cortez, Don Freddy Rivera Soria, Roxana Rivas, Antonio Laime, with whom I explored Apolobamba and, of course, Alcides Imana and his family, who made me welcome in Pelechuco. I would also like to offer my thanks to all at the Hostal Austria, which has been my home away from home in La Paz over the years.

Thanks, too, to Lisa Seaman and Clare Stallworthy for sharing some memorable peak ascents and to Sue Savege for allowing me to use her piece on the first ascent of Cerro Yaypuri, Quimsa Cruz; not forgetting Tony Barton and Andre Geissler for their photos of Illampu and Cerro Castillo respectively. Thanks, too, to Susi Paisley for letting me visit her in her Jucumari project.

Finally I would like to remember Ian Carpenter, who was involved in a tragic fatal road biking accident. He accompanied me on three trips to South America and I shall always remember and value his warmth, enthusiasm, humour and relaxed attitude to life.

Kate Harper

CONTRIBUTORS

Additional text contributors: Dr Rachel Bishop and Dr Jim Litch (Health and Safety, pages 185–6); Kate Harper and Mario Nina (Tiwanaku, page 89); Stuart Holmes (Puyehué Volcanism, page 61 and The Andean Environment – Geology, pages 178–80); Steve Razzetti (Mountain Photography, pages 183–4); Sue Savege (Cerro Yaypuri, page 84).

Additional photographic contributors:
Tony Barton (page 105); Bruce Coleman Collection (page 106); André Geissler (page 48); Lindsay Griffin (pages 166, 171, 173, 174, 176); Kathy Jarvis (page 132); Richard Lindsay (page 142); Katie Moore (pages 66, 144 bottom); Patty Roozendaal (pages 121, 122); Sue Savege (page 84).